open &
distance
learning
series

Second Edition

Delivering Digitally

MANAGING THE TRANSITION
to the Knowledge Media

Alistair Inglis, Peter Ling & Vera Joosten

**KOGAN
PAGE**

First published in 1999
Second edition published in 2002

Kogan Page Limited
120 Pentonville Road
London N1 9JN
UK

Stylus Publishing Inc.
22883 Quicksilver Drive
Sterling VA 20166-2012
USA

British Library Cataloguing in Publication Data

A CIP record for this book is available from the British Library.

ISBN 0 7494 3471 6

Typeset by JS Typesetting, Wellingborough, Northants
Printed and bound in Great Britain by Biddles Ltd, Guildford and King's Lynn
www.biddles.co.uk

Delivering
Digitally

Open and Distance Learning Series

Series Editor: Fred Lockwood

Activities in Self-Instructional Texts, Fred Lockwood
Assessing Open and Distance Learners, Chris Morgan and Meg O'Reilly
Changing University Teaching, Terry Evans and Daryl Nation
The Costs and Economies of Open and Distance Learning, Greville Rumble
The Design and Production of Self-Instructional Materials, Fred Lockwood
E-Moderating, Gilly Salmon
Exploring Open and Distance Learning, Derek Rowntree
Flexible Learning in a Digital World, Betty Collis and Jef Moonen
Improving Your Students' Learning, Alistair Morgan
Innovation in Open and Distance Learning, Fred Lockwood and Anne Gooley
Key Terms and Issues in Open and Distance Learning, Barbara Hodgson
The Knowledge Web: Learning and Collaborating on the Net, Marc Eisenstadt and Tom Vincent
Leadership for 21st Century Learning: Global Perspectives from Educational Innovators, Colin Latchem and Donald E Hanna
Learning and Teaching in Distance Education, Otto Peters
Making Materials-Based Learning Work, Derek Rowntree
Managing Open Systems, Richard Freedman
Mega-Universities and Knowledge Media, John S Daniel
Objectives, Competencies and Learning Outcomes, Reginald F Melton
Open and Distance Learning: Case Studies from Education, Industry and Commerce, Stephen Brown
Open and Flexible Learning in Vocational Education and Training, Judith Calder and Ann McCollum
Preparing Materials for Open, Distance and Flexible Learning, Derek Rowntree
Programme Evaluation and Quality, Judith Calder
Reforming Open and Distance Learning, Terry Evans and Daryl Nation
Supporting Students in Open and Distance Learning, Ormond Simpson
Teaching with Audio in Open and Distance Learning, Derek Rowntree
Teaching Through Projects, Jane Henry
Towards More Effective Open and Distance Learning, Perc Marland
Understanding Learners in Open and Distance Education, Terry Evans
Using Communications Media in Open and Flexible Learning, Robin Mason
The Virtual University, Steve Ryan, Bernard Scott, Howard Freeman and Daxa Patel

Contents

Series editor's foreword

Alistair Inglis, Peter Ling and Vera Joosten have assembled a book that provides managers and administrators, teachers and technicians, in fact anyone associated with the move to delivering teaching or training material digitally, with an invaluable resource. The need for such a book is clear. An inspection of the educational or training press will reveal increasing numbers of organizations in industry, commerce and the public services delivering material via the new technologies; the growth in this form of teaching and training is phenomenal. This book will make the transition from conventional teaching to digital forms of delivery less traumatic; it will identify the many aspects worthy of your attention and for you and your colleagues to resolve. The division into four self-contained sections will allow you to decide what is most relevant to you and let you decide the order in which you want to study the contents. Indeed, the detailed contents list, index and glossary will help you focus on the particular aspects that interest you most; even though I suspect you will find all of it interesting and that it repays any investment you make in its study.

This is not a book for technophobes. It does use the language of Communication & Information Technology (C&IT) and makes a strong case for the exploitation of the knowledge media. However, its clear focus is teaching and learning – using the knowledge media when it is most appropriate and to best effect. The authors' concern with assessing the cost effectiveness of any proposed investment in C&IT, of the required infrastructure to support it, investment in colleagues via staff development activities and its stringent evaluation sets them apart from most C&IT evangelists.

Alistair, Peter and Vera have displayed the best features of a team; combining their talents and providing a product that is broad in its scope, sufficiently detailed to address the main issues and yet packed with concrete advice. The models, frameworks and principles they offer, and the phases they describe in the transition to the knowledge media have emerged from careful research studies and some hard lessons in delivering digitally to adult learners in Australia – lessons from which we can all learn. With direction from these authors you have a better chance of getting there.

Fred Lockwood

Preface

This book has been written for those with responsibilities for managing the transition from traditional approaches to education and training – whether face-to-face or at a distance – to forms of digital delivery. This includes everyone with responsibilities for the transition, from the chief executive officers of educational and training organizations to heads of departments, course co-ordinators and technical and educational specialists.

This is not a book that needs to be read from cover to cover. We recognize that educational managers are busy people – especially those whose primary role is to act as change agents. We have therefore tried to make the contents of the book as accessible as possible. We have divided the book into four sections. Each section more-or-less stands alone. It may be read in isolation from the others and it may be read in a different sequence from that in which it is presented.

The first section is for those who, as we do, like to put their policy and practice in *context* and to be able to support it with a theoretical position. The section provides a history of the emergence of knowledge media, an understanding of the social and educational contexts in which the knowledge media are being adopted and an understanding of learning and pedagogics appropriate to use the knowledge media in education and training.

The second section deals with the practicalities of *implementation*. We start by examining one of the most important factors driving change at the present time – the matter of costs. We then contrast the implications for decision-making of treating expenditure as an investment rather than treating it as a cost. We move on to elements that require attention to effect the transition. These include re-engineering the technological infrastructure, re-skilling and supporting staff, re-orienting the teaching programme, and re-designing learner support services. We provide guidance on developing an evaluation strategy that can be applied throughout the process. We conclude the section by indicating a sequence for effecting the transition.

The third section, *quality improvement*, provides a framework and a tool for implementing quality improvement processes across all aspects of a delivery system.

The fourth and final section, *the future*, takes a brief glance over the horizon, trying to predict some of the new developments with which decision-makers will soon have to deal.

Terminology in this rapidly developing field is still being established. In keeping with other books in this series, we have used the term 'knowledge media', originally coined by Marc Eisenstadt, Director of the Knowledge Institute at the Open University, to refer collectively to the digital delivery media, principally the World Wide Web and CD ROM. In places, we use the term 'new learning technologies' to refer specifically to the technologies supporting the use of the knowledge media, such as Web servers, and conferencing systems.

This is the second edition of *Delivering Digitally*. The original idea for this book arose from a research project undertaken by us for the Higher Educational Council in Australia – New Directions in Resource Based Learning: Quality, Costs and Access. The investigation was commissioned to inform the Council in offering advice to the Minister for Employment, Education and Training. A synopsis of that advice was published as the booklet, *Quality in Resource Based Learning* (National Board of Employment, Education and Training, 1997).

From our work on this project and from our experience in providing policy advice in institutions that are themselves in the process of making the difficult transition to online delivery, we became aware of the challenge that many senior educational managers were facing. They had to manage a change process in an area of which they may have had only a layperson's understanding. It seemed that there was a need for a book that provided an easy-to-assimilate account of the major issues that arise and the key activities involved in making the transition to the knowledge media. We considered that such a book ought to set the advice it offered within the relevant educational framework. Notwithstanding the breath-taking pace at which change is occurring, it is important that education and training managers base their decisions on soundly based rationales.

That was the concept. Fortunately Fred Lockwood and, in turn, Kogan Page, shared our conviction. However, as we got more deeply into the project we began to realize the enormity of the task we had set ourselves. The domain over which we needed to range covers an extraordinarily wide range of topics, some of which have been the subject of whole books in this series. Unlike the authors of these other books, we have not been able to benefit from the work of years of research and practice. Educators are breaking much new ground in making the transition to delivery via the knowledge media.

The first edition of *Delivering Digitally* sold more quickly than either our publishers or we expected and had to be reprinted before a second edition could be produced. A paperback edition of the book was released at the same time.

The first edition has been substantially rewritten for this, the second. There have been many developments in online and multimedia delivery since the first edition was produced. And, many of those developments have implications for education and training managers. Perhaps the most important of these developments has been the marked shift to online delivery. Multimedia is today much more likely to be used in an online than in a stand-alone environment and this trend is certain to continue as the capabilities of the Web are further enhanced.

The book also includes two important additions. The most obvious is a set of case studies that serve to illustrate some of the more important points that we have attempted to make. The second is a section identifying a range of useful online resources. The Web is so dynamic that we have had to restrict these resources to sites that are likely to remain accessible for a considerable time. However, we believe that they will prove useful to those who are just starting to venture into this area.

We are keen to receive feedback from you, our readers, on how adequately we have met your needs and where you would have wished we had said more (or, for that matter, had said less). We welcome any suggestions you might like to make and encourage you to make contact with us if you have specific changes you would like to see incorporated into a future edition.

We would like to thank those colleagues and organizations whose innovative initiatives have provided the basis for the case studies we have included in this edition. We would particularly like to thank Ron Oliver for information supplied in relation to the ANTA Toolbox Project and Tony Bates for the additional information on the UBC-ITESM collaboration.

We would especially like to thank those who have taken time to read and comment on successive drafts of portions of the book: Mike Brooks, Gail Crawford, Paul Fritz, Vincent Harkins, John Kenny, Anne Lennox, Brian Livingston, and Kate Patrick. We have greatly valued their comments, criticisms and suggestions. We want also to express our appreciation to Fred Lockwood for his constant encouragement and valuable advice. We wish to thank the staff of Kogan Page for their forbearance when we have failed to meet our deadlines and for their helpful advice.

Part 1

Context

Chapter 1

The origins of the knowledge media

In this chapter we trace the several pathways of development that have led to the explosion of activity in delivery of courses by means of the knowledge media. We show that contrary to popular perception, the sudden spurt of activity is not the result of some unexpected breakthrough or breakthroughs but the result of a succession of developments dating back over more than three decades.

Revolution or evolution?

Every so often, a breakthrough in technology is achieved that transforms the way in which a particular function is performed. The development of the compact cassette is one such breakthrough. Within a few years of its first appearance, the compact cassette had made reel-to-reel recorders obsolete. In doing so, it set the scene for the emergence of the new lifestyle concept of 'music on the move'.

The CD is another example of a breakthrough technology that, as it happened, emerged from the same industry as the compact cassette. The CD made the vinyl disk obsolete and opened up a new range of storage functions for disk media.

Yet, today in the information industry we are seeing changes that dwarf those brought about in the music industry by the compact cassette or the CD. Whether the magnitude of these changes is measured in terms of their speed or their extent, their impact can only be described as far-reaching. It is now felt in every part of society.

In the popular press, these changes are being attributed to the 'digital revolution'. However, this rather abstract and evocative term is actually a shorthand way of referring to a rapid succession of technological breakthroughs.

The World Wide Web has for the first time provided the general public with a convenient access to the resources of the Internet in a visually appealing format. In doing so, it has begun to change the way in which people search for and access information.

The education and training community has been quick to grasp the significance of the Web's development. Educational innovators have begun to explore the Web's possibilities. However, perhaps the most remarkable development has been the way in which education and training providers have rushed to exploit the potential of the Web for delivery of their courses and programmes. In an industry not noted for its willingness to embrace change, the enthusiasm with which the concept of online learning has been taken up by both teachers and administrators marks this as a watershed period.

Yet, is it accurate to describe what is happening as a 'revolution'? Certainly, the pace at which change is occurring would suggest that it is. Although closer examination of the changes themselves may lead us to a different conclusion.

The shift to digital delivery of education and training programmes has been made possible, more than anything else, by the establishment of the World Wide Web. To anyone who is not familiar with the history of computing and the Internet, it may seem that these developments have come upon us without warning. Yet, if we trace the origins of each of these developments in turn, we soon see that the seeds of this so-called revolution were planted more than three decades ago.

The creation of the World Wide Web

The idea of the World Wide Web was the brainchild of Tim Berners-Lee at CERN, the European Laboratory for Particle Physics. Berners-Lee conceived of the Web as a convenient way of sharing documents over the Internet. The Internet was already well established by this time. However, it was being used as means of interconnecting large computers to carry electronic mail, provide remote access, and transport data files. Berners-Lee's concept transformed the Internet into the transport medium for retrieval of hyperlinked documents.

The initial manifestation of the Web still required a certain amount of technical familiarity with computers and networking. What allowed people without a lot of technical knowledge to gain access to the Web was the release of the first Web browser, Mosaic. Mosaic was developed by Marc Andreeson at the National Supercomputer Laboratory (NCSA) in the United States. It was made available to the public for downloading over the Internet at no charge. The first alpha version of Mosaic – for X Windows, the windowing user interface for Unix – was released in February 1993. In September 1993, working versions of Mosaic were released for Windows and Macintosh. Even though it was slow and had very few of the features we all expect of Web browsers today, it immediately became popular.

The importance of Mosaic was that it gave the general public – even those with little knowledge of computing – the opportunity to glimpse what the World

Wide Web might have to offer. By December 1993, major articles analysing the likely significance of the World Wide Web had appeared in *The New York Times*, *The Guardian*, and *The Economist*.

In March 1994, Andreeson left NCSA to found the Mosaic Communications Corporation, which subsequently became Netscape Corporation. Two months later the first international World Wide Web conference was held at CERN in Geneva.

Laying the foundations for the Web

The creation of the World Wide Web was quite a simple concept. It depended only on the development of a universal set of standards to enable a document created on one machine to be displayed on another and for locating the document in the first place. The standards that were needed were embedded in two new protocols developed specially for the Web: Hypertext Mark-up Language (HTML) and Hypertext Transfer Protocol (HTTP).

HTML defines a set of commands for formatting documents. If the format of a document is specified using HTML commands, then the document can be displayed on different machines using different operating systems and different types of displays, provided that each machine has a suitable browser installed. The browser interprets the commands according to the characteristics of the particular computer and displays the document in the way that best suits the machine.

Definition of the initial set of HTML commands was one of the most critical steps leading to the establishment of the World Wide Web. Yet, creation of such a standard language was not a completely new idea.

HTML is an application of Standard Generalized Mark-up Language (SGML). SGML has been in existence for many years. It is a system for encoding electronic texts so that they can be displayed in any desired format, originally developed to enable text documents to be reproduced on different printers and typesetters. SGML was just starting to be incorporated into word-processing and page layout software just at the time that the idea of the Web started to take hold. SGML was therefore used to create HTML.

The concept of hypertext

Creation of the World Wide Web depended on adoption of the concept of hypertext – a way of structuring text, which permits the text to be expanded not just in one or two dimensions but in many dimensions. In the case of the World Wide Web, the hypertext concept is given expression through the use of links that connect locations in one document with other documents. The document to which a link points may be located on the same computer or on another computer, which may be located just across the corridor or on the other side of the world.

The concept of hypertext is not a new idea either. The term 'hypertext' was coined by Ted Nelson more than three decades ago. Nelson believed that the conventional methods of publishing could not continue to meet the needs of academia. He argued that the pressure on academics to publish was exhausting both the throughput capacity of academic publishers as well as the financial resources of academic and research libraries. He believed that the paper-based method of publishing would eventually be replaced by electronic methods.

Nelson's concept of hypertext was not original. It was based on an earlier idea that had been described by Vannevar Bush, science advisor to President Roosevelt during the Second World War (Bush, 1945). Bush believed that the vast amount of information that had been produced as a result of the research into the war effort should be made available to scientists. He conceived of a device that could make links between related text and illustrations in different research publications. He called this 'memex'.

Nelson established the Xanadu Project to develop his concept of a worldwide hypertext system. Several prototypes of the Xanadu system were produced. For a time, the Xanadu Project was support by Autocad Corporation. When Autocad Corporation decided to divest itself of projects not related to its core business of computer-aided drafting systems, Nelson was invited to move to Japan to continue his research. However, the Xanadu system was never fully commercialized. The development of the World Wide Web therefore constitutes the first fully implemented hypertext system.

The World Wide Web violates a number of the principles that Nelson enunciated for the design of a robust hypertext system. For example, Nelson considered that every document in a hypertext system needed to be individually identified. On the Web, only the locations of documents are individually identified. Nelson also believed that, to ensure reliability, copies of documents needed to be stored in several locations. However, documents on the Web are not required to be duplicated. The effects of these and other differences are now starting to be felt. We shall return in the last chapter of this book to examine the main differences between Nelson's original concept of hypertext and the way hypertext has been implemented on the World Wide Web, and consider the implications that these differences are likely to have for the way the Web evolves.

The expansion of the Internet

The concept of a distributed hypertext database can only be implemented if there is a physical network linking the distributed servers. The physical network that supports the World Wide Web is what we now know as the Internet. The Internet is not an integrated network like the type of local area network an organization might install within a building. It is a myriad of links that, like a spider's web, criss-crosses the world interconnecting sites everywhere. It comprises data connections of all types: wire cables, optical cables, microwave links and even satellite links. It interconnects telecommunication companies, universities, research organizations, government departments, Internet service providers and private individuals.

The origins of the Internet can in fact be traced back as far as 1969, when the Advanced Research Projects Agency (ARPA) of the US Department of Defense set up an ARPANet to connect military, university and defence contractors. Then, with the advent of supercomputers, the US National Science Foundation found that ARPANet was unable to provide the level of service that was then required. It established NSFNet (National Science Foundation Network) in 1986 to provide universities and other research organizations with access to the five supercomputer centres.

Most major developed countries had established the beginnings of their own part of the Internet at least a decade ago too. In Australia, the Australian Academic and Research Network (AARNet) was set up in 1989. In Britain, the Joint Academic Network (JANET) has been providing universities with a similar service for many years.

.In 1987, NSFNet was upgraded in capacity and in 1992 it was upgraded again. In 1995, NSF began moving across to a backbone provided by a commercial network provider.

From this, admittedly brief, historical account it can be seen that the establishment of the World Wide Web represents the convergence of five separate pathways of technological development:

1. origination of the concept of hypertext;
2. establishment of physical transport media – the Internet;
3. adoption of a common standard for communication – HTTP;
4. definition of a common standard for the formatting of Web pages – HTML;
5. development of Web server and Web browser software.

The seeds of these developments were planted more than three decades ago. However, it took the intervening 30 years for these technologies to mature to the stage where the separate pathways of development would start to converge. So, while in the press and in everyday conversation, the World Wide Web and the Internet are often spoken about as if they are one and the same, an understanding of their historical origins makes it clear that they are quite separate entities.

Interactive multimedia

Advances in the area of interactive multimedia have not had the dramatic impact of advances associated with the Web. They could most certainly be more accurately described as 'evolutionary' rather than 'revolutionary'.

The focus of developmental activity in the field of interactive multimedia at present is on delivery of interactive multimedia over the Internet. Indeed, the term 'interactive multimedia' is now often combined with the term 'hypermedia' to signify the merging of interactive multimedia and Web presentation. Producers of interactive multimedia products want to be able to deliver their products via the Web, and developers of tools for interactive multimedia development want to be able to deliver software products that will more easily enable multimedia producers to do this.

However, this has been a relatively recent development, reflective of the Web's growing importance to education, entertainment, and business. Both because the development has been so recent, and because the speed of the Internet is still a limiting factor, Web-based interactive multimedia has not yet displaced the more established modes of interactive multimedia presentation using physical media.

Interactive multimedia is generally understood to be a form of multimedia in which the presentation is carried in digital form and interaction between the viewer and the presentation is supported. The development of interactive multimedia technology was seen as particularly significant for education because it provided the means for learners to participate actively.

Development of the field of interactive multimedia followed closely on the heels of the development of the CD ROM. It has always been possible to move data to the display of a desktop computer more quickly from a local drive than from a file server or a mainframe computer. It has therefore always been possible to do more with data held on storage media attached directly to a workstation than it has with data retrieved remotely across a network. However, the potential of the desktop computer was for a long while limited by the amount of data that it was possible to store on portable storage media. The capacity of floppy disks was quite limited and early hard disk cartridges were not standard media and were relatively unreliable.

With the advent of optical disk technology that situation changed. At the time that the CD ROM first became available, not only did its capacity exceed that of 200 standard floppy disks, but its capacity also exceeded that of a standard hard drive. The greatest disadvantage of the first CD ROMs was that they were not re-recordable. The rate at which CD ROM drives could transfer data was also considerably less than the rate at which hard drives were able to transfer data.

Optical disk technology

In the home entertainment market, DVD players are currently replacing VCRs as the preferred technology for watching movies at home.

When the first edition of *Delivering Digitally* was published, no DVD player had yet appeared in Australia. There are now more than a dozen different models and the price of a typical DVD player has fallen from Aus$1,000 to Aus$400. This is the pattern that is generally seen when a new consumer electronic technology initially appears on the market. Manufacturers of both the consumer product and the component technology try to recoup their development costs over the first two years while competition is not intense. Later, when the research and development costs have been stripped out of the cost equation the price falls to about a third of what it was initially.

DVD is the latest manifestation of optical disk technology. Here are some advantages of the DVD disk:

- It is read by a higher frequency laser than is used to read a CD ROM with the result that it is possible for data to be packed more densely.
- It can store data on both sides.
- Each side of the disk can have two recording layers.

Together, these differences give DVD disks a maximum capacity of 17 gigabytes compared to 0.6 gigabytes for a CD ROM. It is this additional data capacity, together with technology for compressing and decompressing digital video data that has enabled DVD drives to replace VCRs in the area of home entertainment.

The arrival of DVD players on the market is the harbinger of an even more significant development. In the first edition of *Delivering Digitally* we also predicted that DVD drives would replace CD ROM drives in desktop computers and that that would bring about a further convergence of computer and video technologies. Our prediction is now being fulfilled. Apple has introduced recording DVD drives into its high-end Macintosh desktop computers and Powerbook laptop computers. It can be expected that as the cost of DVD drive mechanisms falls, Apple will change over to DVD drives right across its product range. Apple has been a leader in this area because of its stake in the multimedia industry. However, the same trend can be seen right across the personal computer field.

The physical medium of the CD ROM is the same as that used to produce CDs. However, the format in which information is recorded on that medium is different. The fact that CD ROMs and audio CDs share the same physical medium has been critical to the success of CD ROM technology because it enabled CD ROMs to be reproduced on the same presses that are used to manufacture audio CDs. This led to the cost of CDs falling at a much faster rate than would have been the case had optical disks been used for storage of computer data alone.

The physical medium of the CD ROM has also been used as a video recording and playback medium. Video compact disc (VCD) technology combines the optical disk technology with MPEG video compression technology to provide over an hour of video on a standard disk. While the VCD format is popular in Asia it is less well known elsewhere in the world. Yet it is an excellent example of a transitional technology, bridging the gap between DVD and CD generations of optical disk technologies. VCD disks can be replayed on DVD players, computers equipped with CD ROM drives and special-purpose VCD players.

The laser technology used to read optical disks dates back to an earlier development – the laser videodisk player. Laser videodisk technology, developed by Phillips and Sony, was targeted at the home entertainment market. The product was intended to allow high quality reproduction of movies in the home. However, the videodisk never caught on in the home entertainment market. It faced too much competition from the videotape recorder, which offered the advantage of being able to record as well as replay.

An industrial version of the videodisk player produced by Pioneer, which could be interfaced to a computer, did achieve some success. It was seen as offering the first practical means of incorporating video segments into computer-assisted instruction. While this hybrid technology was somewhat clumsy to use, it was nevertheless taken up by many education and training providers for the development of interactive multimedia programmes.

Authoring systems for interactive multimedia

The widespread interest that has developed in interactive multimedia is due in part to the development of authoring software that allows courseware developers who have no expertise in high-level programming languages such as Pascal or C to produce polished interactive multimedia products.

Most interactive multimedia courseware being produced today is developed using courseware authoring software. Courseware authoring systems have taken a number of different approaches to the structuring of presentations. Macromedia Director presents courseware as the interactive multimedia equivalent of a video production. Some may not classify Macromedia Director as a true courseware authoring system because it does not provide support for the full range of course authoring functions. Nevertheless, Director is used widely in education and training for courseware production. Authorware takes the different approach of structuring courseware as a series of instructional events. This way of looking at courseware development is derived from instructional systems design. However, amongst the most popular of the authoring systems are those that are based on the metaphor of a set of cards or the pages of a book.

The first authoring system of this type to appear was Apple's Hypercard. This was joined not long afterwards by Supercard, a clone of Hypercard that added the ability to handle colour as well as a range of other features. Asymetrix adapted the concept that had been applied in Hypercard to Windows with Toolbook, replacing the card metaphor with the metaphor of a book. Later still, Metacard was developed as a cross-platform authoring system. Apple ceased development of Hypercard some time ago. However, Supercard and Metacard are both still actively being developed.

In tracing the development of courseware authoring systems, one finds that the labour cost of developing interactive multimedia courseware has not fallen at the same rate as the hardware cost of computer technology. Consequently, educators and trainers have not been able to enjoy the full benefits of the improvements in technology.

Computer-assisted instruction

The idea of using computers in place of teachers to deliver instruction originated from the pre-war development of teaching machines, mechanical devices that presented the learner with 'frames' of information and required the student to respond to multiple-choice items by pressing buttons corresponding to their choices. The design of teaching machines was based on the behaviourist theories then in vogue in educational psychology that emphasized the importance of practice and feedback. While teaching machines were able to provide basic support for practice and reinforcement they essentially supported a linear model. It was recognized that because they had the potential to retrieve information at random, computers had the potential to deliver instruction much more effectively.

However, in the early days of computing, the cost of computers was high and the capabilities of computers were quite limited. Just about the only places where computers were used in education or training were in the military or in the well-endowed universities that were doing research on computer technology.

The PLATO Project at the University of Illinois at Urbana was one of the best known early examples of the use of computers in instruction. The success of the PLATO Project was largely due to its highly innovative use of technology. At a time when character-based screen display units were just beginning to become commonplace, the PLATO Project used purpose-built graphics display terminals incorporating touchscreen technology. The PLATO Project employed a team of dedicated programmers to develop the software upon which operation of the system depended. This project represented a scale of investment that was beyond the reach of most universities. Many universities and schools were nevertheless able to make use of the PLATO system by dialling into it or accessing it via dedicated connections. The PLATO system was eventually commercialized and when personal computers became widely available, a PC version, lacking the touch screen capability, was developed.

PLATO was a particularly ambitious attempt to substitute teachers with computers. However, during the 1960s and 1970s many other systems were developed.

Computer-managed learning

By the late 1970s, a number of educators were beginning to argue that while the cost of computers still kept computer-assisted instruction (CAI) out of the reach of most teachers, most of the benefits that computers promised could still be obtained if their use was limited to those functions that they performed best. Computers were already being widely used to maintain students' enrolment records and to record their results. However, computers could also be used cost-effectively to administer tests and to track their progress and manage their learning, as in computer-managed learning (CML).

CAI and CML therefore represented two distinctly different approaches to the use of computers in supporting teaching and learning.

Computer-mediated communication

'Computer-mediated communication' is a collective term that refers to all forms of two-way interaction via computers. It includes:

- electronic mail (e-mail);
- asynchronous conferencing;
- synchronous conferencing;
- desktop audio conferencing;
- desktop video conferencing;
- audio-graphic computer conferencing;
- networked virtual environments.

The creation of the World Wide Web has focused attention on the Internet's potential for supporting person-to-person interaction. The greater connectivity of telecommunications networks has led to an expectation amongst teachers and trainers that what they have been doing in the classroom they can now do at a distance and that this ability to extend the classroom across the country and across the world has, all of a sudden, made teaching at a distance more practicable. Yet, computer-mediated communication was used widely in distance education long before the World Wide Web was conceived and in some ways the development of the Web has been an (albeit temporary) backward step.

The first examples of the use of e-mail in education and training employed the MAIL facility that forms part of the Unix operating system. MAIL was intended to allow computer programmers working on the same computer in the days of mainframe computers to communicate with each other. However, with additional software, the capabilities of Unix MAIL were extended to allow mail to be delivered to other mainframe computers also using Unix MAIL, employing a store-and-forward method that worked like a 'bucket brigade'. Mail was passed from machine to machine along the most suitable route until it reached its destination.

When telecommunications authorities began developing commercial e-mail services, gateways were established between these commercial services and the network based on Unix MAIL. Later still, as the Internet expanded, standards were developed for communication between dedicated mail servers.

As most users of e-mail are only too aware, problems still arise in the passing of mail between different types of mail systems, particularly in cases where mail messages have other items such as text documents or images or spreadsheet files attached. However, the reliability of mail systems continues to improve and the capabilities of mail systems are also being increased.

The main direction in which e-mail is now evolving is towards integration with other functions. E-mail capability is now a standard feature of Web browsers. For business users, e-mail is being combined with scheduling software in groupware systems such as Lotus Notes or Novell Groupwise.

Asynchronous conferencing is conferencing that does not require participants to be involved at the same time. An asynchronous conference can be set up using e-mail by having participants create a mail list in their own mail client of all other participants. However, a range of specialized systems for supporting asynchronous conferencing is now available and these offer many features that make conferencing more convenient.

The first example of the use of computers for conferencing was a simple tool built into the PLATO computer-assisted instruction system. The tool became known as PLATO Notes. Software developers who worked on PLATO Notes subsequently adapted the concept to the business communication environment by developing Lotus Notes.

Lotus Notes became a leading example of groupware. However, Lotus Notes is a business application. It lacks many of the features required for educational use. Recognizing the potential size of the education market, Lotus Corporation adapted Lotus Notes for education as Learning Space.

In 1976, Murray Turoff established the Electronic Information Exchange System (EIES) at the New Jersey Institute of Technology. EIES was initially set up to allow classroom discussion to continue throughout the semester. However, it subsequently gave rise to an online educational delivery system called the Virtual Classroom. This still operates today.

PLATO also gave birth to the first synchronous conferencing system. The most widely used example of synchronous conferencing is Internet Relay Chat (IRC).

Another group of synchronous computer-mediated communication systems are the networked virtual environments (NVEs). These offer a more sophisticated form of computer-mediated communication than either IRC or chat systems. NVEs attempt to create Internet-based virtual reality environments.

The development of integrated electronic learning environments

One of the most important recent developments in the shift to online delivery has been the creation of a new type of system for mediation of learning. These are systems that combine the range of functions needed to offer students a complete range of learning experiences as well as to provide the administrative support needed to ensure students' progress through a course. These systems include such products as Blackboard, FirstClass Collaborative Classroom Gold, LearningSpace, The Learning Manager and WebCT. There is, as yet, no widely accepted term for referring to these systems. We use the term 'integrated electronic learning environments' throughout this book.

While, as software products, the emergence of these systems has been a recent development, in concept they simply represent an integration of functions that previously have been performed by separate products. The creation of the World Wide Web has contributed to this process of integration. Some of the products, such as FirstClass Collaborative Classroom Gold and The Learning Manager, represent the latest incarnations of systems that started life as products offering much more limited functionality long before the Web came into existence.

The convergence of technologies

The World Wide Web, interactive multimedia and computer-mediated communications represent the three main streams of development in instructional technology. However, to continue to speak of these as if they represent completely separate technologies is to maintain distinctions that are becoming increasingly false. For as the technologies represented by these three streams of development have evolved, they have also converged.

Migration of computer conferencing to the Web has only been achieved with considerable compromise. The original concept of the Web was of a network of document servers. A Web browser requests transmission of a resource, no further connection is maintained between the browser and the server.

For many years, computer conferencing technology was based on a client-server model in which a purpose-designer conferencing server communicated with conferencing client software designed to interoperate with the server. This is similar to the design of e-mail systems. The central server collects, sorts, stores and distributes messages. The client lets participants compose and upload messages to the server, or view and print messages that have been posted.

However, the focus of development of conferencing systems has shifted to the Web. Existing conferencing systems have been migrated to the Web and new conferencing systems are being designed to operate within Web browsers.

The way in which Web-based conferencing systems achieve interactivity is by using the same protocol that is used to handle the submission of forms. The result is that Web-based conferencing systems are much less responsive than earlier dedicated conferencing systems.

The trend towards technological convergence is also apparent in the area of courseware authoring. Word-processing and desktop publishing applications such as Microsoft Word and Adobe Pagemaker now offer the option of translating print documents to HTML. Similarly, multimedia authoring packages such as Asymetrix Toolbook and Macromedia Director offer the option of producing multimedia segments that can be delivered via the Web.

Today, many types of high capacity storage media are available for distribution of computer data. Recordable media include disk cartridges, ZIP disks, JAZ cartridges, write-only CD ROMs, magneto-optical disks and now DVD ROMs. Any of these media may be used for distribution of courseware.

Whether local or online delivery is more appropriate in a given situation depends on a number of factors: for example, the speed and reliability of the communication links between the distribution point and the student; the prevailing telecommunication costs compared with postal costs and the amount and type of interactivity that has been designed in the courseware.

However, the choice is not necessarily between one and the other. Courseware developers are increasingly recognizing that the best results are often achieved by combining local and online resources.

Distance educators, having started out with the concept of combining several media in a single package, are moving to the point of combining several functions in a single medium. Multimedia is becoming 'unimedia'.

Summing up

The remarkable interest being shown in the potential of the knowledge media for use in the delivery of education and training cannot be explained in terms of a single key technological breakthrough. Rather it is explained in terms of a series of developments that can be traced back over more than three decades. The most important of these developments have been:

● invention of the concept of hyptertext;
● building the physical network connections that have given rise to the worldwide Internet;
● international adoption of standards for formatting and distribution of documents on the Web;
● development of more versatile software tools for courseware authoring;
● development of systems for supporting the range of teaching and learning activities of which a complete educational programme is comprised;
● improvements to microprocessor, computer memory and disk storage technologies that have increased the sophistication of the tasks that can be performed by computers.

It is the cumulative effect of all of these developments, rather than a single major breakthrough that has given rise to the situation we see today.

Chapter 2

Forces driving educational change

In this chapter we examine the educational and social context in which the shift to knowledge media is taking place. We identify a variety of views about the distinguishing features of the current era and suggest some implications that acceptance of these may have for educational institutions. We analyse the emerging expectation that digital media will enhance learning and accommodate the preferences and needs of the new clientele of post-school education and training. We conclude by identifying some educational policy implications with a focus on the use of knowledge media.

What is new in the world?

Post-secondary education operates in an era that has been characterized as a period of change to the point of disjunction with the structures and predictability of the 'modern', post-Enlightenment period of Western history. Features of the current period include:

- dynamic and continuous change and transformation;
- the failure of grand theories such as Marxism to locate and predict directions of change;
- the discontinuist and erratic rather than evolutionary nature of social change;
- the juxtaposition of various images of social, economic and political life and the transformation of images like Disneyworld, TV sports and Web pages into the realities with which we deal.

There is the rise of new social movements that have given a voice to those who were previously marginalized. There is the emergence of multiple new discourses, some arising directly from developments in information and communication technologies, with terms such as 'synchronous and asynchronous communication', 'cyber cafés', 'netiquette', 'user groups', etc. As a consequence, the era can be seen as one in which people and institutions search for a new identity.

Is the current era different?

You will have heard it said many times that: 'This is the age of change. Nothing remains constant but change itself.' Yet is the type of change we are seeing today fundamentally different from that which has gone before?

Radical change has surely been with us and with our forebears ever since the Enlightenment. The agrarian and industrial revolutions brought about upheaval in the day-to-day social life, in economic life and in politics of the time. Now, as we move into a new millennium, can we say that the types of change we are experiencing are any more radical than those which were experienced when steam, electricity and petroleum replaced manual and animal power at the beginning of the twentieth century? Is it more radical than moving from local self-sufficiency to national and international specialization?

Some would claim that we are experiencing a qualitatively different change – significantly different in pace. The current era is a period marked by restructuring and transitions. It is an era in which social institutions are undergoing dynamic transformation. Education and training providers are amongst those institutions being most affected by change.

Many labels have been given to the period. It has been called 'post-modern', 'post-Fordist', 'post-structural', 'post-capitalist', 'disorganized capitalist', 'post-industrial' and 'post-traditional'. Each of these labels carries the suggestion that the current era does indeed depart from the preceding era. As Anthony Giddens (1991) has put it: 'Modern institutions differ from all preceding forms of social order in respect of their dynamism, the degree to which they undercut traditional habits and custom, and their global impact.'

A period of transition

However, for some social commentators not all is adrift. Patterns and directions are emerging. The major features of the period are globalization and the breaking down of political boundaries as the borders for personal, corporate and institutional transactions. In the process of globalization, Western culture, particularly the market economy and Western science, have been penetrating all societies (Giddens, 1991; Drucker, 1993; Wagner, 1994) and all social systems including higher education. Giddens has labelled the current era a period of high modernity, indicating a continuing if tenuous attachment to the modern era rather than the arrival of post-modernity.

Peter Drucker, the well-known analyst of business and social change, also does not see the quest of the West as being lost. Rather, what he sees is that some of the cherished forms are undergoing change. Drucker (1993: 195) talks about the 'post-capitalist' society. He sees this as being a society centred on knowledge. He argues that in future all work and all social interaction will have a cerebral dimension.

One consequence of this change will be the demise of the working class. Post-capitalist society will require leadership by educated people who have access to the great heritage of the past and who have acquired a range of 'knowledges' that allows them to live in an increasingly globalized and yet tribalized world.

Does it matter how we see the social context?

What is at issue is the way the world is perceived. Some people may perceive it as a modern, enlightened (in the sense of the Enlightenment) world, susceptible to reason, to the determination of cause and effect and to predictability of outcomes. On the other hand, other people may perceive it as being only known through variable and personal interpretation in which image conflates with reality, boundaries cannot be maintained or even defined and discontinuity marks patterns and flows.

How we view the social environment makes a difference to our understanding of institutions, the way in which they function and their susceptibility to planned change. If one holds a modern view of social institutions, it makes sense to study organizational psychology and to engage in scientific management. If one holds a post-modern view, one is not able to define scientific principles of organizational behaviour. To effect change one would have to grasp the changing meanings, understanding and motivations of all those who constitute particular organizations.

The view we take in this book may lie somewhere between the modern and post-modern. We start from the premise that social institutions are not entities with a life of their own. They are not entities whose functions may be explained and controlled in terms of simple causes and effects. Rather, organizations are concepts. They are constituted in the minds of people. They are therefore subject to different and variable interpretations and impressions and differing intensities of interest. At the same time we recognize that there is a good deal of commonality in the understanding we each have of social institutions, their physical environment, and of the way in which they operate. Our sharing of meanings allows us to proceed as though cause and effect are understandable and predictable.

The social analysis offered here suggests that we should not be surprised in the current era to find ourselves pulled in contrary directions. However, it suggests on the other hand, that it is valuable to work with common understanding, for instance, understandings of best practice in a field. It also suggests that it is not appropriate to simply abandon the old in favour of the new. A vision of worthwhile outcomes for education and careful consideration of the advantages and disadvantages of the various modes of attaining the outcomes provide a way to proceed. However, best intentions and best practice are subject to the whims, understandings and actions of all players and the actual outcomes of our endeavours may surprise us. There is no one best solution that will fit all circumstances and be able to stand for all time. Rather there are some useful frames of reference for making judgements and informing actions.

Technology and the current era

Technology, particularly information technology, is the key component of the change that characterizes the period. Globalization demands the breaching of time and space limitations and draws upon information technology. At the same time, technological development drives globalization. In arguments about whether we are in a period of late modernity or whether we have entered a post-modern period, information technology contributes to both sides.

On the one hand, information technology is creating a break with the modern era. It is upsetting the types of relationships that previously existed in time and space. It is breaking down borders. It is increasing the frequency of faceless encounters. Yet information technology relies on science from the modern era for its development. It is in turn a vehicle for the dissemination of scientific knowledge. The pursuit of order and of 'scientific' explanations still continues. The mission of modernity is therefore not yet dead.

Educational institutions in the current era

In educational institutions, as in other institutions in society, traditional purposes and modes of operation are being challenged and changed. In the process of this change, the people who define and constitute institutions are caught up in a transition between eras that can lead to widespread confusion, alienation, anger and, in some cases, apathy. It can also have the effect of excitement and challenge, sparking creativity and the development of innovative approaches and strategies. Both of these responses apply to the last decade of the twentieth century. In this context, it is not surprising that education, along with all other sectors of society, is undergoing major transformation, rationalization, restructure and redefinition. In a transition period such as this, social processes such as education are dynamic, disjointed and discontinuous in their development.

The changing character of post-secondary education

In higher education, institutions currently styled as universities share a common origin. They are based on models as diverse as Oxford and Cambridge universities, the Scottish universities, the German universities, technical colleges, schools of mines, working men's colleges and other quite plebeian institutions. They may soon be headed in different directions again in response to changing circumstances, including changing teaching and learning technologies.

> The traditional view that higher education services are best provided on a campus, to a student body resident nearby, via a narrow set of delivery methodologies. . . will come under increasing scrutiny. . . as the new technologies continue to expand the possibilities for location-independent interactions between teachers, between teachers and students, between students, and between students and the providers of academic support services.
>
> (*Higher Education Review*, 1997: 9)

The idea of the university has changed over time. Cardinal Newman, writing from the Oxford perspective, saw the university of the 1840s as the vehicle for the conservation of knowledge and its transmission to an elite. Research was a matter for some other institution (Newman, reprint 1947).

Abraham Flexner, writing in the 1930s about American, English and German universities, saw the role of the universities as advancing knowledge and studying problems as well as engaging in 'training' at the highest level. (Flexner, reprint 1968).

Clark Kerr, reflecting in the 1960s on the writing of Flexner, saw the university as a pluralistic organization: 'Flexner did not realize how many functions can be combined into a single university – even apparently inconsistent functions' (foreword by Kerr in Flexner, 1968: xviii).

From the nineteenth century, as Glenys Patterson pointed out, universities faced pressure for 'increasing democratization of access [and] pressures to be more responsive to the requirement of the industrial age' (Patterson, 1989: 5). Flexner had denied a place for practical training, admitting only the learned professions of medicine and law and denying 'the make believe professions' (Flexner, 1968: 45). How far we have shifted! Universities now are expected to demonstrate a strong commitment to 'enabling our graduates to play a productive, wealth creating role in modern, outwardly oriented economy' (*Higher Education Review*, 1997: 3). It is hard to justify activities that do not satisfy a practical economic end. They have moved from being elite to becoming popular institutions. They will move further to serving the needs of a mass market.

Kerr observed that Flexner did not appreciate the populist drive for education nor 'the desire of a technological society for knowledge'(Flexner, 1968: xix). Now the desire of a technological society for knowledge is translating into an arrangement for technologically acquired knowledge. This is the new imperative:

> . . . our eyes are being opened to extraordinary possibilities in the provision of education through ever expanding technological advance. . . New learning

technologies must be eagerly embraced to cater for a far more diverse – and more discriminating – student body.

(*Higher Education Review*, 1997: vii)

Kathy Tiano has described the changes taking place in higher education as a 'paradigm shift', contrasting the features characterizing the new paradigm with those characterizing the old (see Table 2.1).

Table 2.1   *Old and new paradigms of higher education, Kathy Tiano (cited in AVCC 1996:9)*

Old Paradigm for Higher Education	New Paradigm for Higher Education
Take what you can get	Courses on demand
Academic calendar	Year-round operations
University as a city	University as idea
Terminal degree	Lifelong learning
University as ivory tower	University as partner in society
Student = 18- to 25-year-old	Cradle to grave
Books are primary medium	Information on demand
Tenure	Market value
Single product	Information reuse/info exhaust
Student as a 'pain'	Student as a customer
Delivery in classroom	Delivery anywhere
Multi-cultural	Global
Bricks & mortar	Bits & bytes
Single discipline	Multi-discipline
Institution-centric	Market-centric
Government funded	Market funded
Technology as an expense	Technology as differentiator

Collaboration, internationalization and globalization

In the context of the breaking down of national boundaries, universities and other educational providers are responding by:

- creating competitive units;
- designing and developing programmes that can be offered beyond national boundaries;
- operating off-shore.

Forming bigger units within national boundaries that can better meet infrastructure, design and development costs and take advantage of economies of scale, can allow institutions to better compete with other providers, be they national or international. A number of possibilities present themselves including the merger of like entities such as universities, the merger of complementary entities such as universities and other post-secondary education providers, and working in collaboration with other providers or agencies on particular projects. Prospective partners for collaboration include not only other education and training providers but groups of knowledge experts such as professional societies and communications experts such as Internet service providers and publishers.

Designing and developing programmes that can be offered beyond national boundaries is a process sometimes referred to as internationalization. It involves the development of tuition materials and forms of communication that are relatively culturally neutral or have a wide cultural applicability. With careful design, the processes of internationalizing curricula can be combined with enhancing the educational value of materials by calling upon learners to contribute instances relevant to their own contexts and experiences. Internationalized materials can be used locally with international students, deployed internationally by distance modes, and/or offered on remote campuses.

The process of extending the reach of the provider beyond national boundaries is referred to as globalization, turning institutions into global rather than national entities. Globalization is often achieved by the establishment of campuses or branch offices in various locations around the world or by entering into consortia with providers in various countries. Case Study 1 outlines one approach to developing a consortium of providers. Competing consortia have also been established.

Increasing flexibility in education and training

The new paradigm suggests that educational institutions need to be more responsive and flexible in their dealings with their environment and their clients. It suggests the use of new technologies in the process.

In the new world of education and training there has developed a conventional wisdom about the capacity of the digital media to enhance learning or to accommodate learner convenience and preferences. Digital courseware, by which we mean tuition materials developed for delivery by digital media such as CD ROM, DVD or the Internet, in conjunction with digital communication media such as e-mail, chat facilities and computer conferencing, has the potential to offer increased flexibility with respect to:

- place;
- time;
- pace;
- entry;
- exit.

Case study 1: Universitas 21

The initiative

Universitas 21 is an international consortium of 18 universities spanning 10 countries. The consortium is incorporated as a company registered in the United Kingdom. Members of Universitas 21 are institutions of high repute. Inaugural members were: Albert-Ludwigs University Freiburg; Fudan University; Lund University; McGill University; National University of Singapore; University of Auckland; University of Birmingham; University of British Columbia; University of Edinburgh; University of Glasgow; University of Hong Kong; University of Melbourne; University of Michigan; University of New South Wales; University of Nottingham; University of Peking; University of Queensland and University of Toronto.

Features

- a means for the member universities to offer programmes and engage in other academic activities beyond the individual capacity of any one of the members;
- a means for universities to market courses internationally through the consortium;
- a means for member universities to market higher education products and services through third parties in partnership with the consortium.

Stakeholders

The member universities and associated corporations.

The initiative at work

Universitas 21 is one of a number of consortia of universities planning to offer programmes online internationally. Another is the Cardean University, developed through the Illinois company, Unext.com, and incorporating business programmes of Columbia University, the University of Chicago, Stanford University and the London School of Economics, among others. The Global University Alliance being formed by NextEd based in Hong Kong is yet another.

These enterprises are backed by the repute of their members but at the same time insulate the member universities from business difficulties and the possibility of devaluing their reputations by distancing themselves from the expected inflation in enrolments.

The early drive for the establishment of Universitas 21 came from Professor Alan Gilbert, Vice-Chancellor of the University of Melbourne, who became the initial chair of the corporation. Universitas 21 was established to develop international curricula with credentials that are internationally recognized and portable. To help facilitate the process the company initiated a 'Teaching and Learning Technologies' project to assist member universities to exploit new teaching and learning technologies and to co-operate in providing mutual access to multimedia courseware.

The consortia allow member universities to compete in an environment in which publishing interests such as Pearson, the large British media group, indicate that they will enter the higher education market through online provision, not necessarily in partnership with universities. Universitas 21 envisaged providing partnership opportunities for major new providers, including corporate universities wishing to access the fast-growing inter-national market for higher education. Its experience provides an interesting instance of the interest of major new players in entering the field of provision of university programmes using the new knowledge media. Within its first year, proposals to work in partnership with Universitas 21 were received from News International and Thomson Learning.

Rupert Murdoch's News International company proposed to set up a joint-venture company with Universitas 21 through News International's London-based subsidiary, TSL Education Ltd. News International apparently saw the Internet as the prominent medium for information and communi-cation and education as an important component. However News Inter-national did not pursue direct involvement in the venture and one could speculate on whether this reflected second thoughts on the market value of packaged knowledge online even where it originates from reputable sources.

On the other hand Thomson Learning has entered an arrangement with the consortium under which it develops international higher education and advanced training courses, and provides delivery platforms and an inter-national assurance structure, while Universitas 21 awards degrees, diplomas or certificates to students. This initiative indicates a new and optimistic view of the commercial value of products that can be delivered by the knowledge media. The universities involved can be viewed as providing a reputable product to the publisher along with a system of rewards for students, the clients of the publishers, in return for the students' investment of time and money. Universitas 21 sees itself as bringing international recognition and legitimacy to such partnerships.

Further information

<http://www.universitas.edu.au/>

Place

Web-delivered courseware, audio, video and asynchronous and synchronous computer conferences, CD ROMs and DVDs may be accessed in libraries, in laboratories, in the workplace, in the home – anywhere where the appropriate information and communication technologies are available.

Time

Digital storage media such as hard disks and floppy disks, CD ROMs, DVDs, Web sites and e-mail may be accessed at a time convenient to the learner. Time flexibility is limited by the desirability of synchronous communication. Optimizing time flexibility is a matter of considering what can be dealt with through one-way communication, what can be dealt with through asynchronous communication and what needs to be dealt with synchronously. One-way presentation or stand-alone materials maximize time flexibility. Asynchronous communication gives greater flexibility than synchronous. Of course, there are considerations other than time flexibility in deciding upon the form of communication to be employed. However, if time flexibility is important then we might adopt as our default position stand-alone materials or asynchronous modes of communication.

Pace

Learning programmes utilizing electronic storage systems, like print-based materials before them, allow learners to proceed at their own pace. There may be reason to limit this flexibility, for example to accommodate time-constrained elements of the learning programme such as group activities, or for occupational requirements. Sometimes having a limited period of time to respond is seen as important to meeting assessment requirements or as important to simulating real world conditions. Nevertheless the use of digital media will usually allow the user greater freedom in pace than class attendance modes of study.

Entry

If education and training programmes are designed so that they incorporate pre-tests and offer alternative entry points and different paths through programmes based upon them, learners can obtain credit for prior learning.

Exit

If programmes are designed so that a topic or a sequence of topics can be pursued to different depths or levels of proficiency, learners can exit when their needs have been met and can receive credit for the segments they have completed.

Changing delivery modes contributing to flexibility

In a modified Delphi study of experts in information technology (Hesketh *et al* (1996)), forces for change in education at the turn of the century were identified as:

● student need for flexible delivery to fit in with lifestyles;
● competition amongst universities in attracting undergraduate, postgraduate, and continuing professional education students;
● perception that other competing universities have a technological edge;
● opportunities to export education more readily to overseas countries;
● expectations from the business sector and professional bodies that students will be literate in the use of technology;
● possibility that the Federal Government will provide incentives for computer-mediated communication in teaching;
● students' level of expectation that computer-mediated communication will be used in teaching;
● the threat to Australian universities from the marketing by overseas universities in Australia;
● the potential for computer-mediated communication to provide more equitable access to education for some disadvantaged groups;
● the possibility that industry and professional bodies will provide accredited degrees if universities do not meet their needs.

In the same study the investigators asked which technologies were most likely to be adopted pertinent to the forces for change. Respondents replied:

● Students will have the facility to log on remotely and conduct online searches of libraries and other research databases.
● E-mail will serve as a communications medium between staff and students.
● Courses will be delivered using traditional methods.
● Students will have online access to course materials – lecture notes, overheads, computer-based learning materials.
● Traditional lectures will incorporate widespread use of computer-mediated presentation techniques.
● Electronic communication will be used to facilitate collaborative group work.

The striking feature of this list is that the predictions it offered have materialized. In a field noted for hyperbole, it is, to say the least, surprising to find that the champions of the digital delivery media saw a future that was not greatly different from what we all expect anyway.

The key issues facing post-secondary education

A number of national and international reports have flagged the major issues facing post-secondary education in the USA, Europe and Australia in the current era (National Information Infrastructure Taskforce, 1994; National Board of Employment, Education and Training, 1996; OECD, 1996). The three key issues that keep reappearing are:

1. the cost-effectiveness of different modes of delivery;
2. the quality of education and training available;
3. access and equity.

The demand for education and training is expected to increase beyond the capacity to provide for it by traditional means. Even if it were desirable to respond to increased demand through the construction of traditional institutions it would be neither practical nor economic to do so.

The demand stems in part from the knowledge explosion. The more the use of technology is expanded to provide access to knowledge the more rapid and far reaching the knowledge explosion. There is an associated need for global information infrastructure standards and conventions and possibly a need for national or global assessment via networked services.

New forms of access are required to provide time and place flexibility, especially for adults as they try to adjust to changes in work and social life. As these are adopted some traditional distinctions in forms of provision of education and training are breaking down. The distinction between distance and on-campus modes of delivery is blurring. These modes themselves are being redefined to allow flexible responses to education and training demands. The distinction between public and private providers will blur or be redefined with the privatization or quasi-privatization of public institutions, and the growth of substantial enterprise-based providers. As public institutions embrace new modes of delivery, including online delivery and workplace-based delivery, the roles they are performing are changing. Some are moving towards becoming service brokers or accrediting agencies rather than providers.

Approaches need to be found to transform individual and small-scale initiatives involving the new learning technologies into institutional and systemic change. There has often been a failure to move innovations from the innovators and early adopters of innovation to institution or system-wide application. On the other hand, the desirability of applying technological educational innovations more widely cannot be taken for granted. Many innovations are not systematically evaluated. Evaluations are most often conducted and reported by people with a vested interest in the innovation. The quality of some evaluations that have taken place is dubious. Most investigations of new learning technologies indicate no significant difference in learning outcomes where new technologies are employed.

The implications of trends for policy-making

The study from which the idea for this book originally arose attempted to derive a set of policy implications for educational decision-makers from current social and educational trends. Descriptors of the current social and educational context and descriptors of best practice in technology-mediated resource-based learning were located in the print literature and from sources published on the Web. These descriptors were validated by submitting them to a panel of approximately 30 experts in technology-mediated resource-based learning. A set of policy implications were then derived from the descriptors and validation of the descriptors was sought from the same group of experts. Tables 2.2, 2.3, 2.4 and 2.5 show the descriptors and policy implications that were arrived at through this process.

Table 2.2   *Premises and policy implications relating to the current context*

Premises	Policy Implications
Economic and social change is generating new demands for lifelong learning that will not be satisfied in terms of quantity, quality or convenience by traditional attendance programmes.	Adopting new approaches to the provision of education and training, including the utilization of new learning technologies, is not an option – it is an imperative.
Public educational providers are becoming market-driven. There is no longer a monopoly on education provision. End-users of post-secondary education and training are demanding services more responsive to their requirements.	Education providers in the public sector, like those in the private sector must be concerned with competition, costs and productivity.
The demand for electronically delivered education and training will grow exponentially over the next decade as technological and market developments alter workforce requirements with increasing rapidity.	The pace of developments in the use of educational technologies is such that universities and colleges risk losing relevance if they wait for the results of longitudinal research before making an investment in electronically mediated learning; rather they need to rely upon understandings of best practice.
The distinction between on-campus and off-campus programmes continues but is diminishing. Off-campus programmes employ, as they have done for some time, face-to-face tutorials and laboratory work, and residential sessions. Now programmes for attending students increasingly employ	Institutional organization, policies and procedures need to adapt to the learner as client who will sometimes wish to learn on-campus, sometimes wish to learn in the workplace and sometimes wish to learn free of a pre-specified location. The learner may wish to use educational resources of

Table 2.2 *(Contd)*

Premises	Policy Implications
strategies with time and place flexibility such as syndicate work, use of distance education materials for attending students, use of television and video materials and of computer-mediated instruction programmes. They also use the World Wide Web, e-mail and groupware. Workplace-based education and training provides a new definition of campus.	the provider without having to attend timetabled classes. This has implications for student administration as well as for the provisions for learning. It may suggest new approaches to organization.
The availability and use of new technologies for the provision of education and the extent of change in educational processes can be overstated. The US National Information Infra-structure Task Force (1994) found that the way Americans teach, learn, transmit and access information remains largely unchanged from a century ago. Face-to-face classes, many of them large lectures, remain the mainstream form of tuition.	While contextual factors suggest an imperative for rapid and substantial change, institutions need to be wary of adopting procedures and approaches to learning that are untried, that are not accessible to potential learners or that are not demanded or preferred by clients.

Providers may attempt to lead the market. Those who wish to follow the more cautious approach of responding to the market need to research both the demands of the market and the capacity of clients to take up the educational technologies envisaged. |
| Client expectations and government policies and procedures demand greater accountability and reporting. | Given public accountability and market expectations, universities must find ways to evaluate qualitative and quantitative outcomes of electronically mediated learning. Quality outcomes cannot be assured by quality inputs such as campus facilities nor can universities rely on high tertiary entrance scores of school leavers to ensure quality outcomes. |

Table 2.3 *Premises and policy implications relating to technical developments*

Premises	Policy Implications
Where the resource material supplementing face-to-face teaching and learning has been largely print-based (eg textbooks, reference books and journals), accessed through purchase, libraries and photocopying, students and teachers will increasingly make use of network-based means for sharing knowledge.	The provision of on-campus facilities for access to print-based materials needs to be de-emphasized and provision of electronically accessed materials such as databases on CD ROM or online needs to be emphasized. The definition of libraries may need to change along with the relationship between libraries and computing services.
	The applicability of any copyright fair dealing concessions (which apply to print) to digitized material requires clarification along with copyright and intellectual property rights for material developed by a provider.
Much greater use can be made of digital technologies in post-secondary education than at present. Strategies employing the new knowledge media can contribute effectively to most learning situations.	Design, development and operational arrangements for digital learning resources need to be such that desired learning outcomes are clarified, an appropriate educational design and media mix is employed and learner support services are provided.
	Development of digital learning resources must be driven primarily by educational principles, rather than by technological capacity.
Technology alone will not solve the problems of increasing access to higher education.	Education and training institutions need also to provide for flexible admission policies, recognition of prior learning, communication with potential clients and the appropriate sharing of cost burdens.
In many institutions developments in the new knowledge media are ad hoc, occurring through individual creative endeavours rather than as a consequence of strategic and systematic planning.	The demands for a significant shift in the modes of education and training provision suggest institution-wide or substantial changes are made rather than generating change through individual initiative. The record of producing substantial change through encouragement of small-scale innovations is not good.

Table 2.3   *(Contd)*

Premises	Policy Implications
	Committed leadership and the development of staff are essential to integrate the new technologies into mainstream teaching and learning.
Existing university and inter-university information technology infrastructure will not accommodate the development of good quality digitally based programmes on a large scale.	The implication of large-scale use of new knowledge media for infrastructure requirements needs to be determined. Decisions about communications hardware and software within institutions providing education and training need to be taken in conjunction with decisions about educational infrastructure requirements.

Table 2.4   *Premises and policy implications relating to cost and benefits*

Premises	Policy Implications
It has been proposed that digital educational resources are heavy on development costs and light on delivery costs while traditional face-to-face education is light on development costs and heavy on delivery costs. This proposition should not be accepted at face value. Costing studies suggest the economies of scale for use of the new knowledge media plateau after a critical enrolment is reached. The development and operational costs do not suggest that the new knowledge media offer a cheaper means of providing effectively for the current levels of enrolment.	Providers need to cost digital media carefully, taking into account processes for educational effectiveness, such as direct or indirect interaction between teacher and learner and between learner and learner, which constitutes a continuing operational expense additional to development costs.
While digital media offer prospects for improvement in the quality of higher education and for the capacity to deal with larger enrolments in higher education subjects, most research into knowledge media initiatives has failed to find any significant difference in learning outcomes between traditional and digitally based innovations.	A policy to adopt new knowledge media needs to be based on a premise other than improvement in the quality of education and training provision unless a case can be made for the particular form of media to be adopted.
Development and operational costs for digital technologies can be high.	In an increasingly competitive market-place educational providers need to collaborate in the development of digitally based resources and in their utilization.

Table 2.5   *Premises and policy implications relating to access and equity*

Premises	Policy Implications
The benefits of utilizing the new knowledge media include a capacity to customize programmes, the accommodation of individual learning styles and individual student goals, and time and place convenience for both students and staff.	The imperative to provide flexibility in the delivery arrangements for education and training suggests the development of educational provision policies which specify the potential benefits of the new knowledge media.
The effects upon equity target groups of the introduction of new technologies into education and training programmes are not clear but the limited access which these target groups have to personal computing in the home indicates that they may be relatively further disadvantaged.	Policy and provision arrangements need to provide for learners who do not have home, work or community access to the hardware and software required to use the new knowledge media.
Access to university programmes for students reliant upon these being offered by digital media is limited by the bias in the range of courses available toward humanities and business rather than science and technology.	Education and training providers may need to make special provision to encourage the development of digital educational resources in technological and scientific areas.

Summing up

We live in an era of great change, but every era since the Enlightenment has been seen as such. What makes this era different is the nature of the change.

The key factor now driving change is technology. Technology is creating a break with the modern era, breaking down borders and increasing globalization. Globalization relies on technology, and therefore developments in technology are also driven by globalization.

As society changes, education and training providers are also being required to change. In both education and training there is a shift to offering greater flexibility – in relation to time, place, pace, entry and exit.

Education and training providers are also being expected to accommodate increased demand for education and new forms of access in the context of a rapid explosion in knowledge. They must contend with a blurring of the distinction between public and private providers and a blurring of the distinction between distance and attendance modes of tuition.

There are policy implications arising from this changing education and training environment. The digital age requires change at the institutional and system level if the current providers of education and training are to survive. Accountability considerations and market expectations demand responses to the needs and preferences of learners and quality assurance mechanisms. A focus on flexibility in provision needs to be accompanied by a determination to employ sound educational principles in the design and development of learning resources.

Chapter 3

Learning in an electronic environment

In this chapter we examine what we mean by 'learning', arguing that for learning to be effective it needs to involve the active participation of the learner. We specify what our understanding of the nature of learning implies for the way we should view teaching. We also consider the implications of our conception of effective teaching for the types of components that need to be built into an electronic learning environment if it is to support the learner adequately.

What is learning?

In the traditional model of the classroom, the teacher is the focus, standing in front of a group of students and presenting information. What the teacher does in these situations is sometimes described as 'communicate' knowledge. However, this explanation betrays a misunderstanding of what is actually taking place. Knowledge, skills and behaviours cannot simply be transmitted from teacher to student. Knowledge, in the sense of 'that which a person knows', is not able simply to be absorbed. Nor are skills or the propensity to act in certain ways. What a teacher transmits is information. When learners receive that information they construct knowledge from it.

The approach to teaching described above is often referred to as conforming to the 'transmission model' of teaching. The transmission model is not, of course, a formally enunciated model of teaching. It is a model that is implied by a widely prevalent pattern of practice. The transmission model of teaching has been severely criticized on educational grounds because, when practised in conjunction with forms of assessment that require recall, it encourages rote memorization. In so doing, it leads to surface understanding, a type of understanding in which more attention is paid to the words that are being spoken than the underlying significance of what is said.

Teaching by presenting verbal information can lead to rote memorization and surface learning but it need not necessarily do so. David Ausubel made the important distinction between rote memorization and meaningful verbal learning, either of which, he pointed out, could result from expository teaching. According to Ausubel, the key to enabling learners to engage in meaningful verbal learning is to present information in such a way that they can use the information to extend their knowledge structures (Ausubel, 1963). Expository teaching, which is sequenced to support meaningful verbal learning, reflects a somewhat different 'information transfer' conception of teaching. This conception arose from information processing theories that originated from the research into the way human memory functions.

The limitation of the 'information transfer' conception of teaching is that teaching in accordance with this conception supports the construction of only one type of knowledge – what we might call 'theoretical' knowledge. The learner integrates subject matter information communicated by the teacher into a conceptual framework for modelling the world. Where the 'information transfer' conception of teaching goes wrong is that it assumes that the only knowledge worth acquiring is theoretical knowledge. It may go further – it may assume that the only theoretical knowledge worth acquiring is that which is coincident with some particular 'expert' interpretation.

What does it mean to be expert?

Education and training is concerned with enabling learners to progress towards becoming expert in particular fields of endeavour. An expert is a person who has a detailed understanding of a field. However, this is not the most important distinguishing characteristic of an expert. An even more important characteristic is that an expert has expertise. By that, we mean an expert is able to act appropriately in all situations that they encounter in working in the field, including novel situations. This view eschews the idea of understanding of a field as being finite and emphasizes process in meeting new challenges. Thus, teaching in a world of change involves inculcating expertise – skills and propensities to act constructively in furthering exploration of a field of study.

A person's expertise may be judged by their actions. However, it cannot be assumed that a person who is able to act appropriately in one situation will be able to act appropriately in all situations. Expertise is related to context. So a person who is expert in one field of endeavour will not necessarily be expert in another.

Acting without thinking is not the mark of the uneducated person. On the contrary, one of the characteristics of an expert is that he or she is able to act quickly without thinking about what they need to do. Their actions, too, are largely automatic. Their competence has reached a level at which their actions are no longer sourced directly from tacit theoretical knowledge.

What do we mean by 'theory'?

A theory is a way of understanding how the world and the things that comprise it work. The value of theories is that they enable us to make sense of information available to us and to anticipate events rather than having them unfold in unexpected ways. By anticipating events, we can act in ways that are more appropriate than the ways in which we are likely to act simply from intuition.

Until recently, the accent in formal education has been on the acquisition of theoretical knowledge. This has been the case especially in universities.

Theory and action

While the possession of theoretical knowledge may be accorded status as an indicator of achievement, theoretical knowledge is ultimately valued if it can be, and is, appropriately applied in action. The value of theoretical knowledge is that it is able to guide our actions when we move into a new context or when the circumstances in the present context change. Having a well-developed theoretical understanding of the way in which the various factors impacting a situation interrelate can enable us to determine how we should act in the situation to produce a particular result.

In much formal education, a taken-for-granted assumption is made that, by simply acquiring a sound theoretical understanding of a situation, a person also acquires the ability and the propensity to act appropriately in that situation. However, we know in practice that that often isn't what happens. We can all think of situations in which we have had the information base to act in a particular way but we have done something else. We have acted against our best judgement. The fact that we *know* how we should act in a particular situation does not guarantee that we will act that way. Our use of newly acquired theoretical knowledge has to compete with long-established behaviour. This is why, when a person returns to acting in the real world after having completed a course of study, they will often revert to their old ways of doing things.

Tacit knowledge

Purposive action that is not sourced from theoretical knowledge is sourced from tacit knowledge (Polanyi, 1958, 1967). Tacit knowledge is not the sort of book knowledge that is acquired through formal education. Tacit knowledge is the knowledge we acquire through our experience of acting in the world. It is the type of knowledge that lets us recognize the face of someone we know. It is also the type of knowledge that gives rise to intuition and imagination. The value of tacit knowledge is that it is available to the person even without their having made the decision to acquire it or to act upon it.

In everyday life, we rely on tacit knowledge most of the time. We act automatically, without thinking, in response to the world as it occurs for us. We rely on it in going about our daily lives, in driving, in playing sport, and also in performing routine tasks in our professional work. The problem with relying on tacit knowledge is that our 'automatic' behaviour may not always be appropriate. Once it has become automatic, we will continue to exhibit it even in situations where a different response is needed.

When a person acts in a way that runs contrary to their thought-out understanding of a situation, their actions are usually being sourced from their tacit knowledge.

'Espoused theories' and 'theories-in-use'

The fallacy of assuming that people invariably act according to the theories they espouse was highlighted by the noted management theorists Chris Argyris and Donald Schön (Argyris and Schön, 1974). They said that it was important to distinguish between the theory a person claims to embrace and the theory that was implied by their actions. They termed the latter a 'theory-in-use'.

The distinction between espoused theories and theories-in-use shifts the focus from the information that a person has been given to the knowledge they have acquired. An espoused theory is a theory that a person is able to describe. It constitutes a part of their explicit knowledge. One might assume that it would also be a theory that has gained acceptance amongst relevant experts. However, this need not necessarily be the case. It may be a misconstruction of an accepted theory or it could be a theory generated by the person him or herself.

A 'theory-in-use' is not an actual theory – that is, a theory that has been thought through and enunciated – but a theory that may be inferred from the person's actions.

Action-oriented learning

The attention given to the importance of tacit knowledge in attainment of professional competence by Schön (1983) and others has in more recent times led to a shift in professional education towards the adoption of action-oriented modes of learning. These include action learning (McGill and Beaty, 1992), situated learning (Seely, Brown, and Duguid, 1989), and problem-based learning (Boud and Feletti, 1991). Each of these teaching approaches emphasizes the importance of the learner gaining practical experience in authentic learning situations. What is of primary importance, pointed out the advocates of these approaches, is that the learner is given opportunities to act as a professional in the particular field would act.

Acquiring the ability to act in the way a professional in the field would act is important. However, such approaches have often been adopted at the expense of theoretical knowledge. Learners may become very capable at dealing with everyday situations but may not acquire sufficient theoretical knowledge to deal with situations of which they have little or no practical experience. Theoretical knowledge can be built up from practical experience, but for that to happen the practical experience needs to be of an appropriate kind and it needs to be appropriately structured. Furthermore, the learner needs to reflect on his or her experience and to use that reflection deliberatively to extend their existing theoretical knowledge.

To enable people to act appropriately in many situations it is often necessary, therefore, to begin the process of aligning or challenging their tacit knowledge of the relevant context with their new-found theoretical knowledge. This restructuring of tacit knowledge is accomplished by applying the theory in practice. Such application of theory therefore constitutes part – indeed, it could be argued, the most important part – of the educational process.

Education therefore involves an interplay between theory and practice whether we are preparing for a vocational task or engaging in the study of literature or philosophy. The acquisition of theory informs the development of practice and the experience provides an opportunity for aligning tacit with theoretical knowledge. Education can go wrong where it separates theory and practice and/ or places a barrier between them so that this interplay can no longer occur.

What constitutes good teaching?

While there have been many attempts to describe what constitutes good teaching, it is possible to define good teaching quite simply as that which supports effective learning. We can therefore judge the quality of teaching by looking at the ways in which it supports learning.

If learning involves the acquisition and application of tacit and theoretical knowledge, then teaching must include the creation of opportunities for the development of both of these types of knowledge.

Considered at one level we can say that teaching should be directed at creating the types of opportunities to develop the ability to act appropriately within a particular domain of action. Considered at a deeper level, we could say that teaching ought to involve providing the contexts in which learners can acquire both the tacit and the conceptual knowledge from which appropriate action arises.

In the case of the acquisition of theoretical knowledge, learning will involve acquisition of the theoretical frameworks in terms of which real-world situations are described. Good teaching will involve explicating these theoretical frameworks in ways that are meaningful, given the learner's already-acquired theoretical knowledge, and providing the learner with the opportunity to relate these theoretical frameworks to practical experience.

In the case of tacit knowledge, learning will involve gaining experience at acting in authentic situations. Teaching will involve providing the student with situations in which such experience can be obtained. This practice is what confers on learners the ability to put their newly gained theoretical and tacit knowledge to use. These experiences may be provided by creating opportunities for engaging with problems, issues and situations. They may also be provided by supplying rich learning environments created with multimedia.

One implication of the conclusion that knowledge is constructed is that learners will construct their knowledge differently. They come with differing understandings, experiences and interests and their own interpretations and behaviours will emerge. This makes the design of stand-alone learning materials difficult. It implies that good teaching will also make provision for some degree of ongoing teacher–learner interaction, whether at a distance or face-to-face.

The historical development of distance education

The way teaching is conceived of in distance education has been strongly influenced by the historical developments in the field.

The way in which distance education was originally practised accorded with what was known as a 'correspondence model'. Students were supplied with printed notes that were equivalent to what the lecturer presented in the lecture (in some cases they were transcriptions of the lecture) and tutoring was undertaken by correspondence. Correspondence education was characterized by high attrition and drop-out rates and as a result this was seen as very much a 'second-best' mode of acquiring a qualification. However, the establishment of the UK Open University changed people's understanding of what was possible in distance education.

The Open University was conceived of as an institution serving those who had missed out on the opportunity to obtain higher education. Its planners realized that not only would it be necessary for the University to deliver its courses in ways that matched the needs of students who were working while they studied, but if the University was not to repeat the failings of correspondence education, then it needed to deliver its courses in an entirely different way. Instead of employing low-quality correspondence materials, it needed to take full advantage of all the available media. The Open University therefore adopted a model that combined print, television, radio, with local study centres and residential schools. The Open University model still employed a resource-based learning approach. However, the resources used to support this approach took full advantage of the presentation media and the self-study materials were supported by a modest amount of face-to-face interaction.

The approach taken by the Open University in the UK quickly proved successful and the success of the Open University led many countries to establish national distance education universities based on the Open University model. Examples include the Fernuniversitat in Germany, Sukhothai Thammathirit Open University in Thailand, the Indira Ghandi Open University in India and Athabasca University in Canada.

The two countries that represent the most notable exceptions to this trend have been Australia and the United States. Australia had a long history of involvement in distance education before the Open University was established. It did not follow other countries in setting up a national open university, although this possibility was the subject of a government enquiry at the time (Committee on Open University, 1975). Instead, Australia extended its dispersed model of dual-mode institutions. Even when the Australian government took steps to rationalize the provision of distance education in Australia, 11 major distance education providers still operated in a country with a population of only just over 25 million people. Nevertheless, the scale of operations of most Australian major distance education providers is such that, with the methods of delivery they use and production values they adhere to, they are still able to operate efficiently.

The United States does not have a strong tradition of involvement in distance education. There, participation in distance education at the higher education level has, until recently, been limited to a small number of providers such as Penn State University and the University of Wisconsin. However, with the rapid development of satellite and cable technologies in the 1980s, many educational institutions saw the opportunity for entering the field of distance education through the use of audio, audio-graphic and video conferencing. Consequently, in the United States distance education has tended to be conceived of in terms of a 'remote classroom' model. In other words, distance education delivery involves linking together students located in multiple sites in real time, which is still reflected in the use of online delivery platforms that transit video of teachers and electronic whiteboards and provide for online responses all in real time.

Conceptions of teaching reflected in traditional distance education

Distance education obviously uses different delivery methods from face-to-face classroom teaching. The physical separation of teacher and learners imposes constraints on the range of options that are available for the delivery of programmes and courses. For much of the time, students may work independently. If they interact at a distance then the interaction is mediated by technology and this influences the extent and nature of the interaction. Even when they are engaged in face-to-face interaction, it is for short intensive periods at weekends or in residential schools or in study groups. Despite these differences, the way distance education and training programmes are delivered indicates that those engaged in teaching at a distance display the same range of understandings of teaching as are displayed by those engaged in face-to-face teaching.

On the one hand, one major group of distance educators sees the most important element of a distance education programme as being the learning package. Of these, there are some who still manifest the 'knowledge transfer' conception of teaching. The learning packages they provide typically comprise mainly subject matter information, but the information often displays comparatively little structuring. Fortunately, this group is shrinking in size. Those members of this group who manifest the 'information transfer' conception of teaching produce learning packages that are also substantially made up of subject matter information. However, in their case the information is carefully sequenced and extensive use is made of textual clues such as a hierarchy of headings and subheadings, typeface variations, and other forms of signposting to reinforce the structure that is implicit in the text. Finally, there are those who consider that learning occurs primarily through doing. These distance educators build extensive interaction into their materials. Their materials are oriented towards having the learner attain defined learning outcomes and these outcomes are frequently expressed as competencies.

The other major group of distance educators sees the most important element of a programme as the discourse that occurs both between the tutor and the student and amongst the students themselves. For them, the most important component of the teaching is the opportunities that are provided for students to interact. Amongst this group, it is again possible to discern three subgroups. There are those who see interaction as supporting the personal construction of knowledge (Garrison, 1993, 1995). Secondly, there are those who see knowledge as being constructed in a social context and interaction being necessary in order to provide that context (Evans and Nation, 1989). Finally, there are those who see interaction as challenging students' existing understandings, opening the way for students to make conceptual shifts (Laurillard, 1993).

The distinctions that have been drawn here reflect marked tendencies rather than clear divisions. While those who favour the use of learning packages consider that ideally the learning package ought to be self-contained, they nevertheless acknowledge that in practice this ideal can seldom be attained. They accept that the learning package must therefore be backed up by a range of other means of delivery, such as tele-tutorials, weekend and residential workshops, local study groups and individual access to tutors. This group of distance educators tends to see learning as the development of a student's capabilities in directions defined by the teacher. For them, the learning package serves to provide the resources needed to achieve this result.

Meanwhile those who favour the use of interactive modes of delivery neverthe-less generally accept the practical and economic necessity of making use of learning resources. They argue, though, that learning materials need to be used in such a way as to construct a dialogue between the teacher and the student.

In connection with this, it is important to distinguish between the physical delivery of the package and metaphorical delivery of the course. In print-based distance education all the materials are assembled into an integrated package and the package mailed to students at the beginning of the study period. From the point of view of the physical package, delivery is mainly one-way. Yet experienced distance educators are acutely aware of the importance of incorporating activities into the design of learning packages. What happens to the physical package therefore tends to disguise a complex set of interactions that are engendered between the teacher and the student. Through the medium of the package, opportunities for interaction can be incorporated into programmes that are carried via a one-way delivery medium such as print. Even the language that is used in the package can help to create the experience of interacting with the tutor, rather than simply being the passive recipient of information.

At the other end of the spectrum are programmes oriented entirely to project work, where the package serves simply as a means of guiding the student to start and pursue the work.

So the quality of the student's learning experience resides more in the way a medium has been used than in the characteristics of the medium itself.

The resource-based and classroom-based models of distance education delivery

The differing ways of seeing distance education can be characterized as two distinct models. One, exemplified by the UK Open University and institutions that have followed it, might be termed the 'resource-based' model. The other, exemplified by the remote classroom approach adopted by many distance education providers in the US and some providers in Canada, might be termed the 'classroom-based' model.

Conceptions of electronic learning

If you browse through the recent literature of distance education and open learning you will notice the distinction that has been drawn above between the use of the delivery media to support the communication of information and the use of the delivery media to support person-to-person interaction. There are those who see the role of online learning in terms of the delivery of Web-based materials. Others see the value of technology in its capacity to support interaction between teacher and student and between student and student.

When institutions consider moving to online delivery they generally apply the model that they have been adopting in the traditional mode of delivery to the new delivery mode. If they are currently operating within a resource-based delivery model they will generally adopt a resource-based delivery model when moving into online delivery. They will conceive of online delivery in terms of Web-based learning. If they currently operate within a classroom-based model they will generally adopt a classroom-based approach to online delivery and will centre their programmes on the use of synchronous and asynchronous conferencing.

These differing approaches lead to two distinctly different models of delivery using the knowledge media, one the resource-based model and the other the classroom-based model. However, when we use the term 'classroom' in this context, we do not necessarily mean teaching in a physical space; we also include 'remote classroom' and 'virtual classroom' teaching. We also need to be aware of the differing ways in which the term 'virtual classroom' is used in different parts of the world. In the US, the term 'virtual classroom' refers specifically to teaching by means of synchronous conferencing, whereas in other parts of the world it refers also to teaching using asynchronous conferencing and that is the way in which we use the term here. Table 3.1 shows a breakdown of delivery methods by mode and approach.

Table 3.1   *Examples of delivery methods employed in resource-based and classroom-based programmes*

Mode	Pedagogical Approach	
	Resource-based	**Classroom-based**
On-campus	Computer-aided learning	Lectures Tutorials Practicals
Traditional off-campus	Print learning package Audiotape Videotape Practical kits	Teleconferences Videoconferences Telelectures
Digital off-campus	Web learning package CD ROM	Asynchronous learning networks

As in the case of traditional distance education, there are staunch advocates for both approaches. While programmes involve a combination of both approaches, they also tend to favour one approach or the other.

Our view is that there is no single best approach to online delivery. The approach that is most appropriate in each situation will depend on a range of factors such as the nature of the subject, the backgrounds of the learners, the outcomes being sought and the context in which the programme is being offered.

The approach a teacher chooses to use in a particular situation will depend in part on the range of options that are available. It will generally only be possible to consider using a particular delivery method if the systems and procedures to support that method have already been put in place. The implication for providers of the adoption of a balanced approach to digital course delivery is that they need to be planning to support a spectrum of delivery options. We shall return to look more closely at what this might entail in Chapter 8.

In moving to embrace the knowledge media, providers need to devise policies, systems and organizational structures that encourage teachers and trainers to adopt good practices and discourage them from adopting poor practices.

How should technology be used to support learning?

The way in which we see technology being used to support learning depends on how we conceive of learning. If we conceive of learning as the acquisition of book knowledge, then we will tend to view technology as providing a means of transmitting and presenting information. We will compare different technologies in terms of their ability to present information or their cost and the speed with which information can be moved from place to place.

If we conceive of learning as occurring principally through the interaction between teacher and student and of students amongst themselves, then we will tend to view the value of technology in terms of its potential to support such interaction.

The role of information technology

Using the term *information technology* to describe aspects of the delivery of education and training programmes can be misleading. It suggests that the function of the technology is to transmit information.

In the education and training literature, one sometimes finds information technology being used in an educational context referred to as *educational technology*. This terminology is also misleading. The word 'technology' in the term *educational technology* does not refer to hardware or software but rather to sets of principles used in designing materials.

Choosing the right term to describe information technology when it is applied to education and training is probably less important than recognizing that the role of information technology in education goes well beyond the mere delivery of information. Even when the technology is serving to transmit information, the information being transmitted is structured in particular ways to achieve educational purposes. It is the way that the information is structured that is of greatest importance here, not the speed or accuracy with which the information is carried from point to point.

It is unfortunately the case that many educational multimedia programmes do not conform to sound pedagogical principles. Many do little more than present large volumes of information – much of it textual. There is little reason to believe that students are motivated more strongly, or learn more effectively by reading information from a screen than by reading information from print. Simply from the point of view of cost, the use of multimedia for 'electronic page turning' needs to be challenged. This constitutes a very extravagant use of a particularly expensive medium. It would be much more economical to provide this information in print or even to include a copy of the document on a CD ROM in a form ready for printing.

However, the fact that many productions do little more than transmit information should not be regarded as a limitation of the medium itself. Rather, it is a matter of an inappropriate use of the medium.

Alternatives to the information dissemination model of electronic delivery

Over the past 20 years, a number of instructional models have been developed for the design of courseware in computer-assisted learning. These include:

- drill and practice – learners respond to questions;
- tutorials – presentation of information via computer;
- simulations – learners are presented with a real-world situation to which they are required to react;
- problem solving – learners are given a problem situation and asked to find a solution.

All of these models have now been adapted for use in interactive multimedia. However, up until recently, the range of instructional models that it was possible to implement in an online environment was limited by the range of software available for Web-based delivery of interactive multimedia products. As server systems become more sophisticated and Web browser plug-ins for interactive multimedia authoring systems become available, these facilities are quickly being exploited by courseware developers.

However, it is important to recognize that the delivery of distance education programmes involves much more than the delivery of learning resource materials.

What functions does an electronic learning environment need to support?

Educational institutions and training providers that have not had experience in delivering programmes at a distance often conceive of what constitutes an adequate delivery system too narrowly. They focus on the most obvious aspects of course delivery, such as the presentation of Web pages and the structure of threaded discussions and ignore the ancillary support functions such as the provision of a rapid response system for dealing with problems that helps to ensure that learners complete their courses of study.

Yet delivery of a programme at a distance no more stops with the provision of the courseware or the conduct of online conferences than the delivery of a programme taught face-to-face stops with the conduct of the lectures and tutorials. A programme is not complete without appropriate assessment, tutorial, library, and administrative support and all of these functions need to form part of a comprehensive delivery system.

In making the transition to the knowledge media it is also important to consider how functions that previously would have been performed on a person-to-person basis ought to be conducted online. A system for supporting online learning therefore needs to support both teaching and learning functions and administrative functions. The most important functions that need to be considered include:

- enrolment/registration of students;
- provision of course advice;
- provision of course materials;
- provision of access to library resources and services;
- provision of feedback on progress;
- provision of responses to administrative and academic queries;
- conduct of assessment and provision of results;
- support for communication among teachers and lecturers.

Those education and training organizations that already offer programmes by distance education based on traditional media will have systems and processes in place for performing each of these functions. In moving to delivery via the knowledge media it is quite likely that some or all of these systems and processes will need to be rethought. Delivering programmes digitally offers opportunities for improving the responsiveness of some services and reducing the cost of others. However, obtaining the benefits that may potentially be available depends on taking advantage of the strengths of the particular technologies being used and perhaps bringing functions together in different combinations. Migrating to technology-dependent systems also carries risks. Making the transition successfully therefore depends on being aware of the risks and building safeguards to protect the overall operation when the inevitable technical failures occur.

Cost is a very important determinant of which technologies have reached a sufficient level of maturity to be considered for use in a production environment. It is always more expensive to conduct the trial of a technological innovation than it is to put the technology to use on a day-to-day basis. However, there are high ongoing costs in the adoption of some technologies.

With the escalation in the pace of innovation, the time that elapses between when a technology first appears and when it is ready to be taken up by education and training may be reducing. Nevertheless the basic principle remains.

Why switch to the knowledge media?

Why might education and training providers want to make the transition to the knowledge media? Essentially there are three reasons. The knowledge media offer the possibility of delivering courses in ways that are:

- cheaper;
- faster;
- better.

Cheaper

Many education and training providers are starting to make the transition to delivery via the digital media because they believe they can save on costs. In Chapter 4, we shall examine more closely the issues that govern the costs of delivery in resource-based learning and how these are likely to be affected by a shift to the Web and multimedia. We will point out that whether it is cheaper to deliver via the digital media is not clear-cut. However, we go on to explain that we believe the costs are certain to decrease with time and we explain why. Therefore, although it may not yet be cheaper to deliver courses digitally, it will be before too long. The cost benefits of making the transition will accrue within the life of materials that are presently being developed.

Faster

Communication via the Internet has the potential to be almost instantaneous. When a hot link on a Web page is activated, it can result in an HTTP command being issued to the server on which the relevant document resides to download the document immediately. The server may be located halfway around the world.

This factor is important if you are delivering to students who are very distant – especially to students who are located in other countries. In this case the time taken for delivery of materials and especially for delivery and return of assignments can be very considerable. Use of the Internet can eliminate this delay.

Better

The primary reasons most education and training providers are shifting to the knowledge media may be to save cost, or to reduce delays in delivery. However, experienced distance educators consider that the most justifiable reason for considering such a shift is to improve the quality of the programmes that are offered.

The factors that affect the quality of a programme may be associated with the presentation of the learning materials, with the academic and administrative support provided to students, or with the type of interaction that is possible between teacher and student and amongst the students themselves.

Quality can also be interpreted as being related to the range of variation that is possible in the presentation of learning materials. Multimedia and Web-based material may be judged by some teachers as better because they offer a much more diverse range of presentation options including:

- colour;
- high-quality half-tones;
- animation;
- video;
- multimedia interaction;
- interaction between individuals;
- group interaction.

Avoiding the risks of being oversold on technology

The success of innovations owes much to the pioneering work of early adopters. An early adopter sees an opportunity for a new way of accomplishing some outcomes and sets out to demonstrate that it is possible. Early adopters gain satisfaction from being early and from having other people follow their example.

Early adopters feel that they can afford to take the risk of pursuing innovations that do not work out as expected. Indeed, part of their success comes from finding ways through the many barriers that pioneering a new application throws up. However, early adopters tend to highlight the advantages of innovation and to downplay the disadvantages or limitations.

A technology that is ripe for exploration by early adopters may still be too immature for incorporation into a full production system. A favourite saying in the information technology industry is that the first users of a new piece of software become the test group that finds the software 'bugs'. The fact that a technology is capable of performing a particular function should not be taken to imply that it will be effective in performing that function from an educational point of view.

Recent advances in computer and communications technology are throwing up many exciting possibilities for improving the way in which education and training programmes are delivered. Yet managers of educational delivery systems require technologies that are functional, reliable and above all cost-effective. The technologies that are most effective in performing a particular delivery function are not necessarily those that are perceived to be most 'glamorous' or 'hi-tech'. Often it is the simpler technology that, because of its greater reliability and lower cost, does the job.

The fields of education and training have generally not been at the forefront in the take-up of new technologies. Throughout the history of instructional technology, the technologies that have proven to be most successful have first found a market elsewhere. The compact cassette, the VHS cartridge, the overhead projector are all technologies that became established in entertainment or business first. Once they had secured a market there, educators saw the potential for adapting them to educational functions. The reason for this pattern is that widespread market adoption of a technology drives the cost down. Early adopters of a technology funded the recovery of the initial investment in research and development. With a few notable exceptions, fields of education and training have seldom had the resources to support the research and development investment costs needed to bring a new piece of technology on to the market. Moreover, education and training providers generally look for technology that is reliable and can be applied with some confidence.

For technology to support learning effectively it needs to support the full range of delivery functions. These include administrative functions such as enrolling and re-enrolling, provision of examination information and query handling. Supporting these functions requires the provision of a wider range of support functions. Distance educators are accustomed to thinking of the development of support systems holistically. However, teachers who are exclusively involved in teaching face-to-face are not accustomed to thinking in that way. They tend to be more focused on the teaching–learning aspects of delivery. They do not have a lot to do with other support functions such as enrolment, examination, counselling. Yet all of these other functions need to be catered for by a system.

How effective is electronic delivery?

Distance educators have worked hard to overcome distance education's early reputation for high drop-out and high failure rates. The key to reducing the incidence of drop-out and failure, it was found, was to improve the quality of the learning environment. It would be unfortunate if, in making the transition from print-based to electronic delivery, these hard-fought-for gains were lost. It was not that print was an inappropriate medium for distance education but that print was not being used in a way that was appropriate to the needs of distance learners.

The development of interactive multimedia follows on from three decades of experience in computer-assisted instruction and computer-managed learning. During this period, a considerable amount of research has been undertaken into the effectiveness of computer-delivered education and training. An assessment of the early studies of the effectiveness of CAI concluded that computer-delivered instruction could be as effective as traditional instruction (Kulik, Kulik and Cohen, 1980). Later studies by the same researchers supported these early findings (Kulik and Kulik, 1986; Kulik and Kulik, 1991).

Multimedia does, of course, offer a range of more powerful capabilities than traditional computer-assisted instruction and computer-managed learning. It would therefore be reasonable to expect interactive multimedia to be potentially more effective.

In the short time that the World Wide Web has been functioning there has not been the opportunity for well-designed studies to be undertaken into its effectiveness compared with other forms of computer-based delivery or indeed compared with other forms of resource-based learning.

As was explained in Chapter 1, while the systems of computer conferencing being used today may be quite new, conferencing via computer was first introduced into education in the mid-1970s. Since then it has become widely used.

Roxanne Starr Hiltz has undertaken extensive research into the effectiveness of computer conferencing in education in her work with the Virtual Classroom™ at the New Jersey Institute of Technology. She argues that, to be effective, computer conferencing needs to be tightly integrated into the curriculum (Hiltz, 1997). If use of the conferencing facility is not made part of the 'required', graded curriculum, then the majority of the students will not use it. Even those students who do start to use it will quickly conclude that 'there is nothing going on there' and will stop using it. On the other hand, if conferencing is tightly integrated into the teaching programme then this mode of delivery can be as or more effective than more traditional modes of delivery.

One of the major advantages of electronic learning is that it enables students to learn in their own time, at their own pace, and in their own location. Print-based distance education offers these advantages as well. However, electronic delivery offers a greater range of presentation options as well as the possibility of tutor–student and student–student interaction. The importance of these advantages will depend on the extent to which an education or training programme is designed to exploit them.

Summing up

Learning is concerned with acquiring the capacity to conceptualize and to act appropriately in a particular context. Teaching is about facilitating the acquisition of that capacity. The way in which a person acts reflects their tacit and explicit knowledge of the situations in which they find themselves from moment to moment. However, a person's tacit and explicit knowledge of a situation will not always give rise to the same response. In that case, a person will often act one way when they know they should have 'done something else'. Developing the ability to act appropriately in a particular situation involves engaging in activities that bring one's tacit and explicit knowledge into alignment. This is accomplished through acting in authentic situations.

The knowledge media hold the promise of delivering education and training more effectively by providing students with a much richer environment in which to learn. Whether that promise is realized depends on how the media are used. Thinking of the knowledge media simply in terms of the transmission of information is likely to foster an approach to learning that accentuates the acquisition of explicit knowledge. For the electronic delivery of courses to be effective, it needs to enable learners to engage in associated practice.

The delivery of education and training programmes involves much more than simply the delivery of instruction. It also involves the creation of the type of environment in which the full range of academic, administrative and support needs of the learner are met.

Part 2

Implementation

Chapter 4

Counting the cost

In this chapter we provide a framework for understanding cost relationships; describe a basic method of estimating costs; explain how savings in the costs of delivery are achieved through economies of scale; suggest some strategies for managing costs and consider the likely costs of delivering programmes digitally. We go on to examine the question of whether shifting to digital delivery is likely to yield overall cost savings.

The cost motive for going online

One of the main reasons why education and training providers originally became so interested in using the knowledge media for the delivery of courses was to obtain what they saw as significant cost savings. Delivering courses electronically *seems* less expensive than delivering them in print; communicating with students via e-mail *seems* less expensive than communicating by telephone or letter.

Twigg (1994), in outlining the case for a national infrastructure for online education in the United States, argued that because of changes in the types of students undertaking higher education and changes in where students were undertaking their learning, the existing means of delivery would be incapable of meeting the educational needs of the country in the 21st century at reasonable cost.

To contain costs while at the same time expanding access, she argued, institutions needed to embrace the new learning technologies. Yet how realistic are these expectations for institutions engaging in distance education and those wishing to adopt more flexible approaches to programmes concurrently offered face-to-face? In order to answer that question it is necessary to understand how cost savings are achieved in distance education.

When the Open University was being planned, it was recognized that the way to recoup the substantial initial costs of design and development of learning materials was by taking advantage of the potential for economies of scale.

Economies of scale

'Economies of scale' are economies that result from an increase in the size of an operation. The concept of economies of scale originated from the development of mass production.

Economies of scale originate because the costs of production do not increase proportionately with output. The reason for this is that some costs are fixed, or relatively fixed – that is, they do not vary directly with the number of units produced – whereas other costs are variable and do increase in proportion to the number of items produced. Economies of scale are therefore economies that accrue as a result of the fixed costs being spread over a greater number of units of output.

Economies of scale can be achieved in most production operations. However, the scope that exists for obtaining further economies of scale depends on the proportion of the overall costs of production attributable to fixed costs compared with the proportion that is attributable to variable costs. If a large proportion of the overall costs of production is attributable to fixed costs, then there will be considerable scope for obtaining economies of scale. If fixed costs account for only a small proportion of unit costs then the scope for obtaining economies of scale will be modest.

Economies of scale can be achieved in education and training by increasing the number of students taught. The potential that exists in education and training for obtaining economies of scale depends on the proportion of the costs of delivering a programme that represent fixed costs.

Cost differences between resource-based and classroom-based delivery

One of the most important factors that influences the costs of delivery of courses is the pedagogical approach, ie whether delivery is by a resource-based approach or classroom-based. Each of these approaches may be applied to the three main delivery modes: on-campus, traditional distance education or digital delivery.

The two approaches exhibit quite different distributions between fixed and variable costs. The types of costs involved in delivering a programme can be subdivided into capital costs, materials costs, labour costs and service costs. Table 4.1 shows examples of the costs involved in face-to-face classroom-based delivery. Table 4.2 shows examples of the costs involved in resource-based delivery.

Resource-based and classroom teaching approaches exhibit quite different cost structures. In classroom delivery, most of the cost of delivery is accounted for by variable costs – the costs of staff time, the costs of the resources used by students, the costs of maintenance of classrooms.

Resource-based delivery, on the other hand, involves a substantial component of fixed costs. The largest fixed cost is usually the staff time involved in the initial development of the learning packages from which students learn. This is the reason that moving from classroom delivery to resource-based delivery greatly increases the potential for obtaining economies of scale.

Table 4.1 *Examples of the costs involved in face-to-face classroom delivery*

Cost Categories	Fixed	Variable
Capital	Classrooms; long-lasting equipment	
Materials		Laboratory supplies; photocopying
Labour	Core academic and administrative staff	Short term & casual staffing
Service	Building & grounds maintenance	Facilities servicing

Table 4.2 *Examples of the costs involved in resource-based delivery*

Cost Categories	Fixed	Variable
Capital	Computing infrastructure	
Materials		Printed matter; CD ROMs
Labour	Tuition materials design & development	Tutorial support; non–automated assessment
Service	Infrastructure maintenance	Marketing [costs of extending the market]

The effect of size of intake

It is commonly believed that it is possible to continue to reap economies of scale indefinitely with increasing student intakes. This is a misconception.

Figure 4.1 shows the relationship between the cost per student and the average annual intake for a hypothetical subject. It is assumed that the costs of development of the learning package for this subject were $50,000, the costs of providing tutorial,

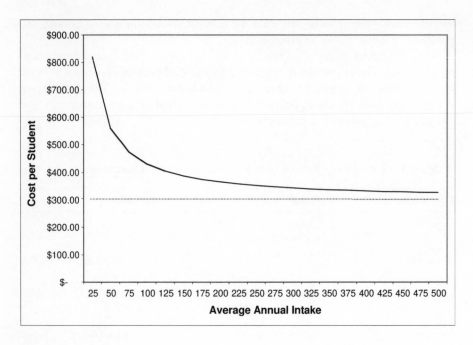

Figure 4.1 *Economies of scale curve*

assessment and administrative support were $300 per student. It is also assumed that the effective life of the learning package is five years.

The actual figures used here are unimportant. What we are interested in is the trend. We can see from the graph if the annual intake is low, doubling or tripling the size of the intake can greatly decrease the cost per student. Fixed costs such as the costs of teaching staff time required for the design and development of the learning materials represents a substantial proportion of the total cost per student of offering the course. As the size of the intake increases, the scope for obtaining further economies of scale declines. Variable costs such as the costs of tutoring, examining students and provision of administrative support make up an increasing proportion of the total cost per student.

However, the rate of decline in the cost per student is not constant. Initially it is quite rapid. Then, as the fixed costs are spread over a growing number of students, the rate of decline slows. Eventually the point is reached that the additional savings resulting from increasing the number of students are scarcely worth pursuing. There is even the possibility of diseconomies of scale if some of the variable costs rise with increased scale (for example, if scarce labour had to be purchased at penalty rates or if market costs rise as addressed below) or if a further fixed cost arose when the scale passed a certain point (for example, if new infrastructure or administrative systems are needed).

The effect of varying the ratio between fixed and variable costs

The total cost per student shown at each point on the curve in Figure 4.1 represents the sum of the contribution to fixed costs plus variable costs. Increasing the average annual intake reduces the contribution of fixed costs to the total costs of delivery. As the curve flattens out it approaches (but never actually reaches) the horizontal straight line representing variable costs per student.

It is possible to see from the graph the effect of increasing either the fixed or variable costs. If the variable costs are higher, the curve will still have the same shape, but the curve will lie higher up the y-axis. If the fixed costs are higher, then the tail of the curve will extend further to the right. A higher average annual intake will be needed to be able to offer the subject at that same cost per student.

However, there is one other factor we need to take into account – the cost of recruitment of students.

The contribution of marketing costs

The graph shown in Figure 4.1 does not take into account the costs of marketing. In the past, the costs of marketing programmes were often not taken into account in estimating the costs of programme delivery. There were two reasons for this. Firstly, the marketing of an institution's programmes was commonly the responsibility of a central department handling enrolments. The amount spent on marketing was governed by the size of the department's annual budget. Secondly, there were always more students wanting places than there were places available. Institutions did not need to market heavily in order to fill their quotas. Institutions competed for the best students rather than for any students.

As competition amongst institutions increased, the amount spent by institutions on marketing grew. Also, the role of marketing changed. Institutions spent more on marketing in order to attract more students.

Teaching departments also began to recognize the importance of actively promoting their programmes. In the devolution of responsibility that has been the hallmark of economic rationalism, responsibility for marketing was formally handed over to the teaching departments and marketing then appeared as a cost item in their budgets.

However, many institutions still treat marketing as an off-budget item. Similarly, most of the studies of the costs of distance education provision have not identified the costs of marketing as one of the specific costs of delivery.

In a competitive market environment, creating and maintaining the market for a product requires continual investment in advertising and promotion. In a highly competitive market, the costs of marketing can represent a significant proportion of the overall costs of doing business. The investment that needs to be made in order to increase sales depends on how close the market is to reaching saturation.

Making a shift to online delivery allows a distance education provider to extend its reach internationally. This is seen as providing the opportunity to increase intakes, thereby generating greater returns on investment by increasing economies of scale. This possibility exists if moving online enables a provider to tap into a new market that is not yet being adequately served. However, the shift to online delivery, as well as opening up new markets for programmes, also exposes institutions to increased competition.

Nevertheless, it can be seen from the graph that there must be some level of intake at which the saving made through economies of scale for every additional student recruited will be counterbalanced by the additional investment that needs to be made in marketing to attract that student.

In consumer markets, the way in which producers respond to this situation is to buy out their competitors. By buying out competitors they both increase their market size and reduce the level of competition. However, publicly owned institutions generally do not have this option available to them. Amalgamations do occur – but usually because of government policy initiatives rather than market forces. What this indicates is that educational institutions seeking to expand their markets need to be prepared to compete on more than price alone.

Shifting to online delivery may give access to new markets. However, those markets will only be worth tapping if the cost of promoting to those markets does not completely erode the savings made through achieving greater efficiencies from increased economies of scale.

The relationship between efficiency and effectiveness

Efficiency is concerned with minimization of the call on resources. If we relate the concept of efficiency to the curve shown in Figure 4.1, we can say that a distance education provider is operating efficiently if all its subjects are operating in the flat part of the curve.

Effectiveness, in the context of teaching, refers to the extent to which teaching results in changes in a learner's understanding, skills, competencies, attitudes and dispositions.

The aim in education and training is to deliver in ways that are both efficient and effective. However, these goals sometimes compete. Increasing efficiency does not imply improving effectiveness. While the concept of efficiency implies having the desired effect, it does not imply maximizing effectiveness. The pursuit of efficiency can compromise effectiveness and effectiveness can be pursued at the expense of efficiency. For example, increasing the extent of tutor–student interaction can increase the effectiveness of student learning. However, it also increases the cost per student of delivering the course. The aim is therefore to strike an appropriate balance within the limits of available resources.

The scope for cost savings

Cost savings may be obtained through increased economies of scale and achieving greater efficiency. The scope for obtaining cost savings depends on the extent to which economies of scale have already been realized. If substantial economies of scale have already been realized, then the scope of obtaining additional economies of scale through a change in delivery mode may be small.

If programmes are already being delivered efficiently, then increasing the intake into a course or programme may not generate much in the way of additional economies. However, if a course or programme is not being delivered efficiently, then moving online may allow a larger market to be tapped and greater efficiency to be achieved as a result. Alternatively, being able to tap into a larger market may allow greater efficiency to be achieved. Alternatively, being able to tap into a larger market may allow courses to be offered that otherwise simply could not be offered at acceptable cost.

The Monterrey Institute of Technology in Mexico has developed a strategy of using online delivery to tap into highly dispersed niche markets. The Institute identifies potential market opportunities and then enters into contracts with institutions that have subject matter experts in the relevant fields of study to undertake the course development (see Case study 3, page 82).

Taking advantage of economies of scale to manage costs

This highly simplified explanation of the way in which economies of scale are achieved ignores the many complexities that emerge in the delivery of actual programmes. In the first place, it doesn't take into account further economies of scale that can also be achieved at the institutional level.

Ashenden (1987) pointed out that economies of scale could be obtained at the institutional level as well as at the course level. At the course level, as we have explained, economies of scale are achieved by spreading the fixed costs of learning materials development over a larger intake into the course. However, Ashenden pointed out that further economies of scale could be obtained at the institutional level through spreading the fixed costs of the infrastructure needed for the development and delivery of distance education programmes over a larger distance education cohort. Ashenden argued that institutional infrastructure is not used efficiently until the annual student intake across all courses rises above 3,000 equivalent full-time students.

Ashenden's estimates related to print-based delivery and the intake level at which efficiency is achieved would be different for other modes. The number varies with the amount of capital investment in infrastructure so the figure could be expected to be much higher for programmes delivered online.

The explanation doesn't take into account, either, the fact that programmes typically become much more specialized in later years. Consequently the number of students enrolled in later-year courses is usually much lower than the number enrolled in first-year courses. Annual intakes fall from hundreds or even thousands of students to, in some cases, single-digit figures.

Nevertheless, the explanation does give us sufficient understanding of economies of scale for us to be able to predict, in general terms, the way in which costs will be impacted by changes in delivery mode. If one wishes to drive variable costs down, then the options available for achieving this result are to eliminate cost components or to make delivery of those components more efficient.

It can be appreciated that making learning packages more self-contained will have the effect of reducing students' reliance on tutors and administrators, and will reduce ongoing staffing costs though it may increase development costs.

Eliminating any of the variable cost components may, however, impact the quality of students' learning and as a consequence push up failure and drop-out rates. This approach is sometimes adopted as a short-term expedient to manage funding cuts. However, it carries a longer-term cost. If more students drop out in the early years of a programme, then the number of students subsequently graduating from those cohorts is likely to fall. The reputation of the programme is also likely to be adversely affected.

Turoff (1997) argued that once a body of subject matter is so well understood that it can be delivered entirely by resource materials, it was no longer sufficiently up-to-date to be suitable for university-level courses.

The only way to reduce the variable costs associated with distance education delivery without running the risk of increasing failure and drop-out rates is to improve the efficiency with which services are delivered.

The potential for achieving economies of scale with online delivery

In Chapter 3 it was pointed out that the two developed countries that did not move to establish national open universities following the successful establishment of the Open University were Australia and the United States.

In Australia, some rationalization of distance education provision did occur in the mid-1980s. However, this reduced a field of more than 40 providers down to 11 major providers plus about the same number of much smaller specialist providers that were required to operate in conjunction with one or more of the other specialist providers. This rationalization, instituted by government legislation, was aimed at reducing duplication and increasing efficiency. However, the reason such a dispersed model of distance education remained viable was that each of the major providers was able to attract sufficient students to achieve efficiency using the low-cost production methods that had become the norm in Australia. Current thinking, based on the concept of a competitive market, has removed government protection of distance education providers and assumed that competition will generate efficiency. Protection of distance education providers became difficult to sustain due both to the rise of economic rationalism and the convergence of on-campus and off-campus teaching techniques and technologies.

The fact that the United States did not move heavily into distance education at the time that other countries did, combined with the fact that when it did, it adopted the 'remote classroom' model, meant that institutions in the US did not reap the economies of scale that the national distance education providers were exploiting. Institutions in the US were not faced with the cost pressures that institutions in other countries faced and they had better access to the types of communication technologies needed to support their higher cost delivery model.

When Twigg (1994) presented the case for a National Learning Infrastructure, therefore, she was writing against the background of a higher education system that has been very strongly geared to on-campus, residential delivery and in which distance education has principally been used for the delivery of continuing education programmes. The savings that she suggested were potentially available by moving to online delivery were expected to come, not from switching from face-to-face to distance learning, but rather from switching from classroom-based to resource-based learning.

Greatest interest in the potential offered by the World Wide Web and interactive multimedia for lowering the costs of delivery is being shown in the United States. It is there that we have witnessed the establishment of the Western Governors University and the ill-fated California Virtual University (see Case study 2, pages 64–65). It can now be appreciated that the main reason for this is that the potential for achieving cost savings through economies of scale has yet to be fully exploited in that country. The scope for cost savings is consequently much greater. However, the factor that will be responsible for generating cost savings will be the switch from classroom-based to resource-based delivery. The shift to online delivery is merely the means by which that switch will be achieved.

In countries that had already established a national infrastructure for distance education, the economies of scale that can accrue from shifting from a classroom-based to a resource-based delivery model had already been achieved from establishment of a distance education system based on use of the print medium. Shifting from print-based distance education to online distance education does not offer the same potential for achieving economies of scale and indeed may end up being more costly.

The potential for achieving economies of scale with delivery of interactive multimedia

As in the case of print, the use of interactive multimedia reduces variable costs in relation to fixed costs and therefore offers the potential for obtaining economies of scale. However, the cost of development of multimedia materials is typically very much higher than the cost of development of textual materials. A rule of thumb that is often used in making rough estimates of the costs of multimedia materials is that 100 hours of development time are required to generate one hour of instruction. Obviously, the actual ratio will depend on the type of multimedia product that is being produced. If a high degree of sophistication is

Case study 2: The rise and demise of the California Virtual University

The initiative

The California Virtual University is an example of the type of collaborative venture that governments, corporations and institutions are coming up with in order to capture world markets for online learning. It is also an illustration of what can go wrong when grand ideas are built on weak foundations.

The California Virtual University was the brainchild of California Governor Pete Wilson. Wilson had earlier declined to allow his state to participate in the formation of the Western Governors' University. In 1997, he announced the formation of the new University by executive decision. The online university would not award its own degrees but would have its own administration. Wilson established a 22-person task force, with delegates from the four sectors of higher education – the University of California, California State University, the community colleges, and the private campuses. The University was established with much fanfare in September 1997.

In proposing the concept of the CVU, Wilson was counting on his ability to secure start-up funding from the Democrat-controlled state legislature and also on his ability to secure matching corporate sponsorship, which would, in turn, be added to by grants from charitable foundations. He expected that as demand for CVU courses grew the university would become self-sufficient.

The initial Web site attracted more than 100,000 enquiries in 60 days and 1,500 people asked to receive a regular e-mail newsletter. There were originally to be 10 founding partners, but only five came forward – Oracle, Sun Microsystems, Cisco Systems, Pacific Bell and International Thompson Publishing. Each gave $75,000. However, these contributions were not untied grants. In return for their funding, the participating corporations were expecting to take a share of the profit from the activities of the University.

The Californian governor was much less successful at attracting endowments from the private foundations. The Alfred P Sloan Foundation contributed $250,000. However, most private foundations were reluctant to participate. The institutions themselves were not required to make any commitment of funds.

Meanwhile, the Governor lost interest in his creation. He removed staff and computer support, expecting the participating institutions to fill the gap, but the institutions did not respond.

Stanley Chodorow, who had previously been provost at the University of Pennsylvania, was appointed as CEO. Not long after Chodorow had arrived to take up his position, he realized that the University had no financial support and could not survive without an injection of funds. He immediately set about to try to salvage this situation.

Chodorow turned to book sales as a way of generating income. The CVU signed a contract with Barnes and Noble. However, this antagonized the institutions as they saw textbook sales as one of their own income sources. Next Chodorow tried to sell online courses overseas. He sent a delegation to Japan and China and the prospects looked promising. However, the time that would be required to produce a cash flow from this source was too great.

In a last ditch attempt to save the organization, Chodorow persuaded the CVU board to accept a revised business plan based on selling advertising space in the online catalogue and attracting matching grants from the foundations. However, the three education sectors could not be persuaded to support the plan and it collapsed.

In March 1999, Chodorow returned $250,000 to the Sloan Foundation and returned to the UC San Diego History Department. The University of California made a commitment to maintain the CVU Web site. However, the administrative structure was dismantled.

What can be learnt from the CVU's demise?

Perhaps the most important lesson is that visionary ideas need to be underpinned by sound business models. The CVU had no proper business plan, indeed no real means of financial support.

In collaborative ventures institutional politics can easily scuttle the most visionary initiative. The universities did not really understand the nature of the organization they had created, didn't know what would be involved in getting it to the point of self-sufficiency and at the end of the day, weren't committed to seeing it survive.

The second lesson is that for a consortium to succeed, its members must be fully committed. When the fledgling organization began to founder, the consortium members walked away.

Further information

Downes S (1999) 'What happened at California Virtual University?' <http://www.atl.ualberta.ca/downes/threads/column041499.htm>

being looked for in the design of materials, then the ratio will be much higher. If particular efforts are made to contain costs then the ratio may be lower. However, the magnitude of the indicative figure shows that the cost of multimedia development is much higher than the costs of development of textual materials.

One implication of the high development cost is that to supply multimedia materials at a cost per student that is comparable to the cost per student of print materials the cost must be spread over a very much larger student intake. As we have noted in this chapter, obtaining and administering a large student intake can incur other costs more than proportionally.

Use of interactive multimedia does not generate cost savings in delivery; if anything, it tends to increase costs. The justification for employing interactive multimedia in distance education needs therefore to be made in terms of the educational benefits that result.

We need to be cautious about accepting at face value many of the claims made for the effectiveness of interactive multimedia in teaching. Interactive multimedia can offer means of teaching when the material that is being taught can take advantage of the attributes of the media. However, it is misleading to suggest that simply by using interactive multimedia the quality of teaching is enhanced. The most important benefits that interactive multimedia can offer are related to the quality of teaching, arising from the capacity of students to grasp new concepts, to understand processes and procedures – particularly where these involve motion. However, many interactive multimedia products do little more than present text and graphics on screen. In these cases, the multimedia presentation is doing little more than 'page turning'.

For the reasons given above, interactive multimedia is best used to target small parts of the curriculum for which it offers a clear advantage. The World Wide Web provides a means of integrating short interactive multimedia segments into learning materials.

The scope for obtaining cost savings through moving to online delivery

The scope that exists for achieving savings in making the shift to online delivery depends not just on the model that will be adopted for online delivery but also the model of delivery that is currently being used.

If a course is currently being delivered at a distance via print, then the scope for obtaining additional cost savings may be quite small. If the course is already being delivered at maximum efficiency, then the potential for obtaining further economies of scale by increasing the size of the intake may be quite modest. Indeed, the fixed costs of online delivery may even be higher than the fixed costs of print-based delivery.

It cannot therefore simply be assumed that a shift to online delivery will necessarily result in savings. Whether or not this will be the case is going to depend on whether there is any scope to increase the intake into the course without undue expense.

When online learning is conceived of as learning via self-instruction with resource materials distributed over the Internet, the same principles that govern the costs of print-based delivery apply. The potential for obtaining economies of scale depends on the magnitude of the fixed costs of delivery.

When online learning is conceived of as learning through the direct interaction between teacher and students and between student and student, the fixed costs of delivery are much lower and very little potential exists for obtaining economies of scale.

Advocates of the use of the remote classroom model argue for this model on the basis of improving the quality of student learning rather than saving costs. A variety of strategies may be used to manage the costs of activities involving group interaction. These activities include:

- having students work on team projects without the assistance of a moderator;
- using discussion forums rather than direct e-mail to staff and encouraging peer feedback to reduce the need for staff input;
- combining the use of online conferencing with the use of resource materials;
- providing students with answers to frequently asked questions to reduce the demand on tutor's time;
- providing automated responses from a database to student responses to assessment tasks and to frequently asked questions.

Some assumptions underlying expectations of cost savings

The expectation that there are savings to be made from shifting to electronic delivery is based on a number of assumptions, some of which have not been fully tested.

One of the most important assumptions is that the savings made by eliminating or at least reducing printing and mailing costs will not be fully eroded by the additional costs attributable to maintenance of the infrastructure needed for electronic delivery. A number of new costs are incurred in moving from print-based to online delivery. These include:

- overhead costs of Web server and mail server storage;
- staff costs of Web site maintenance;
- staff costs of registration of students;
- staff costs of provision of help-desk services;
- initial and ongoing costs of delivery software.

It is commonly assumed that these costs are negligible. However, analysis of the costs shows that they can be comparable with printing and mailing costs.

It appears that the item that makes one of the greatest contributions to the cost of learning online are the communication charges. In Australia, the costs of communication charges will, in many cases, exceed the costs of printing and dispatch of print packages. Most institutions consider these as costs that should be passed on to students.

Will shifting to online delivery reduce overall costs?

As indicated in Chapter 2, one of the major reasons education and training providers have been shifting to online delivery has been to save costs. However, given what has been said about costs in this chapter, we need to ask ourselves whether this expectation is realistic. The answer depends to a considerable extent on the mode or modes of delivery that a provider is presently using.

For universities that have not previously been involved in resources-based learning, such a shift offers the possibility of achieving considerable economies of scale just as the shift from face-to-face delivery to print-based distance education offered in the past. The costs of establishing communication infrastructure can be offset against the cost of buildings that would be required to increase on-campus enrolments to a similar extent.

For institutions other than the major national distance education providers, the outcome is difficult to predict. It will depend on a host of factors, including the experience of staff, the size and location of target markets, the nature of the courses offered and the precise manner in which a programme is to be delivered.

The conclusion to be drawn from this analysis is that the decision to shift to online delivery ought to be made as much on the basis of the educational and marketing advantages to be gained from such a move as on the expectation of savings.

What are the likely costs?

Rumble (1997) pointed out that one of the difficulties that distance education providers encounter in managing their budgets is that line-item budgeting often conceals critical cost relationships. Rumble argued that distance education providers would be better able to manage their budgets if they moved to activity-based costing.

In activity-based costing, the costs of delivery are subdivided according to the major activities involved in offering a course off-campus. The major activities involved in offering courses off-campus are shown in Figure 4.2. The breakdown is different from that suggested by Rumble, reflecting the just-in-time approach to the reproduction of learning packages that is more typical of Australian distance education providers. The nomenclature used in the figure has been chosen to be applicable across media. Other terms are in some cases more commonly used with reference to particular media.

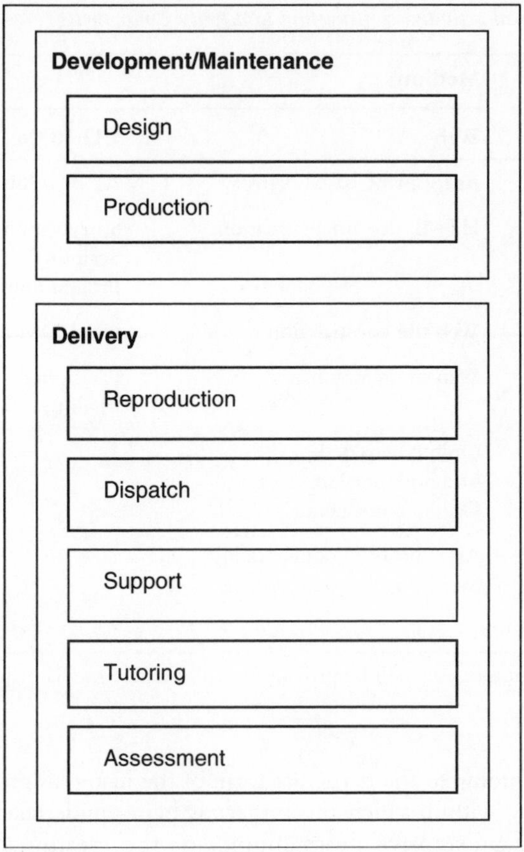

Figure 4.2 *Breakdown of activity components*

While the delivery of courses via digital media involves the development of quite different resource materials, many of the activities involved are the same or similar to those involved in the development of print materials. It is therefore possible to draw quite close parallels between the costs of print-based distance education delivery and the costs of online and interactive multimedia delivery.

Table 4.3 compares the activities involved in Web-based and interactive multimedia delivered via CD ROM with the activities involved in print-based delivery. In the case of interactive multimedia delivered via CD ROM, support, tutoring, submission, and return of assignments will not be specific to this medium.

In using an activity-based costing approach to estimate the costs of a project, the resource requirements of the project are quantified and a total cost is calculated by multiplying each component cost by its corresponding unit cost.

Table 4.4 identifies the typical cost components for print, Web, and interactive multimedia projects. The actual costs of a development project are likely to vary

Table 4.3 *Typical activities contributing to activity components*

Activity Component	Medium	
	Web	**CD ROM**
Design	As for print-based delivery	As for print-based delivery
Production	HTML document creation	Storyboarding Scripting Programming
Reproduction	Web site construction	CD ROM duplication
Dispatch	Web site maintenance	Packaging Mailing
Support	Online help desk Online library services Online counselling	*
Tutoring	Asynchronous conferencing Synchronous conferencing	*
Asssessment	*	*

*Typically these components will be provided via alternative media or in other ways

quite widely according to the particular form of the materials produced as well as with the country within which the project is being undertaken. For example, projects involving extensive programming or the creation of sophisticated animations will be much more costly to produce than projects that provide an interface to a range of existing print, illustration and video resources. Attempting to provide indicative costs for multimedia projects would therefore be more likely to mislead than to inform.

If a more sophisticated analysis of the costs of delivering distance education and training via the World Wide Web is required, then the cost/performance model developed by Bloniarz and Larsen (1997) for the costing of the provision of government information services offers a possible methodology.

What about the 'hidden' costs?

One of the difficulties experienced in estimating the costs of a new mode of delivery is that some cost components can remain unaccounted for or 'hidden'. Paul Bacsich and his colleagues at the Sheffield Hallam University have been investigating the hidden costs of online delivery in universities in the UK (Bacsich *et al*, 1999). They have identified three types of hidden costs: costs to the institution, costs to staff and costs to students.

Table 4.4 *Cost elements in resource-based learning projects*

Activity Component	Cost Contributor	Units	Print	Web	CD
Design	Subject specialist	hours	✓	✓	✓
	Teaching-learning specialist	hours	✓	✓	✓
	Multimedia producer	hours			✓
Production	Subject specialist	hours	✓	✓	✓
	Teaching-learning specialist	hours	✓	✓	✓
	Scriptwriter	hours	✓	✓	✓
	Editor	hours			✓
	Camera operator	hours			✓
	Audio producer	hours			✓
	Narrator	hours			✓
	Graphic designer	hours	✓	✓	✓
	Photographer	hours	✓	✓	
	Desktop publisher	hours	✓		
	Web publisher	hours	✓	✓	✓
	Production manager	hours			✓
Reproduction	Printing	pages	✓		
	Binding	volumes	✓		
	Storage	volumes	✓	✓	
	Web database integration	Mbs		✓	
Dispatch	Packaging/postage	packages	✓		✓
	Mail label production	packages	✓		✓
	Stuffing	packages	✓		✓
	Delivery to PO	packages	✓		
	Web delivery	Mbs		✓	
Support	Communications support	students	✓	✓	
	User support	students	✓	✓	
Tutoring	Subject specialist	hours	✓	✓	
Assessment	Examination supervision	centres	✓	✓	✓
	Examiners	students	✓	✓	✓

Amongst the costs to the institution, Bacsich *et al* (1999) have identified the cost of costing, the costs of collaboration, the costs of monitoring informal staff–student contact and the costs of copyright compliance. Amongst the costs to staff, they identified the costs of time spent out-of-hours in development of learning materials and the costs of use of privately purchased computers and consumables. Amongst the costs to students they identified the costs of ink jet cartridges needed to print out learning materials.

One of the reasons institutional costs can stay hidden is that institutions may not have had previous experience of resource materials development and may not be organized to manage the types of activities involved. Institutions that have had a long history of involvement in print-based distance education are likely to be much more alert to the types of costs that arise in the team-based design and development of resource materials.

Who pays the cost?

The proportion of the total cost of offering a course or programme paid by the student differs greatly from country to country and even from programme to programme. In some countries, the total cost is born by the student, in other countries, students pay only a small proportion of the cost. In many countries, private institutions operate alongside public institutions and some of the private institutions exist to make a profit. In these countries, the proportion of the delivery costs borne by the student will depend on the type of institution at which the student is studying.

Not only may moving from print-based to online delivery shift costs to the student, it may also increase costs so that the costs the student is asked to bear may be higher than would otherwise be the case.

Over the past decade, the production of print-based distance education materials has been made highly efficient. Furthermore, the advent of fast, economical courier services has considerably reduced the time and cost to deliver print-based learning materials to students. If the first action students take upon downloading electronically delivered learning materials is to print them out on slow, inefficient laser printers then any expected savings to be made from delivering courses online will indeed be illusory.

Moving to online delivery may also alter the distribution of costs between different cost centres within an institution if full-cost budgeting is not being practised.

The possible impact of increased costs on course enrolments

The increased costs imposed on students as a result of moving to online delivery may have the effect of restricting the market for a programme. One way to avoid this possibility is to offer programmes for a time in parallel forms. For example, a programme might be offered both in print-based and Web-based versions.

The strategic approach to dealing with the penetration of information technology into homes is to target professions that are known to have a high penetration of computers first and to target postgraduate programmes before undergraduate programmes.

Summing up

One of the major reasons education and training providers showed such considerable interest in delivery of courses online and via multimedia was because of the perceived potential for obtaining economies of scale. The potential for obtaining greater economies of scale can be increased by lowering variable costs.

The costs of delivery can be managed more effectively by switching from a line-item costing to activity-based costing. The costs of development of Web-based delivery are comparable to the costs of print-based delivery. However, the costs of development of multimedia materials are typically several orders of magnitude higher. Multimedia materials are therefore best used selectively in situations where their particular advantages compensate for the much higher development costs involved.

Chapter 5

A cost or an investment?

In this chapter we pose the question: is it appropriate to regard expenditure on the design and development of courseware and the implementation of delivery systems as an investment rather than simply as a cost? We then examine the implications of adopting an investment orientation to the way the design and development of courseware is managed. We examine in particular the implications for:

- protection of intellectual property;
- return on investment;
- responding to competition.

We conclude by discussing the importance of being able to monitor the real costs of development and maintenance.

The importance of seeing learning materials and delivery systems as assets

In the last chapter, we explained that the costs of mounting a distance education programme could be divided into upfront expenses and ongoing expenses. The upfront expenses include the costs of design, development and pre-production of learning materials as well as the costs of establishing the infrastructure needed to support the ongoing delivery of programmes. Providers of traditional print-based distance education programmes have tended to treat these expenses merely as costs. The literature dealing with the economics of distance education has also generally dealt with them in this way. Yet, in other industries they would be treated as investments.

The way one thinks about expenditure affects the way one manages it. The tendency to regard expenditure on the development of courseware simply as a cost is one of the main factors that has discouraged many higher education institutions in the past from entering the field of distance education. The high upfront costs involved in the development of courseware were seen as a barrier to entry in the field of distance education. Managers in institutions could not see the justification for such large costs when they were not incurred on programmes taught entirely with an annual budget period. In many cases, it has been a belief that delivery of courses online largely avoided these upfront costs that led many institutions to venture into this field.

However, courseware has a value that lasts for several years. Courseware should therefore be seen as an asset. This value also subsists in the knowledge derived from the research that went into the development of the materials. Consequently, the expertise of the staff who were responsible for developing the materials is also an asset. This expertise may be drawn on again for the development of related materials. The expense involved in developing the learning resource materials should be seen as an investment rather than simply a cost. The same reasoning can also be applied to the expenditure on new delivery systems.

What difference does it make to treat an expense as an investment?

In the commercial world, the profitability of a company depends on the return it makes on its assets. In the public sector, the health of an organization depends on the use it is able to make of its assets. The financial viability of an organization therefore depends on the success it has in building up and protecting its assets.

In the past, distance education providers often did not display the same concern for their investment in courseware and delivery systems as a manufacturer does for its assets in product designs. Once a product has been launched, efforts will be made to preserve the value of the resulting asset. The types of action include:

- protecting the intellectual property that gives to the product its unique position in the market;
- marketing the product appropriately and adequately;
- updating the appearance or image of the product regularly to ensure that it does not become tired or outdated.

Making the investment decision

Making the investment decision involves making a judgement as to whether the return that is likely to be generated justifies the size of the investment. While it is a mistake to spend too little on the development of a new course, it is obviously also a mistake to spend too much or to invest in a course for which there is insufficient demand. Yet, how should you decide what is an adequate return? The answer will depend on the nature of the project.

A general rule used within the investment community is that the rate of return should reflect the level of risk being taken. A riskier investment should hold the promise of a higher rate of return. If one applies this rule to the provision of offerings in distance education, then one should look for a higher rate of return from courses and programmes that do not have a guaranteed intake than from those that do.

One aspect of risk management is spreading risk across a range of different types of projects. By combining different types of projects, the risk that several projects will run into trouble all for the same reasons is reduced. However, combining projects of different types carries another type of risk. This allows losses on loss-making projects to be offset against the higher returns on profit-making projects. The factor that most determines where best to seek a market is the margin you can achieve between the unit cost of supply and the revenue you can obtain. The greater the margin the more attractive the investment opportunity. Nevertheless, achieving small margins on products that achieve high sales figures can still make profits.

In the case of government-funded courses, budgeting is directed towards producing the best result with the funds provided. There is no call to achieve a surplus and the funds available are often less than one would ideally like to commit.

The situation can be different for full-fee courses offered by government-funded institutions. In this case, it may be expected that the conduct of courses will generate a surplus to provide for growth or to support other activities in which the institution is engaged. In this case, the cost of offering the course needs to be looked at against the potential income. Some projects may be worth undertaking because of the size of the market. Other projects will be attractive because they offer the prospect of better than average margins. The factors that are critical in making a good investment decision are that you have adequate knowledge of the particular market and that you have a good understanding of what your costs will be in entering that market. The most common mistakes are to overestimate the size of the market for a particular product and to underestimate the costs of development. It is therefore advisable to allow for a wide margin of error in making your estimates.

Marketing

One of the major attractions of online delivery for educational institutions is that it offers access to a much wider market. Courses that might not be viable if they have to rely on a local market can attract students from around the world. Of course, whether a programme is suitable for online delivery to an international market will depend on the extent and nature of the practical work that is required or whether there are ways in which the requirements for practical work can be accommodated in other ways.

The marketing of education and training programmes is a topic that is becoming of increasing interest to educational institutions as competition for students increases and globalization brings threats or perceived threats to existing markets from overseas providers. Some of the avenues through which you can promote your programmes include:

● World Wide Web;
● professional associations;
● government and non-government organizations;
● advertising;
● word of mouth.

When promoting your programmes via the World Wide Web, it is important to make your promotional literature accessible to search engines. This is accomplished by adding metadata tags that will be picked up by the search engines. If you ensure that your promotional literature is appropriately tagged you may be able to generate up to 20–30 per cent of your enquiries from the Web. It is also important to ensure that you include the information that prospective students are likely to be seeking:

● What will it cost per course and what will it cost per semester?
● What are the minimum specifications for a computer to access the learning resources and to participate in online discussions?
● What methods are used to solve students' problems?

Some of the questions that you need to be asking yourself include:

● Are you looking for a mass market or a niche market?
● Do you want the best students or most students?
● Do you want students who are looking for your traditional products or are you wanting to design new products to meet the new opportunities that are opened up by moving to online delivery?

It is important not be misled by the rate at which enquiries come in. Even some of those students who are prepared to pay the enrolment fees may not meet your entry requirements. Perhaps as few as 10 per cent of enquiries will lead to actual enrolments. It may be preferable to refuse enrolment from an applicant who is not ideal rather than accept the enrolment and then find that you are involved in costly remedial courses or individual tutoring later.

If you are in the workplace training sector, your customer is likely to be a business unit manager rather than a student. Marketing in this case takes on a different meaning. It entails convincing the business unit manager that using your product will be a worthwhile investment. In the training sector, the business case for training has traditionally been made by providing estimates of return on investment (ROI). However, Cross (2001) suggests that when it comes to e-learning, business unit managers deciding whether to make a particular training investment are placing more weight on their intuitive judgement rather than on ROI estimates. The reason for this is that business unit managers have begun to realize that in an area that is so little understood as e-learning, ROI estimates are likely to prove overly optimistic.

Keeping courseware current

Maintaining distance education offerings, like maintaining a home, is an ongoing expense. The fact that courseware can be so easily reproduced makes reusing it very tempting even when it is out of date. Yet, failure to maintain the currency of courseware can cost real money, not just a provider's reputation.

As students bear an increasing proportion of the cost of their education, they are likely to become more discriminating when judging what they regard as acceptable quality. In a competitive environment, providers that are able to claim they are offering the most up-to-date training are likely to attract a larger clientele.

Regular revision of courseware involves significant additional expense. If this task is to receive adequate attention, specific budget provision needs to be made for it. Budget provision should also be made for conducting the evaluations that should inform the revisions (see Chapter 10). The cost of evaluation, updating of courseware and systems and marketing should be budgeted on a year-by-year basis. While this might seem like an optional expense, failing to allow for it will eventually affect the competitiveness of your products and show up on the 'bottom line'. As in the case of owning a home, regular maintenance generally ends up costing less than major reconstruction necessitated by neglect.

Keeping systems up to date

If you are making a substantial investment in courseware maintenance then it represents poor economy to allow the infrastructure needed to deliver courses to slide into obsolescence through failure to make adequate budget provision for its maintenance.

It is not uncommon for public institutions to adopt the attitude 'If it ain't broke, don't fix it.' Commercial providers tend to be more aware of the hidden costs of outdated and inefficient infrastructure, probably because their attention is focused more closely on the impact that that strategy has on the 'bottom line'. Yet systems that have been in use for several years without ever having been reviewed can become inefficient and barriers to innovation. Even more importantly, systems based on information and communications technology become out of date through technological obsolescence.

Regular updating of infrastructure requires a specific budget allocation. A strategy that may be worthwhile considering is to make specific annual provision for the updating of systems and to apply this to the tasks that have highest priority. In this way it is possible to maintain a priority list for system upgrading in the safe knowledge that at least the most important items will receive timely attention.

Planning for the investment

Making the transition to online and interactive multimedia delivery involves a major investment in the development of new courseware. It also requires a substantial investment in infrastructure – in upgrading communication networks, acquiring and installing new servers and acquiring licences for new software. There will also be a substantial investment in training staff. Making the right investment decision calls for the development of a plan as a basis for first deciding whether it is prudent to proceed with the project as it has been initially conceived or whether the proposal needs to be further developed.

The plan may take a form similar to that of a business plan of the type initially prepared before starting up a new business venture. The plan should detail the changes proposed, the sequence in which the changes would be undertaken, the benefits anticipated from the changes and the risks that the project entails.

The most important part of the plan is the financial information. This needs to detail not only the costs that would be involved but also the expected return on the investment. The overall returns may be derived from several income streams. For example, as well as course fees, some, or all of the courseware may be sold as a product on its own. In addition, the rights to use the courseware in another course may be sold to other education or training providers. Even if no money is to change hands, a notional estimate of income and expenditure should be prepared as part of the justification for the project.

Protecting the intellectual property component of courseware

The intellectual property of courseware is protected via copyright legislation. Copyright legislation differs from country to country. It is therefore important to be conversant with the provisions of the copyright legislation in force in your own country and to be aware of the extent of the protection that the law gives to the materials you are producing.

Copyright protects the expression of a work, not the ideas that led to the creation of the work. The value of the intellectual property subsisting in the courseware has hitherto been more closely associated with the subject matter content than with the pedagogical approach. Pedagogy does not advance as rapidly as most other fields of study. Thus, the frequency with which courseware needs to be updated is determined more by currency of the subject matter than by the currency of its pedagogical approach.

However, in the case of multimedia courseware visual presentation assumes considerable importance. Because copyright subsists in the expression of ideas, there is significant scope for enhancing the value of multimedia courseware by encouraging creativity in visual expression. The life of multimedia courseware is also likely to be greater if it is given a contemporary look and feel.

In Chapter 7, we will discuss the option of outsourcing the production of courseware. Outsourcing the programming of multimedia materials or the design of a Web site may enable the development cycle for a project to be shortened and the cost to be kept low. However, it is important to establish from the outset what rights you will be receiving to the courseware or Web pages. If you employ contractors under standard terms then what you may be paying for is the right to use the courseware or Web pages rather than the copyright over the materials themselves. This will mean that you won't have the right to update the material in future except by employing the same contractor. If you wish to secure copyright over the materials, then you should make explicit provision for this in the contract you sign with the contractor. The costs in this case are likely to be somewhat higher.

Contractors make a living by selling the skills they pick up in one job to a client who needs those skills in another. If you are implementing some innovative ideas in your project and you are employing contractors to execute them, then it may not be many months before your competitors are using the same ideas. Commercial-in-confidence conditions are difficult to define and enforce as a way of protecting such ideas. Obtaining compensation for breaches of agreements may be difficult and will almost certainly take considerable time.

In commerce, most innovation is actually adaptation of ideas. In manufacturing industries, many companies rely on rapid innovation to keep a step ahead of their competitors. One way of dealing with the matter of copyright is therefore to aim to provide the most up-to-date materials and to be known for that.

Responding to competition

While the Internet offers access to new markets, it also exposes providers to much greater competition. The effect of competition is to drive prices (in this case course fees) lower.

In an open market, if competition becomes too intense, the revenue of suppliers may fall below the cost of getting the product to market. When this happens, some suppliers are driven out of the market. The reduction in the intensity of competition eases the pressure on prices and leads to a new equilibrium being established where prices are sufficient to allow a profit margin that is acceptable to at least a few suppliers. The suppliers that remain in the market once this stage has been reached will be those that operate most efficiently.

In a global market for online courses, we should therefore expect that survival would depend on efficiency of provision rather than on price alone. As was shown

Case study 3: UBC–ITESM joint programme in educational technology

The initiative

The strategic partnership between the University of British Columbia and the Monterrey Institute of Technology (ITESM) provides an example of the way two institutions can lower the costs and risks of investment in courseware development and increase the return on their investment by working co-operatively. One of the first initiatives undertaken under the strategic alliance was the development of a joint programme in educational technology. Full accounts of this initiative have been published in a number of journal and conference articles of which the most informative, in this context, is Bates and Escamilla de los Santos (1997).

Features

- UBC developed five technology-based courses with funding support from ITESM.
- The courses are taught via a combination of Web-based delivery including online discussion, e-mail, textbooks and readings, and in the case of one course, a CD ROM.
- UBC provides guidelines and assessment criteria for marking assignments.
- ITESM teaches the courses to students in its own Masters in Educational Technology programme and can market the courses within Latin America.
- UBC offers the courses to its own students and can market the courses elsewhere in the world.

The stakeholders

The University of British Columbia, located in Vancouver, Canada and the Monterrey Institute of Technology, the largest and most prestigious of the private universities in Mexico with 29 campuses throughout Mexico and over 80,000 students.

The factors that made UBC an attractive partner for ITESM were its strong links with Asian countries, its research interests and its expertise in distance education. The factors that made ITESM attractive as a partner for UBC were its location in a region that UBC wanted to become more involved with and its suitability for student exchange.

The initiative at work

ITESM had earlier established a Virtual University as an internal training programme for its own staff. ITESM had begun planning a Masters degree in Educational Technology for its staff and had developed seven of the required twelve courses. However, the Institute still required five courses on technology-based teaching. ITESM's Virtual University approached UBC's Distance Education and Technology Unit to develop these courses under the strategic alliance agreement.

Before commencing development of the courses, the UBC conducted a market survey to assess the likelihood of sufficient demand for the courses worldwide. The survey identified a number of potential competitors including Athabasca University, the UK Open University, Deakin University and the University of Southern Queensland. It was also recognized that there was likely to be increasing competition. However, it was judged that development of the courses would still be viable because of the fact that the costs of development would be shared and UBC's reputation in technology-enhanced learning would help to attract students.

The courses were designed by a team of staff from the Distance Education and Technology Unit at UBC. The team was assisted by an Internet specialist, a graphic designer, a desktop editor and a course administrator. Throughout the development process, course team meetings were held by video-conference between UBC and ITESM.

Subsequent enrolments justified their confidence. Enrolments for the first offering of the first course totalled 120 of which 80 came through ITESM and 40 through UBC. The enrolments for the second course reached 300 of which 240 came through ITESM and 60 through UBC. After four years enrolments reached 1,500 through ITESM and 500 through UBC. UBC and ITESM now plan to develop a fully joint Masters degree in educational technology that can be taken entirely in English or Spanish.

Issues encountered

Problems arose in obtaining the required texts from the publishers and in getting course materials through customs. Problems also arose in collecting payments. Because UBC accepts students from around the world, special arrangements were needed for payment of fees and for purchase of course texts. UBC has since addressed this problem by establishing a single point of contact for all matters to do with the course. Students can now pay for both tuition and materials in a single payment by electronic funds transfer.

UBC had provision for offering courses at Masters level on an experimental basis and this was the basis on which the first three courses were offered.

Further information

Bates, A W and Escamilla de los Santos, J G (1997) Crossing boundaries: Making global distance education, *Journal of Distance Education*, 12, 1/2, 49–66 in the previous chapter, efficiency can be reached with quite modest intakes if the size of the initial investment is not very substantial. Instead of going head-to-head in a global market for online provision of the most popular courses, it is therefore possible to sustain a viable operation by seeking out niche markets where there is under-provision. Meeting a need where there is high demand and insufficient supply allows a greater return.

Institutions that do well in the market for online courses will be those that are able to spot new opportunities, are nimble at meeting those opportunities, and have an efficient responsive operation for supplying their services. This is the essence of an investment approach to course provision.

Maximizing the return on investment

One of the most common reasons for education and training providers to want to move into online delivery is that it opens up a wider market (see Case study 3). It opens the market for students who hitherto have not been able to attend on-campus classes because of work or other commitments and who have not been attracted to traditional modes of distance education. It also opens the door to more geographically distant markets. Yet the fact that an institution gains access to a much larger market does not guarantee that it will be successful in tapping that market. The strategies that have been found effective in the past with the more traditional media may not be appropriate for the new knowledge media. Even if the strategies are appropriate, they may not be effective.

The importance of real-cost accounting

In some organizations, actual costs are not used in transferring expenses between sections. The major reason for this is to encourage particular types of behaviour. However, the effect of pricing services at less than their true cost is for the organization as a whole to subsidize.

An important side effect of using internal transfer pricing that does not reflect true costs is to reduce the ability of the organization to monitor the financial impact of resource utilization. This makes it difficult to determine the effect of strategic decisions. A better way to encourage change is through explicit specific purpose subsidies.

Shifting to online delivery will involve major budget adjustments. The changes may have important implications for the distribution of powers and responsibilities within an institution or organization. Making such adjustments carries significant risks because the effects of the adjustment cannot be fully known in advance. Unforeseen expenses may arise. However, the risks are greatly magnified if the data upon which the effects of the adjustment are assessed do not reflect the effect of the changes on the organization's financial position. The adoption of real-cost accounting practices enables real costs to the organization to be used as the basis for strategic decision-making.

Summing up

Our intention in this chapter has not been to provide a comprehensive treatment of all the factors that need to be taken into account when adopting an investment orientation to entering the online education market. Rather, it has been to highlight the changes in ways of thinking about course development and course delivery that the adoption of an investment approach implies.

Treating the initial expenditure on the development of courseware and the establishment of infrastructure as an investment implies looking for a return that justifies the magnitude of the expenditure. It is important not to rush into an investment. However, the initial investment needs to be sufficient to allow the products and services that are developed to meet the prevailing expectations of the education and training marketplace. Once funds have been committed, it is important to preserve and enhance the value of the assets that have been acquired. As a result:

- courseware is kept current in terms of content, appearance and teaching approach;
- delivery systems are regularly updated to maintain and if possible improve their efficiency;
- opportunities are sought to exploit further the investment in courseware and delivery systems so as to derive additional income.

Chapter 6

Re-engineering technological infrastructure

In this chapter we will examine the changes to technology infrastructure that a major shift to online or multimedia delivery is likely to necessitate. We examine three ways of going about implementing an electronic learning environment and describe the features of a number of commercially available products that perform this role. We also identify the types of changes that will need to be made to communications infrastructure to support the increased traffic that the shift to online delivery will generate and discuss the vexed issue of student access to online resources.

The importance of planning

Making a major shift to delivery online or via multimedia almost invariably requires a substantial investment in ICT infrastructure. The types of improvements that may need to be made include:

- acquisition of servers to hold and deliver courseware;
- installation of new cabling and communication equipment to provide increased access or increased capacity;
- acquisition and installation of more up-to-date workstations for staff;
- acquisition of site licences for applications software for staff and students;
- acquisition of licences for software required for the delivery of courses (eg integrated electronic learning environment software, conferencing software,

computer-assisted assessment software, streaming audio or streaming video software).

The scale and nature of the improvements required will depend first and foremost on the magnitude of the shift being contemplated. Trialing with a pilot group of 30 students in a single course will obviously require very little in the way of additional ICT infrastructure – perhaps only the acquisition of the conferencing software. Shifting all the courses offered by an institution online would require massive upgrading of ICT infrastructure, which, because of the cost, may need to be staged over several years.

Laying the foundations for future developments depends on thinking through the sequence of steps to be taken:

● Are you intending to deliver courses online or are you only intending to deliver courses via CD ROM?
● Are you planning to offer parallel print and online versions of courses?
● Are you planning to use audio or video teleconferencing?

There is now a strong and widely recognized trend amongst distance education providers towards delivering courses online. The convergence of technologies is enabling even interactive multimedia courseware to be delivered online. Authoring software such as Asymetrix Toolbook and Macromedia Director provide the tools to enable courseware developed with these systems to be delivered via the Web. Improvements in streaming audio and streaming video technologies are enabling audio and video materials to be delivered to students in their homes and work places. Nevertheless, the data-carrying capacities of networks still impose severe constraints on what is feasible. The reliability of networks and systems also remains an issue.

The functions that a course delivery system needs to perform

In Chapter 3, we outlined in general terms the functions that need to be supported in order to deliver courses and programmes online. Most multimedia authoring systems are essentially tools for developing presentation. To support the full range of functions needed to deliver courses and programmes online it is necessary to look beyond multimedia courseware authoring systems.

Moving to online delivery results in a further increase in the volume and complexity of the information that needs to be managed. This includes:

● programme administration – student enrolment, fee payments and student progress record systems;
● courseware delivery – provision of access to learning materials comprising text, graphics, photo images, animations, audio or video;

- communication – communication between student and tutor, between student and institution and between student and student;
- collaboration – file sharing, shared workspace, applications sharing, shared virtual whiteboard facilities;
- learning management – online registration, user authentication, online assessment on demand, monitoring of participation and progress of individuals and groups, monitoring of access to learning materials, and providing the student with a path through a course that matches the student's individual needs.

If the intention is to use a basic form of presentation, then little may be required in the way of additional software. Most word-processing and desktop publishing systems offer the option of saving files in HTML format. This approach can be quite economical. Documents will be able to be produced by the teaching staff themselves and only the task of uploading them on to the delivery system will require technical support.

However, it needs to be recognized that producing HTML documents in this way does carry some penalties. The options of inclusion of illustrations are quite limited and the HTML code produced is relatively inefficient with the result that it takes longer for documents produced in this way to be downloaded over the Internet.

The quality of the result obtained using this approach can be improved using templates to standardize the format of Web pages much as templates are used to standardize the layout of print documents.

If the intention is to reach a higher standard of presentation, perhaps making more creative use of layout or making extensive use of graphics and illustrations, then it will be necessary to move to the use of professional Web design tools. Such tools provide much greater control over the design of Web pages and allow more efficient creation of HTML output. In this case, the production of the courseware will need to be placed in the hands of professional Web designers.

If the intention is to go all the way to full multimedia development, then a suite of multimedia development software will be required. Because the development of multimedia materials places much higher demands on the processing capabilities of systems, particularly when it comes to compression of video segments, the decision to move to this standard of presentation will need to be supported by the acquisition of top-of-the-line systems. In this case, the production of courseware will need to be placed in the hands of a multimedia programmer who is skilled in using the particular multimedia authoring system that has been chosen for development.

Alternative approaches to acquiring an online course delivery system

One may take three general approaches to acquiring an online delivery system:

● purchasing an integrated system 'off the shelf';
● assembling a system from commercially available 'building blocks';
● custom building a system from the ground up.

The 'off-the-shelf' option

No generally recognized name has emerged for this category of product. However, we will refer to them here as 'integrated electronic learning environments'.

Integrated electronic learning environments are delivery systems that combine all the components into a single integrated product. The components provided by such a system are selected and designed to support the full range of functions needed by the learner. The components are designed to work together and to share a common look and feel. This integration of the components results in navigation being simplified. For most education and training providers, 'off-the-shelf' solutions are likely to represent the best option. Some of the advantages of the 'off-the-shelf' option are:

● Such systems can be quickly brought into operation.
● The complete system is provided by one supplier – the problem of suppliers refusing to accept responsibility for incompatibilities between separate components is avoided.
● The cost is much less than if the system was developed in-house.
● The software developer takes care of the product research, design of the system architecture, software development and maintenance.
● There is greater consistency in the way the various components function. The need for students to log on to each component separately is avoided.

Some of the disadvantages of choosing this option are:

● One is locked into the supplier's timetable for updating the software – one generally cannot upgrade individual components separately.
● The eventual cost of continuing to use the software may turn out to be somewhat higher than initially expected because of changes in the basis on which licences are priced.
● New servers may be required to support the software.
● One is constrained by the teaching model upon which the product has been designed.
● If the product or supplier turns out to be unreliable, one's whole teaching programme may be placed in jeopardy.

Because of the number of organizations looking for this type of solution, the number of such systems available on the market has grown rapidly in recent times. Examples of commercially available integrated electronic learning environments include Blackboard, The Learning Manager, LearningSpace and WebCT.

A trend that has become evident amongst suppliers of integrated electronic learning environment systems has been to increase the customizability of their products.

The 'building block' option

The building block option allows an incremental strategy to be adopted. While off-the-shelf systems may permit a certain amount of customization, a much greater amount of customization is possible when the building block approach is adopted. In this case, the system is assembled from a set of major functional components, each of which is a commercially available product. For example, the conferencing component may be provided by one supplier, the course delivery system may be provided by a second supplier and a computer-based assessment system by a third. The total suite of software may comprise more than half a dozen components.

The building block approach is made feasible by the fact that the functional components can be brought together behind a common Web interface.

A variant of the building block option is emerging from a new trend amongst suppliers of integrated systems to make provision for third-party components to be integrated into their systems.

The 'custom built' option

Adopting the custom built option will give you a system that is fully tailored to your needs and responsive to emerging requirements – if you can afford the cost of development. If you have the resources to choose this option, it can offer you a substantial comparative advantage in the marketplace as it lets you incorporate features that the systems your competitors are using do not have. You can incorporate exactly the combination of features you require and you can develop the system in directions and at a pace that matches your strategic plans. It will also give you a system that is capable of being enhanced as your needs change or when you want to introduce an innovation in the way your delivery system operates.

The major disadvantages of the custom built option are the cost and the work involved in obtaining what is wanted. The time taken to develop such a system is also considerable. Commercial learning environment producers may employ 50 programmers, graphic artists and media staff. Meanwhile the field is advancing apace. For these reasons, custom building a learning management system is an option that usually can only be considered by large organizations and organizations that are prepared to assign a team of software developers to the task full time. Nevertheless, it should be pointed out that many of the popular 'off-the-shelf' systems have evolved from systems that were custom built by educational institutions. These include Blackboard, and The Learning Manager and WebCT. So custom building is a genuine option given the right circumstances.

Integrated electronic learning environments

Integrated electronic learning environments have different origins. Not all have originated as such. The types of components that an integrated electronic learning environment is likely to offer include:

- a data storage for uploading and holding learning resources;
- links to other available learning resources;
- messaging facilities, such as noticeboards, e-mail, discussion and chat, for one-to-one, one-to-many and many-to-many interaction, including a facility for synchronous many-to-many interaction;
- assessment features such as self-assessment quizzes, online assessment and assignment uploading.

Some 'off-the-shelf' integrated electronic learning environments

Because of the number of integrated electronic learning environments on the market it is not practicable to provide a comprehensive, up-to-date catalogue of such systems in a book like this. Indeed, given the pace at which the market is growing, any such catalogue would soon be out of date. Nevertheless, it is important to be aware of the types of systems available and the types of functions that they support. We shall therefore briefly describe five of the most popular:

- Blackboard;
- FirstClass Collaborative Classroom Gold;
- LearningSpace;
- The Learning Manager;
- WebCT.

Blackboard

Version described: Blackboard 5

Blackboard was earlier marketed as Courseinfo and many people still know it by that name. Originating in the US, the system is more oriented to the classroom-based model of course delivery than the resource-based model. Yet, many institutions that have adopted the resource-based model have chosen Blackboard because of its flexibility, convenience and robustness.

Blackboard now comes in three versions. Level 1, the Course Manager, is the direct successor to Courseinfo. It offers built-in conferencing, content administration and test administration components. These provide quite adequate functionality but provide fewer features than corresponding stand-alone applications. Blackboard Corporation has indicated that it intends to open up its system to third-party suppliers to enable them to add modules to the basic Blackboard architecture.

Level 2, the Course and Portal Manager, adds modules that provide seamless communication with other communication systems as well as allowing institutional branding.

Level 3, the Advanced Course and Portal Manager, adds functions associated with end-user authentication and full integration of the system into an institution's IT environment.

Blackboard can be supported on Windows NT, Windows 2000 and Unix servers.

FirstClass Collaborative Classroom Gold

<http://www.centrinity.com/FCCGold.pdf>

FirstClass originated as an e-mail and conferencing system designed specifically to meet the needs of users in education and training. The early versions of FirstClass were based on a client-server model. However, more recently FirstClass has been migrated to the Web.

As with other groupware products that were migrated to the Web, FirstClass initially lost some of the functionality that the earlier client-server version offered. However, more recent versions of the FirstClass product have taken advantage of the new opportunities that the Web offers for enhancing the students' learning experience.

One of the major advantages of FirstClass has always been its cross-platform capability. It is available in versions for Windows NT and Mac OS servers and can support Windows and Mac OS clients.

The main functions that FirstClass Collaborative Classroom Gold supports are asynchronous and synchronous conferencing, an enhanced shared workspace, highly customizable Web forms, Web publishing and scheduling. FirstClass Collaborative Classroom Gold does not offer learning management features or testing. On the other hand, it does offer sophisticated event scheduling features and the ability to allow easy sharing of multimedia resources.

The major strengths of FirstClass Collaborative Classroom Gold are its cross-platform capabilities, scalability and reliability.

LearningSpace

Version described: 4.0
<http://www.lotus.com/home.nsf/welcome/learnspace>

LearningSpace has been built on top of the groupware product Lotus Notes and the Domino Web server software. Lotus Corporation is now a subsidiary of IBM.

So, LearningSpace is effectively IBM's version of an integrated electronic learning environment. Lotus Notes is considered the leading groupware product for business. LearningSpace takes advantage of the features Lotus Notes offers for conferencing, e-mail and scheduling. However, LearningSpace is not just a groupware product. It is also designed to provide access to a wide range of Web-based interactive multimedia courseware and to support online testing. LearningSpace also provides a range of tools to assist instructors in courseware development, administration, and learning management.

LearningSpace is supported on Unix, Windows NT, and Windows 98 servers. It may be accessed via Lotus Notes clients for Windows and Macintosh.

The Learning Manager

Version described: 3.0

The Learning Manager (TLM) has evolved from the Learning Management System (LMS), one of the leading computer-managed learning systems. LMS was originally developed at the Southern Alberta Institute of Technology (SAIT) as a distributed CML system, which ran on VAX computers. It was one of the first CML systems to develop a strong following, particularly in technical training. LMS was subsequently acquired by Campus America. The Learning Manager was released in 1996 as a microcomputer-based version of LMS. It was subsequently bought back from Campus America by SAIT, which has established a subsidiary company to undertake its continuing development. LMS was one of the first CML systems to be developed.

TLM differs from LMS in that it is able to run either on individual workstations or over the Internet. When it is used over the Internet, it is accessible via a standard Web browser. The major strengths of TLM remain its wide range of learning management and test administration capabilities.

WebCT

Version described: 3.5 Campus

WebCT was developed by the Department of Computer Science at the University of British Columbia. The system's initial popularity was due to the low cost, which was explained by the fact that licence fees were initially pitched at a level to provide funds for further research and development and support costs were kept low.

Notwithstanding its origins, WebCT is a mature product that offers a variety of features including a conferencing system, online chat, tracking of student progress, organization of group projects, student assessment, maintenance and publishing of grades, automatic index generation, course content searches, a course calendar and student home pages.

All users of WebCT, including course developers, students and markers, access the system via a standard Web browser. The system currently runs under various versions of Unix.

Which system should you choose?

The integrated electronic learning environments described above are only some of the growing array of such products available commercially. If you have decided to opt for a commercially available solution and have reached the stage of making a selection, then you will need to review the range of products. There are a number of Web sites that have side-by-side comparisons of these products. One of the most comprehensive is the site maintained by Bruce Landon <http://www.c2t2.ca/landonline>This is regularly updated, covers a wide range of products and provides a very detailed comparison of features.

Having collected the most up-to-date information on what appear to be the strongest contenders you will still be faced with the task of selection. A rule of thumb in the ICT industry is that the selection of software should take precedence over the selection of hardware. In other words, users should select the applications software that best meets their needs and then select the hardware that best supports that software. Of course, much software runs on more than one platform. That situation can either simplify or complicate the selection decision.

Table 6.1 provides a checklist of features to look for in integrated electronic learning environments. However, in selecting an integrated electronic learning environment, it is also important to consider factors other than the functions a system is able to support. Four factors likely to be of major importance are:

- teaching model;
- scalability;
- compatibility with other systems and processes;
- cost.

Teaching model

The first decision that needs to be taken concerns the software that best matches the teaching model you are intending to adopt. Earlier, we distinguished between the classroom-based and resource-based approaches to course design. It is important to ask yourself which of these approaches you are intending to adopt. Are you intending to base your model mainly on group interaction? If so, you will want a learning environment that supports asynchronous and possibly synchronous conferencing. Are you intending to base your model mainly on self-instruction? If so, then you will want a learning environment that supports students in managing their own learning.

Other aspects of the teaching model that you wish to employ may also have a bearing on your choice of learning environment. For example, if you are working

Table 6.1   *Checklist of features to look for in integrated electronic learning environments*

Feature	Notes
Asynchronous conferencing	
☐ Supports threading	Allows students to follow the sequence of a series of messages on a topic
☐ Allows formation of groups by subject/ module	
Synchronous conferencing	
☐ Provides cross-platform whiteboard support	
☐ Supports application sharing	
Mail	
☐ Supports SMTP	Allows exchange of mail with other servers across the Internet
☐ Supports POP	Allows mail to be retrieved by mail clients such as Eudora that use Post Office Protocol
☐ Supports creation of personal mail lists	
Learning management	
☐ Delivers learning materials developed using a range of authoring software	
☐ Tracks progress of students	
☐ Directs students' study route based on their performance on tests	
Testing	
☐ Supports a comprehensive range of item types including algorithmic	
☐ Supports random selection of items	
☐ Allows the timing of tests to be set	
☐ Reports results of a given student on a test	
☐ Reports results of all students on a given test	
Database	
☐ Supports inclusion of interactive multimedia segments programmed in common authoring systems	
☐ Allows open access for import and export of course-related and student-related data	

in the technical and vocational education sector there has been a strong orientation towards competency-based training, then you may want a learning environment that provides support for computer-assisted assessment.

Scalability

Scalability refers to the capacity of a system to expand to accommodate increased demand; for example, to support more students or more courses.

While scalability may not be an important factor when it comes to selecting a system for a pilot project, when it comes to selecting a system for institution-wide use it will be important to establish whether the system can be scaled up to meet increasing demand over its expected life. If the expected life of the system has not been laid down then it is probably desirable to assume a five- to seven-year time horizon with regular updating of the chosen system occurring during that period.

Compatibility with existing systems and processes

Although an integrated electronic learning environment may be designed to be more-or-less self-contained, one will usually find that it is necessary for the system to operate in conjunction with one or more existing systems. For example, it may be necessary to the system to accept class lists from an existing student records system. In selecting an integrated electronic learning environment, it is important to consider which systems will need to operate alongside it and to establish what scope there is for interoperation with those systems.

Cost

One of the most important factors to consider is cost. The cost of a licence for an integrated learning environment is generally based on the maximum number of students to be supported or the number of servers on which the system will run. However, in most cases, the number of students will increase over time and the cost per student may not rise proportionately with increasing numbers of students. It is therefore important to compare costs based on projected student numbers over the expected life of the system.

Upgrading local networks

Most education and training providers now accept that if they are to be able to deliver their programmes online then they are going to have to make substantial investments in the upgrading of the ICT infrastructure and then continue to invest in the maintenance of this infrastructure. However, many education and training managers who do not have a strong background in ICT are experiencing difficulty

Case study 4: IT Alignment Project (ITAP)

The initiative

The ITAP project was initiated at RMIT University in order to integrate developments in information and communication systems with RMIT's Teaching and Learning Strategy. The Teaching and Learning Strategy sought to improve practice across all facets of the learning process.

For some time, improvements in information and communications technology have impacted on the delivery of programmes and the qualitative improvements that the new technology could make to student learning outcomes. It also presented an opportunity for senior management to co-ordinate efforts across the university and develop a consistent corporate Information Technology Framework

The aim was to enhance and augment current teaching and learning processes by exploiting the new technology in the following educationally appropriate ways:

- improve the capability of the existing IT infrastructure;
- refocus staff efforts in the renewal and/or development of learningware and learning environments, to improve quality, access and cost-effectiveness;
- increase retention and progression rates for all students;
- provide online capability to assist the learner in all aspects of their learning experience (enrolment, student records review and progressive assessment);
- improve staff skills in the application of IT to support teaching and learning;
- create a module bank of interchangeable building blocks thereby maximizing the flexibility for structuring individual learning programmes.

Features

- large investment of Aus$16 million (proposed) per year for three years;
- re-engineering of all course delivery processes;
- improving student outcomes, satisfaction levels and career prospects;
- consistent corporate IT framework;
- large-scale change in management processes.

Stakeholders

Faculties, divisions and staff at RMIT, all RMIT students, whether at a distance or on campus.

The initiative at work

The ITAP project leaders recognized that in order to achieve their aims they needed to address issues of cultural and structural change. The following changes were implemented as part of the IT Alignment Project:

Improving staff capabilities

Appointment of learning technology mentors in each of the faculties; offering of a series of educational design and educational technology workshops to build teacher competencies and confidence in the application of online technologies.

Management and administration

Large-scale allocation of central funds for learning enhancement projects and the development of course/subject-specific learningware to identified priority areas; development of IT planning process across the University to ensure the integration of IT with the Teaching and Learning Strategic planning process.

Student and clients

Implementation of a student-focused Student Management information system providing online capability for enrolments, assessment and student progress information; reviewing/re-engineering all the major elements of the student management process to identify appropriate student-centred learning management processes.

Technical and infrastructure modifications

Specification of the IT architecture and delivery platforms to support the integrated framework; adoption of a comprehensive set of relevant IT policies and agreed standards across the university to ensure reliable connectivity and access.

Key success factors

- executive commitment and large-scale investment in the development and deployment of appropriate infrastructure, systems and support services;
- a student-centred teaching and learning focus that would not be compromised or subsumed by the technology;
- a concentrated effort in the planning and change management processes to ensure effective outcomes.

Future developments

The ITAP project is now its third year of operation and some of the goals are being realized. The next phase of the project will be to identify ways to demonstrate and justify confidence in the process and the anticipated return on investment.

Further information

The Web site for ITAP is <http://www.online.rmit.edu.au>

in knowing where to start, what priorities to assign to different tasks and what level of funding to allocate.

The key to understanding the nature of the problem is to recognize the magnitude of the increase in the load on networks generated by Web traffic. Networks that have been designed to cater for traffic comprising e-mail, word-processed files, database transaction data and distributed use of software may not have the capacity to support the downloading of large numbers of graphics files.

Local area networks can become like the streets of Bangkok – so clogged with traffic that the rate of movement slows dramatically. The result is lengthy delays in accessing information held on servers, increased frustration on the part of users and lower productivity on the part of staff.

Just as putting in motorways and roundabouts can get the traffic on the roads moving again, so increasing the capacity of network backbones and upgrading routers and servers can restore networks to an acceptable level of performance. Further improvements can be obtained by distributing servers so that their location reflects their use.

However, getting network traffic flowing again does not guarantee that it will remain that way. Arriving at a design that will continue to provide adequate performance into the foreseeable future depends on being able to anticipate the rate at which network traffic is likely to increase.

The solution to the problem is not to replace complete networks, nor to duplicate them. Rather, it is to identify and relieve the 'bottlenecks' – the points in the network where data traffic is being held up.

The principles of network design are relatively simple. However, the actual layout of design of networks can be quite complex. Furthermore, the fact that most networks are continually being reconfigured to accommodate new or updated equipment adds to the complexity.

The way in which one approaches the design of a network depends very much on the amount of traffic it will be expected to carry, the reliability that will be expected, and these factors depend in turn on the purpose for which the network is being used.

Just as educational managers have difficulty in understanding the significance of bits and bytes, network managers have difficulty in understanding the distinction between facilitating learning and transmitting information.

Updating staff workstations

Many of the problems that beset teachers in the use of IT result from the fact that the equipment they are required to use is not sufficiently up to date. It is unfortunately the case that many educational institutions simply do not make adequate provision in their annual budgets for regular replacement and upgrading of desktop computers. Computers are replaced when they fail or when the cost of maintaining them becomes too high. Yet the annual cost of the staff time that is lost in trying to cope with inadequate equipment may be higher than cost of replacement of the equipment. If this is the case, then an institution's resources are not being well managed.

By the same token, aiming always to have the latest equipment can also lead to problems. In the IT industry it is widely recognized that design faults are commonly discovered in new models within a few months of their release. Early adopters pay a price for the right to be pioneers, in terms of having to find ways of dealing with these new model problems. They also pay a price in the literal sense, because new models are generally priced at a premium. Manufacturers seek to recover the costs of development in the first year.

Upgrading too frequently can also be unnecessarily costly. Changing over workstations requires an investment of time on the part of the user to delete or archive old files, set up a new filing system, gain familiarity with new software, and resolve any compatibility problems that may show up.

Taking into account all of these factors, a reasonable time frame within which to change over equipment is two to three years from initial date of purchase. The equipment purchased should have been available on the market at least six months.

Another problem that commonly arises when teachers do receive new computers is that they do not operate correctly, either because the software has not been correctly installed or because there are incompatibilities between different pieces of software. One of the selling points of Macintosh computers is that they are easy to install. The more open design of Windows-based computers accounts for the greater time required to set them up. However, the requirements of the discipline often determine which type of computer is selected.

The main reason why installation problems occur is that ICT support staff are overloaded and do not follow the sequence of steps recommended by the manufacturers of computers and software. This is even more likely to happen when large numbers of computers are being installed. One way of minimizing the problem is therefore to contract for workstations to be supplied with the applications software already installed. Adopting this strategy will require some prior planning to ensure that the complete set of applications software that will be needed has been fully specified.

Solving the problem of student access

Distance educators have been wrestling with the problem of how to give students adequate remote access to data communications for more than 20 years. The solutions they have come up with have changed as technology has evolved. Institutions first began looking for ways of providing remote access to computer facilities when they began teaching courses at a distance. In these early years, access was provided via dial-in communications. Students were required to use modems and telephone lines. If the student was located at a great distance from an institution, then this mode of access was expensive, slow and sometimes unreliable. Some institutions tried to assist students by placing computers in local study centres and installing leased lines to the study centres. However, this only assisted those students who lived near to a study centre.

With the advent of the Web and of the increasing competitiveness of the telecommunications industry Internet service providers (ISPs) offered a commercial competitive service that was generally much less expensive than using long-distance calls.

By the mid-1990s, most institutions were finding that they simply could not afford to provide the number of dial-in lines needed to service all of their students. Whenever they increased the number of lines, demand rose to meet the new level of supply.

ISPs now provide the points of access for most distance education students. ISPs provide the points of access where they are needed – locally. ISPs are able to respond quickly to increased demand. ISPs also compete with each other to offer the most up-to-date service.

While most institutions initially entered into contracts with a preferred ISP to secure better rates for their students, it now seems that most students prefer to 'shop around' and find their own ISP. Students can often find an ISP that provides them with the type of service they want at a better rate than that offered by the preferred supplier.

Over the past two years, the telecommunications industry has been undergoing consolidation because of the intensity of competition and as a result of the bundling of high-speed data services with cable television. Further significant changes are likely to be seen over the next three years. The general trend will be towards an improvement in service and a lowering of costs. However, these benefits are not available to all subscribers and there is still some way to go before students in remote and isolated areas will all have access to adequate services.

Different issues arise when students need to access material online from overseas. The data communications infrastructure in different countries is not equally reliable and the connection speeds may be quite low. A problem that is frequently encountered when students access from a study centre or company Intranet is that the connection between an intranet and the Internet is so slow that when it is being shared by several users sessions time out before operations are complete. Problems of this sort are often mistakenly attributed to the wrong cause because the technical support staff at the provider institution cannot easily inspect the way the network connection has been set up.

Summing up

Re-engineering technological infrastructure for online delivery should start with the development of a clear set of goals indicating what, it is hoped, will be achieved. The areas in which upgrading of infrastructure is likely to be needed include:

● acquisition and implementation of software and hardware for managing the online delivery of courses;

- acquisition of additional software for courseware development;
- updating of computer and communications infrastructure to support an increased load on networks and systems;
- equipping teaching and support staff with workstations and suites of software that are adequate for them to perform the tasks they will need to perform in developing courseware and teaching students online.

Moving to online communication and course delivery will require the implementation of a system for delivery of courses. Broadly speaking, there are three options for implementing such a system:

1. off the shelf – acquire a licence for one of the commercially available systems;
2. building block – combine components from different suppliers to obtain the best combination of functions;
3. custom build – build a system from the ground up.

The type of system that will be most appropriate for a particular situation will depend on whether a resource-based or a communicative approach is being adopted. It will also depend on whether courses will be designed around topics or around competencies.

Chapter 7

Re-skilling and supporting staff

We begin this chapter by suggesting how to create a work environment suitable for staff working with the knowledge media. We go on to identify the knowledge and skills that staff will require. We suggest ways of assessing and recording the current computer proficiency of staff, thus determining their staff development needs. We then examine the range of alternative forms of staff development and make suggestions for choosing between them when setting up a comprehensive staff development programme.

Creating an appropriate work environment

In any work environment, many factors contribute to staff commitment and to staff acting competently, creatively and responsibly. These include motivation, indications of being valued, interpersonal relationships, sharing goals, and clear and open communication. Here we take up one factor, particularly pertinent to introducing knowledge media: how to create the conditions for staff to work effectively with the new media.

There are some general considerations to be explored when seeking to provide appropriate and satisfactory working conditions for staff engaged in design, development and delivery of courses via the knowledge media. These include:

- location of offices and work areas;
- network access;
- equipment and software access requirements;
- health, safety and comfort requirements;
- recognition and reward systems.

Location of offices and work areas

Physical proximity may not appear to be an important factor when considering where to locate staff involved in the design and development of online courses. However, there remain advantages in co-locating staff: development of common understanding; raising and talking through incidental issues and the adoption of creative approaches and dealing with design problems can be best served by enabling staff to interact in an unplanned, incidental and informal way.

It may not be possible to co-locate all those who are involved in design and development. If that is the case, an alternative option may be to set aside a design and development area with space for those working on projects at the time.

One question that often arises is whether it is preferable to provide open plan offices or individual offices. Separate offices allow confidentiality to be maintained in conversations. This may be important when it comes to discussions between designers and teaching staff. Provision of sound insulation between the course design area and the multimedia development area is also important. The noises produced during the development of multimedia materials can be very distracting, particularly when the same sound effect is being tested repeatedly. However, accommodating staff in separate offices can lessen the advantages of co-location. A compromise is to provide withdrawal areas for private conversations, sound-insulated areas for multimedia development and open plan areas for other activities. It is important to recognize that if open planning is to be used in some work areas, then some staff may need to adapt to that type of environment.

Network access

Providing adequate and appropriate network access is essential for staff working on the design and development of courses that make use of resources and facilities on the Internet or Intranet. Security checks may be needed to protect confidential materials against unauthorized access.

Equipment and software

Staff obviously require access to workstations that have sufficient speed and memory to perform the necessary functions. Staff also require suitable and up-to-date software. It is poor economy to provide staff with less than optimum equipment and software because the cost of staff time lost through inefficiency is likely to be greater than the saving in facilities.

A question worth considering is whether everyone involved needs to be issued personally with each item of equipment and every item of software. The basis of the decision should be the extent of access required. Access needs to be available within a time frame in which the costs of any delays (eg the cost of unproductive staff time, or the costs incurred or income opportunities lost through delayed delivery times) does not exceed the costs of providing the equipment and software. Managers may also wish to use the provision of a better standard of equipment as part of a reward or motivation system.

Health, safety and comfort

Consideration needs to be given to occupational health and safety requirements, including the need for ventilation in areas where electronic equipment, particularly photocopiers and printers, is operating. Ergonomic furniture needs to be provided. If comfort is to be taken into account, it may be necessary to go beyond the minimum health and safety requirements.

Recognition and rewards

The time spent by the teaching staff in the design and development of courseware needs to be recognized in the same way as classroom teaching. This will further encourage participation and innovation, especially where the use of knowledge media is seen as an add-on activity.

Knowledge media may be developed to supplement classroom activities. The development of the digital resources may have taken considerable staff time and initiative but, while the quality of the learning experiences and options may have been enhanced, the number of students taught may remain the same. It can be difficult to arrange appropriate operational recognition in these circumstances. An alternative is to offer one-off rewards such as project funding or including teaching innovation as a criterion for promotion. This, incidentally, raises questions about the desirability of developing knowledge media as a supplement to classroom activities. The phenomenon is not unusual but you cannot afford to continue committing resources to developments that make no difference to costs of delivery or to income. By giving some thought to design, development and delivery, media innovations can replace some of the commitment of resources to the classroom.

What new skills will staff need?

Some of the sets of expertise needed to use digital technologies in the delivery of education and training programmes are very new. Also, the range of expertise is continually changing. This expertise can be acquired by:

- recruitment;
- staff development;
- buying in or contracting out.

Many of the technologies used to support online delivery are so new that established staff may well lack the capabilities needed to exploit them. Recruitment of new staff may be necessary. However, new staff need to be recruited on the basis of their capacity to adapt to technological change, not just their current know-how. You can't recruit experience in tomorrow's technology.

Because the expertise required is of recent origin, it is often in short supply. Development programmes for suitable staff provide a solution where staff with suitable expertise are difficult to recruit. Staff development in a changing environment is necessary but can have a downside. The capabilities that staff acquire through staff development will make them more marketable. There is, therefore, a risk that staff will leave. Technical staff, in particular, are often subject to high turnover. On the other hand, there is an inertia factor, which tends to reduce the frequency of staff movements. Nevertheless, you need to look to ensuring work satisfaction for expert staff and appropriate levels of remuneration or provision of other rewards.

If particular expertise is only required from time to time, the most economical way of acquiring it may be to buy it in or to contract out particular tasks. This approach offers the advantage of making staff turnover and industrial relations somebody else's problem. However, it is important to recognize the intellectual property implications of outsourcing. These were discussed in Chapter 5.

By one means or another, new staff capabilities are required. Which staff need which abilities? Moving to online delivery changes the relationships between staff in education and training enterprises. The degree to which the changes in relationships create the need for staff to specialize is taken up in Chapter 8. What we can say here is that all staff – administrative, technical, audio-visual, library, instructional design and teaching – contribute to design, development and operation of knowledge media and that roles cannot be quarantined. Technicians need a feel for pedagogical principles; teachers need an appreciation of the possibilities and limitations of technologies; student administrators need some appreciation of teaching–learning processes and the rationales for the approaches that have been taken in the design of courses. Teachers and multimedia designers need to work with librarians to optimize access to resources. Different roles have different emphases but the boundaries overlap and each specialist requires the contribution of the others, as indicated in Figure 7.1.

Staffing implications of use of an integrated electronic learning environment

Integrated electronic learning environment software refers to software such as WebCT, Blackboard and LearningSpace, which allow for presentation of materials, discussion, chat, and assessment online. Learning environment software enables teachers to engage in online delivery of learning materials and to support communications amongst students without having to rely on instructional design or technical staff to support them. Two issues arise here: staff inclination and capacity to use learning environment software and the incorporation of instructional design.

Staff use of learning environment software

The challenge here is developing the inclination to use the software. The capacity to use the software can be addressed through some of the usual forms of staff

Zones of Expertise

Expertise in information technologies	Expertise in instructional design	Subject expertise
information systems operation and maintenance	advising on education and training approaches	providing an understanding of the specialist skills, knowledge and attitudes appropriate to the subject and to the likely learners
the operation and maintenance of audiovisual equipment	devising formats effective in supporting independent learning	
scripting audiovisual materials and directing audiovisual productions	devising the channels of communication between teacher and learner	
design of computer and visual graphics and in presentation of material	providing for formative and summative assessment opportunities	
image capture and manipulation design and production of print-based and screen-based presentations of materials		

Activities aligned with the teaching function

Specialisms more removed from the teaching function

Figure 7.1 *Organizing for digital delivery*

development referred to in the section below. If the use of learning environment software is to be adopted widely in the institution it requires a shift in culture from reliance on face-to-face contact and old technologies – overhead projectors, photocopied notes, slides and videotapes – to digital technologies.

One strategy is the lighthouse projects approach – the sponsoring of exemplary use of learning technologies by early adopters of the technology in the hope that others will be inspired. Investigations of the success of this approach are not encouraging. The enthusiastic early adopters move on to their next pet project and others have no ownership of what has been developed. Rather than being inspiring, the projects may be seen as daunting. Often the resources applied to such projects cannot be applied more generally.

Rather than focusing attention on the members of teaching staff with an interest in the use of learning technologies, attention can be focused on communicating more effectively with students through digital delivery. If, for instance, a Web presence is created for each subject, allowing teaching staff to upload digital material from their own computers and to delete or modify material, it can save staff time in photocopying material. It can allow last-minute action, eg uploading lecture notes or slides before walking out the door to the lecture and modifying them straight after the lecture. This can soon become a facility staff rely upon in the same way they do overhead projectors. Positive experiences of their peers and the expectation of students that their learning materials will be available online soon persuades reluctant starters to adopt the methodology.

Other features of Web pages can likewise quickly become a normal form of teacher–student and student–student interaction. These include online noticeboards, discussion and chat. These facilities provide for an incremental change of culture leading to willingness to explore other capabilities of learning environment software and to hone skills.

Learning environment software and instructional design

Where academics have, in the past, required technical assistance to transform print-based off-campus materials, word-processed class notes and graphic materials to online formats, some institutions used the opportunity to incorporate expert instructional design into the process. The use of learning environment software can lead to this component being omitted to the detriment of learning materials and processes.

Most commercial learning environment software encourages a thoughtful approach to materials design and deployment. Teachers are advised to specify their learning objectives and to design materials and communications appropriate to these objectives. They are also encouraged to devise assessment in harmony with learning objectives. Amongst the available learning environment software, The Learning Manager is particularly suited to situations where there is a strong desire to relate the selection of materials and forms of assessment closely to learning objectives.

The limitation to this approach is that the design can be superficial and the approach formulaic. Even with the use of learning environment software there is a role for instructional designers in the identification of learning challenges and the design of appropriate responses. The instructional design component can be handled by having instructional designers work with teachers and trainers before the online deployment of each set of learning materials. Alternatively, instructional designers can take on a staff development role inculcating instructional design knowledge and skills amongst teachers who are to use learning environment software. The latter approach assumes teachers will have the time, inclination and ability to acquire capabilities in instructional design. We anticipate that their ability to do so is likely to be partial and therefore suggest the maintenance of an instructional design process that assists in:

- the definition of the learning tasks;
- determining strategies for assisting learners to acquire the understandings and skills involved and to address associated problems;
- devising valid and reliable forms of assessment of learner progress.

Assessing the computer proficiency of teaching staff

There is, then, no simple answer to the question of what skills and knowledge staff need in order to work effectively with new learning technologies. Nor is there a simple answer to which staff need which skills and knowledge. However, in an organization committed to making greater use of the new learning technologies, there are minimum competencies that teaching staff should be capable of displaying. Table 7.1 is a checklist of the basic computer skills and aptitudes that staff involved in courseware development are likely to require.

The skills, knowledge and attitudes required of staff go well beyond the minimums indicated in Table 7.1. Figure 7.1 gives an indication of other areas in which staff development may be required. The areas that will be appropriate to your situation need to be defined and the required competencies in each area specified. A profile of current competencies can be derived by audit, perhaps using a format similar to that used in Table 7.1. This can then be used to determine your specific staff development requirements.

Forms of staff development

Staff development can take various forms. Those commonly used to prepare staff for teaching via the knowledge media include:

- 'how to' training sessions;
- seminars and workshops;
- mentoring;
- staff-initiated innovation projects.

Some of these staff development activities may be conducted in-house while others may be conducted by outside providers.

'How to' training sessions

Conducting 'how to' training sessions may be an appropriate approach where an enabling skill, such as the ability to operate the basic commands of a particular software package, is required and the skill can be put to immediate use. However, a 'how to' training approach is unlikely to be effective, at least by itself, if application of the skill requires judgement to be exercised, or if conditions for application are uncertain or are subject to change.

Table 7.1 *Computer skills audit checklist*

Key to columns:
1. I am satisfied with my skill level in this area.
2. I would like to (further) develop skills in this area.

NAME _____

	1	2
Environment PC or Macintosh		
Operating in Windows environment or on Macintosh desktop	❏	❏
Organizing files and data, installing programs	❏	❏
Connect to Intranet and the Internet	❏	❏
Transferring files, downloading files and programs	❏	❏
Word-processing and desktop publishing		
eg MS Word, Pagemaker, Quark		
Handling files eg find file, open, save, page set-up, print	❏	❏
Editing eg copy, paste, find & replace	❏	❏
Viewing files eg using toolbars and headers	❏	❏
Inserting eg pictures, dates, annotations, page nos	❏	❏
Formatting eg fonts, borders, bullet points & nos	❏	❏
Using tools eg spell check, auto-correct, macros	❏	❏
Using columns eg two columns, frames, callouts	❏	❏
Using tables eg creating tables, auto format, sort data	❏	❏
Spreadsheets eg MS Excel		
Handling files eg find file, open, save, page set-up, print	❏	❏
Editing eg copy, paste, find & replace	❏	❏
Entering data in worksheets and workbooks	❏	❏
Writing formulas eg add/multiply/etc items, ranges, formulas, statistical functions, scenarios	❏	❏
Formatting eg data as $s, borders, colour, autoformats	❏	❏
Charting data eg pie charts, graphs	❏	❏
Data management eg sort, worksheet management, reports	❏	❏
Linking data to other programs	❏	❏
Automating repetitive tasks using toolbars and macros	❏	❏
Presentation software eg MS PowerPoint		
Handling files eg find file, open, save, page set-up, print	❏	❏
Editing eg copy, paste, find & replace	❏	❏
Viewing eg slides, notes, outlines, toolbars	❏	❏
Inserting eg slides, arts, graphs, movies, page nos	❏	❏
Formatting eg fonts, bullet points, templates, colour schemes	❏	❏
Using tools eg spell check, slide shows	❏	❏
Drawing eg shapes, colouring, grouping, sizing, positioning	❏	❏
Slide show eg animate, transition, build, buttons	❏	❏
Graphics and photo editing eg Paintshop, Illustrator, MS PhotoEditor, Photoshop		
Handling files eg find file, open, save, page set-up, print	❏	❏
Inserting an image	❏	❏

Using graphics tools ❑ ❑
Creating, manipulating and modifying images ❑ ❑
Adding and formatting text elements ❑ ❑
Changing colours and backgrounds ❑ ❑
Creating and using layers ❑ ❑
Saving files in various formats: gif, tiff, pict, jpeg ❑ ❑

Databases eg Filemaker, Access
Handling files eg find file, open, save, page set-up, print ❑ ❑
Designing databases eg fields ❑ ❑
Entering and modifying data in databases ❑ ❑
Formatting eg data as $s, form layout ❑ ❑
Data management eg sort, reports, calculated fields ❑ ❑
Linking data to other programs ❑ ❑

Ideas software eg Inspiration
Handling files eg find file, open, save, page set-up, print ❑ ❑
Editing eg copy, paste, change symbols & links ❑ ❑
Viewing files eg schema, outline, text, headers ❑ ❑
Concept mapping eg ideas, symbols, links ❑ ❑
Formatting eg fonts, colours ❑ ❑
Using tools eg spell check, find & replace ❑ ❑

E-mail eg Eudora, Pegasus, Groupwise, MS Outlook
Sending & receiving mail ❑ ❑
Using lists eg subscribe, unsubscribe, address lists ❑ ❑
Attachments eg sending & receiving attachments ❑ ❑

Web browsers eg MS Explorer, Netscape Navigator
Handling files eg open browser, save, page set-up, print ❑ ❑
Editing eg copy, paste, find & replace ❑ ❑
Searching using search engines ❑ ❑
Searching online eg library catalogue, telephone directories ❑ ❑
Bookmarking ❑ ❑
Options eg fonts, colour, mail preferences, toolbars ❑ ❑
Navigating eg hypertext, forward, back ❑ ❑

Web authoring software eg FrontPage, Dreamweaver
Handling files eg open, publish, import, using templates ❑ ❑
Editing eg copy, paste, find & replace, setting preferences ❑ ❑
Viewing eg toolbars, status bars, hyperlinks, source code ❑ ❑
Using tools eg spelling, hyperlinks, Web settings, debugging ❑ ❑
Inserting frames, tables, layers, images, rollovers, plug-ins, tags and anchors,
library items. ❑ ❑
Modifying page and image property, aligning and arranging items ❑ ❑
Formatting text, using HTML and CSS style sheets, using macro commands,
cleaning up, optimizing image size ❑ ❑
Creating animations ❑ ❑
Opening sites, creating new sites, checking site-wide links ❑ ❑

Case study 5: Flexible learning options

The initiative

Swinburne University of Technology in Melbourne, Australia has a commitment to flexible learning. Flexible learning refers to offering students choices about the time, place and pace of study as well as content, styles of learning, assessment tasks and individual versus collaborative study. This flexibility is achieved through the adoption of specific policies and practices aimed at increasing flexibility. In part, it has been achieved through the adoption of 'multi-modal learning'; that is, the provision of programmes in multiple forms – face-to-face, print, online and by video-on-demand. The educational development challenge in this context is to set up development opportunities, which offer faculty the same sort of flexibility they are asked to afford their students.

Swinburne University, through its Learning and Teaching Support unit has responded by devising CD ROM and Web materials to complement face-to-face staff development. The material is entitled Flexible Learning Options and Assessment Strategies and produced as the 'FLO CD' and 'FLO online'.

FLO online is designed to support decision-making about flexible learning techniques and technologies. In particular, it is intended to assist teaching staff as they make decisions about approaches to teaching, assessment and the techniques and technologies they might employ. It maps flexible learning options against learning and assessment theories, techniques and technologies.

Special features

- a theory and practice compendium for teachers preparing for flexible learning;
- modelling online teaching practices through online staff development;
- examples from within and from outside the University.

Stakeholders

- staff of the university;
- students;
- educational developers of the University.

The initiative at work

The site has multiple uses. For educational development advisers at Swinburne University, it provides support materials in the theory and practice of flexible provision of learning for staff development activities including work with teaching teams and symposia around topics such as supporting online learning or approaches to assessment. For faculty, the site may be used independently to assist them in planning their teaching in ways that utilize new knowledge media and which are pedagogically sound.

FLO online defines the concept of flexibility in the provision of education and training as a matter of offering choice to students. It identifies educational techniques and technologies that assist in providing flexibility along with assessment techniques and technologies that provide flexibility. Theories of learning and theories of assessment are included to help support decision-making about techniques and technologies. The content may be approached from various directions. You can start from:

- desired elements of flexibility such as choice of time and place;
- an approach to learning and teaching such as interactive communication via the Web;
- a learning technique such as role play or technology such as CD ROM-based materials;
- an assessment technique such as case studies or technology such as an electronic laboratory;
- a particular learning theory such as a constructivism.

Whatever your starting point, you can link through to associated elements. For example, if you start with a constructivist approach you can link to an appropriate learning and teaching approach and compatible learning and assessment techniques. From there, you can link to the forms of flexibility they facilitate. The techniques and technologies are illustrated with examples. A glossary of key terms and a map linking to the various screens and to a list of examples is provided.

The site is designed according to constructivist learning principles. It allows users to start from their own point of interest and to add to their understanding by exploring elements pertinent to them. However, exploring the site without a purpose is likely to lead to skidding over the surface. Users are therefore encouraged to start with an element of interest and follow links from there or to explore with a particular task in mind.

For those simply wishing to advance their understanding of flexible learning options, suggested activities are provided. The activities provide orientation for the user. The activities cover:

- How can I make my subjects flexible?
- Can technology help me with assessment?
- Should I use a particular technology?
- Can I be both flexible and educationally sound?

The activities are in PDF format and can be viewed using Acrobat Reader.

Technical requirements

- Pentium PC or Macintosh PowerPC, 32 Mb RAM, 1,024 x 768 pixel display resolution with a 256 colour (8-bit) palette;
- 56Kb dial-up Internet connection or better;
- Netscape Navigator 4.0 or Microsoft Internet Explorer 4.0 or later with Macromedia Shockwave 8.0 player or later, Apple QuickTime 4.0 or later Adobe Acrobat Reader 4.0 or later.

Further information

<http://www.swin.edu.au/lts/ed_dev/flex.htm>

Seminars and workshops

Seminars and workshops provide scope for participants to contribute solutions and exchange ideas. Presentations at a seminar may have some influence but to produce change, seminars need to provide the opportunity to practise skills, to reflect upon the application of information to their work context and to relate theory and practice over time. To have wide impact across an organization, a programme of seminars and workshops needs to be closely linked to an organization's strategic plans and work programme. Seminars and workshops pertinent to and attended by all staff of a department are more likely to generate changes than those attended by a few.

Mentoring

Mentoring can be an effective means of staff development both for newly recruited and for existing staff. In either case, commitment is required of both mentor and mentee. The mentee's commitment may be gained through their recognition of their need to know. The selection of people with an interest in the process is important in obtaining mentors with commitment. This is most likely to occur with a structured and monitored process involving a formal mentoring agreement, with agreed aims and objectives, procedures such as observation arrangements and meeting times, an agreed form of record-keeping, such as a journal, agreed regular forms of communication and an agreed system of monitoring and evaluation of the relationship and its processes.

Staff-initiated projects

Support or stimulation of staff initiatives may also be a means to staff development. Provision of financial or other support for innovative projects, as well as resulting in a product, can also lead to the development of expertise.

The history of generating greater use of the knowledge media is not encouraging. There have been some outstanding successes, but in the cases of many initiatives, more thought goes into the process of obtaining funding support than into the educational initiative. Those who are successful in obtaining funding invariably find the task more demanding in time and energy than anticipated. Many projects never reach completion: systematic evaluation is lacking, and communication of the results of projects beyond the members of teams responsible for execution of projects is limited. When the enthusiasts who have been responsible for initiating a project move on, the project is abandoned. This is not to say that valuable learning and development may not have occurred during the processes, just that more is usually expected of such projects by both sponsors and innovators than is delivered. To maximize benefits it is important to:

- make a realistic estimate of the resources required;
- evaluate systematically;
- ensure the innovation is adopted by selecting or developing projects integral to courses or departments' programmes and that it fits the strategic plans.

Designing a staff development programme

The focus of staff development programmes

A focus on staff development, as a key to the adaptation of education and training organizations to the digital age, is an acknowledgment that staff, along with customers, clients, suppliers and other people who interact with an organization constitute the organization. They not only constitute the organization in a similar way to its buildings and other resources but, through their perceptions of the organization, and hence the way in which they relate to it, they help to constitute what the organization is and how it operates.

Organizational change and adaptation depend on the development of staff. The development of staff changes the perceptions and understandings they have of the organization and consequently the nature of the organization. As an organization changes staff, it changes itself. The changes that take place may be unintended as well as intended.

Staff development programmes, therefore, need to have an institutional orientation to them. They are not only about technical developments and possibilities or even educational creativity. Staff need to have a clear understanding of institutional missions and goals in relation to knowledge media. Staff development should be strategically related to course development and delivery priorities.

Staff development programmes also need to provide staff with a clear understanding of the principles underpinning the use of digital delivery technologies and an appreciation of the potential of those technologies. As a beginning, staff development programmes could use the Quality Improvement Framework identified in Chapter 12 for the discussion of staff development needs.

Tailoring a person's development programme to their role

In devising a staff development programme to enhance digital delivery, the first point that needs to be established is, which staff are to be developed, what are their roles and what are their development requirements. While there may be benefits to all staff involved in the design, the development and the application of knowledge media, of having an appreciation of the processes as a whole, it is important to be clear about the role expected and to focus development efforts upon this. In particular, there is little point in training all teaching staff to design and develop multimedia if specialists are employed to carry out this function. What is required of teachers, apart from keeping up to date in their subject area, is understanding of learning and teaching and the ability to translate the understanding into effective teaching and learning transactions. Thereafter, they might benefit from some attention to the areas of expertise proximate to the teaching function, as indicated in Figure 7.1.

For instructional designers and for technical staff, the focus of their staff development will be their areas of specialization. However, roles are not static. They need to be adapted to accommodate developments in technology. The convergence of audio-visual and computing technologies is leading to marked shifts in what have previously been established and defined role boundaries. For example, a photographer's role once had almost nothing to do with computing. Photographic chemistry is now rapidly being replaced by digital technology and computers are being used to capture, store, manipulate and use digital images. Staff who prepare print-based material must now be able to work with digital templates, if not design them. These changes in work and working environment require staff development responses. It could be argued that as approaches to education and training move toward greater flexibility in time, place and pace for learners, there is also a convergence between education provision and the media and multimedia industry. Traditional educational enterprises are adopting new modes of delivery while media and software corporations market education and training products. This does not necessarily mean that the roles of educators and trainers will be combined with those of media designers and developers. If the enterprises are large enough they will maintain specialist roles.

Selecting the right form of staff development

A staff development programme will utilize multiple forms of staff development. The form of staff development you will find most effective for meeting a particular need will depend on the skills required and the staff member or staff members who require them. Approaches likely to be most successful are those that involve all personnel in a work group, generating a commitment to change and creating a common understanding of the directions of change and the means to attain it. Working with teaching teams or with departments as a whole is likely to be more successful than drawing individuals from across an organization. For new staff, the most appropriate form of staff development may be mentoring.

Should participation in staff development be voluntary or compulsory?

Compulsory participation in staff development is not likely to produce an enthusiastic response. Nor is it likely to lead to a worthwhile development of the staff member's knowledge and skills. On the other hand, leaving participation to individual whim is not likely to serve institutional needs either. Participation in staff development programmes should be strategic – tied to individual performance planning, relating it to position descriptions, and integrating it into promotion and reward systems.

Summing up

In preparing staff to deliver courses via the knowledge media, you should first consider what changes are required to their work environment. Aspects of the work environment that should be examined in such a review include:

- location of offices and work areas;
- network access;
- equipment and software access;
- health, safety and comfort;
- recognition and reward systems.

In proceeding to devise a staff development programme, you should begin by making an assessment of the existing skills of staff against the range of new skills that you know will be needed. This assessment leads to the identification of which skills are 'missing'. The staff development programme can then be constructed using a combination of different strategies:

- training sessions;
- seminars and workshops;
- mentoring;
- staff-initiated innovation projects.

Chapter 8

Reorienting the teaching programme

In this chapter we distinguish between some alternative approaches to teaching that may be employed in delivering programmes via the knowledge media and identify the implications of each approach. We examine the relative merits of designing and developing courseware compared with acquiring courseware produced elsewhere and address online assessment issues. We provide a set of criteria and a checklist for selecting courseware and examine the advantages of entering into collaborative ventures in the design, development and adaptation of courseware.

Approaches to teaching with the knowledge media

There are a variety of ways in which courses can be delivered digitally. Some involve the use of self-contained learning packages and some involve ongoing teacher–learner or learner–learner communication. The self-contained approach tends to maximize, time, pace and place flexibility for both teachers and learners but is relatively static in content and in the learning approach once it is adopted. This approach therefore requires a carefully researched and designed product. Computer-mediated communication between teachers and learners and between learners and learners allows somewhat less time, pace and place flexibility, particularly if the communication is synchronous. It is, however, more dynamic and flexible in its ability to respond to individual and group learning needs as learning progresses. It does not require that the needs of different learners be anticipated. It requires instead an ongoing capacity to generate learning and to react to learning developments.

Table 8.1 *A simple typology of approaches to digital delivery*

	Self-contained Learning Packages	Computer-mediated Communication
Time, pace and place flexibility	High	Lower, particularly where synchronous
Adaptability to learning needs	Low	High
Investment of time	High design and development costs	Higher operating costs

Of course, a combination of these approaches may be adopted to provide for learner needs and organizational requirements. Either of the approaches may be combined with elements of face-to-face tuition to meet learner needs and preferences. Such combinations might be facilitated by the use of computer-managed learning systems. We move on to look at the basic approaches first and then to consider combinations, including computer-managed learning.

Self-contained learning packages

In this approach, the courseware more-or-less stands alone. Typically, the courseware might take the form of a module or series of modules on CD ROM or be presented on a self-contained Web site.

Adoption of this approach assumes that it is feasible to anticipate and provide for all the learning needs of the target group. It is, however, difficult to produce courseware that matches the full spectrum of characteristics of potential learners. Courseware that suits some learners will not necessarily suit others. If a learning package is going to be effective as a self-instructional medium, then considerable attention needs to be paid to its design. The needs and characteristics of the targeted learners should be investigated. Ideally, the package should be trialed during the design and development stages with a pilot group of representative targeted learners. Once their needs have been established, the design process should ensure that:

● the intended learning outcomes are explicit;
● the materials are logically and transparently structured;
● alternative starting points, pathways and end points are offered;
● each segment of the programme incorporates an element of self-assessment;
● the materials are attractive and easy to navigate.

Most of these features are found in well-designed print-based distance education materials. However, the new knowledge media offer possibilities not afforded by print. Using hyperlinks, digital materials can allow the learner to select a starting point from a set of alternatives, to pursue a particular pathway and achieve one of a number of alternative outcomes. They can provide for self-testing and then offer feedback appropriate to the student's response to the test, perhaps personally addressed. The materials are, to this extent, personalized for the student and materials inappropriate to that particular student remain inconspicuous. Utilizing these capabilities of the media, commercially available integrated electronic learning environments software allows users to design and deploy materials incorporating alternative pathways and to incorporate self-assessment items. Some users may require the assistance of a support service. The costs of initial research, design, development and evaluation of courseware is high and must be amortized over the life of the programme. This is especially the case for courseware that incorporates multimedia components. Animations and simulations can be used to convey key concepts in a way that is difficult to achieve with static printed materials. Interaction with the materials can provide immediate feedback.

The development of animations and simulations is likely to require the involvement of a multimedia programmer. Self-contained learning packages are therefore most suited to use with large numbers of students.

The variable costs associated with delivery, on the other hand, can be substantially reduced in the case of fully self-contained learning packages. Self-contained materials imply no tutorial support and the costs of reproduction and distribution of materials are minor components of overall cost. The high upfront costs of design and development may be recouped from the resulting savings. The use of self-contained learning packages, however, cannot completely eliminate variable costs of delivery. There may still be significant costs associated with student enrolment, administrative support and student assessment. Self-contained learning packages are most suited to situations where:

- the potential market for a new course is large;
- flexibility with regard to time, place and pace is of prime importance;
- the characteristics of the learners in the target group are known or can be readily ascertained;
- materials can be trialed during the design and development phases;
- learners in the target group have other learning materials and facilities on which they can draw.

Computer-mediated communication

An alternative approach to using packaged self-instructional materials is to use computers to facilitate online discussion and conversation, and provision of information. Computer-mediated communication was originally limited to text but it can now include sound, graphics and video. The interaction may be:

- one-to-one – allowing the communication to be directed to the needs of the individual;

- one-to-many – allowing economy of communication to the instigator of the communication;
- many-to-many – allowing multiple participants to contribute to or to audit the communication.

Computer-mediated communication has been practised for many years now in the form of e-mail. A variety of means for supporting this form of communication is now available:

- e-mail;
- listservs;
- electronic bulletin boards;
- newsgroups;
- proprietary conferencing systems;
- Web-based conferencing systems;
- Internet Relay Chat;
- desktop video-conferencing;
- audio-graphic conferencing;
- MUDs (Multi-User Dimension, Dungeon, or Dialogue) a text domain, which allows participants to 'chat' or take actions in pursuit of a task;
- MOOs (Multi-user dimension Object Oriented) a graphic or other object domain, which allows participants to manipulate or extend an object or objects on a site.

Communication may be either asynchronous or synchronous. Asynchronous communication (threaded discussions, listserv discussions, e-mail) allows participants to contribute at times that suit them. Synchronous communication (chat sessions, video-conferencing, audio-graphic conferencing) requires participants to contribute at the same time.

Asynchronous communication offers flexibility in terms of time and pace, allowing participants to give considered responses at a time that suits them. On the other hand, asynchronous communication forms can be a protracted means of interaction between teachers and learners, between fellow learners, and between learners and resource personnel. They are best employed where participants are available at different times, where participation in the communication is optional in the learning situation, or where response requires consideration or investigation. Asynchronous electronic communication may also be set up to provide anonymity to participants. This can be of value, for instance in encouraging reluctant learners to participate.

Synchronous conferencing offers a greater sense of participation but demands more spontaneity. Synchronous and asynchronous conferencing refer to two ends of a spectrum rather than being mutually exclusive. E-mail, for example, can be used semi-synchronously. The major advantages of online communication are that:

- It allows teachers to respond flexibly to the changing needs, abilities and understandings of individual learners.
- Teachers and other learners may be used as resources.
- Learners can explore each other's meaning and understanding.

If the use of computer-mediated communication leads to increased interaction between teachers and learners it is likely to result in an increase in costs. However, demands on the time of teachers can be kept down by giving greater responsibility to the learners. Other possibilities for reducing the commitment of teacher time to the communicative process include providing a databank of responses to frequently asked questions, a process that could conceivably be automated, and establishing a protocol where the teacher monitors interactions between learners and intervenes only occasionally, for example to counter misconceptions, to motivate and stimulate learning, or change direction or open new paths for consideration.

Most integrated electronic learning environments, such as LearningSpace, FirstClass and WebCT have built-in support for computer-mediated communication, although not all such systems support computer conferencing. General purpose business communications software or 'groupware', such as Lotus Notes or Novell Groupwise, provide many of the same functions and can also be utilized. Using the same communication software for both teaching and administration has many advantages. It makes fewer demands on institutional infrastructure, and it reduces the amount of training required by both staff and students. On the other hand, it has limitations. Induction to communications software and the operation of software involves the use of metaphors such as mailboxes, documents and bulletin boards. The metaphors employed for administrative purposes, such as filing cabinets, often differ from those used for educational purposes, such as online libraries. Sometimes a metaphor refers to an aggregation of functions, as is the case for the virtual classroom.

Metaphors matter in conceptualizing the uses to which the software may be put and the protocols and conventions that govern their use. While the same software base may be used for administrative and educational purposes, there may be value in using alternative descriptors or icons for at least some functions. There are a number of things to consider when designing for computer-mediated communication:

- *Whether to use synchronous or asynchronous communication forms.* Synchronous forms can give a greater sense of presence and generate spontaneity. Synchronous chat, however, requires immediate response. The conversation may have moved on to another topic if your response is slow. Asynchronous forms give time flexibility and allow for considered responses.
- *Introduction of participants to the communication format.* Arrangements need to be made to ensure that participants are aware of both the technical requirements of the communication method to be used – hardware and software requirements

– protocols, and polite conventions for participation. The style adopted by the facilitator will help to set the pattern, including the pattern for any introductions.

● *The numbers of participants involved.* For communication with individuals, e-mail is appropriate. For groups, discussion allows and tracks contribution by multiple users. It allows the subdivision of a large group into syndicates or the like. The facilitator needs to establish the basis for allocation to groups.

● *The complexity of the subject matter.* For communication on complex topics or topics likely to become complex over time, threaded discussion allows topics and subtopics to be distinguished and contributions to them tracked. Again, the facilitator needs to set up an initial structure for the discussion and indicate to participants rules for participation and for the establishment of new topics.

Use of computer-mediated communication is most suited to situations where:

● the potential market for a new course is small;
● there is a need to respond to the emerging needs of the learner, for instance where the prior understandings, characteristics and learning needs of the learners is not known and the subject matter or the level at which it is pitched arise from the needs and interests of the particular cohort of students;
● responses to individual learners can be provided economically, perhaps by reserving tutor responses until after peer responses are received, posting responses to frequently asked questions, drawing common responses from a prepared item bank.

Combining approaches

The two approaches to course delivery described above – self-contained packages and computer-mediated exchanges – are basic forms. Generally, the construction of a course will involve a combination of the approaches illustrated in Figure 8.1. The use of computer-mediated exchanges alone is seldom sufficient as a means of facilitating learning. Discussion needs to be combined with other types of learning activities and the use of learning resources. On the other hand, difficulty in anticipating learner needs in the development of self-contained packages could be compensated for by providing opportunities for person-to-person interaction. The weight given to each component will determine the character of the course.

In a course primarily delivered via computer-mediated communication or in a course primarily delivered face-to-face, packaged self-instructional materials may be used to:

● illustrate a concept;
● supplement learning experiences appropriate to the skills, knowledge, attitudes and propensities that students are expected to develop;

- provide simulations of learning experiences too expensive, inconvenient or hazardous to provide in reality;
- vary the teaching approach to increase motivation.

In a course that is largely based on self-contained learning materials, computer-mediated communication might be used to:

- introduce learning materials to the particular learners and explain their purposes and procedures;
- monitor students' development of concepts and skills, and to adjust the presentation of a course accordingly;
- respond to learner concerns arising from the materials;
- support learning through peer interaction;
- update or supplement materials.

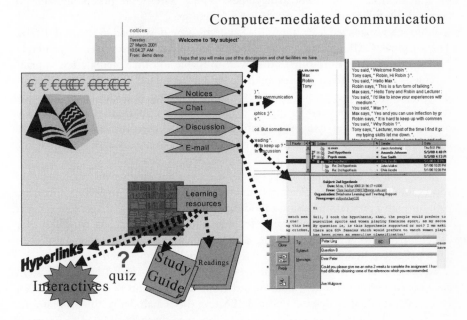

Figure 8.1 *Combining computer-mediated communication and self-instructional materials*

When choosing to combine approaches, economic, pragmatic, competitive and even political issues need to be taken into account. The most important factor to be considered is how the learners are most likely to achieve their intended outcomes. There are differing views but one thing is agreed – the simple presentation of information is not likely to be the optimal approach (see, for example, National Committee of Enquiry into Higher Education (1997)). Approaches likely to be favoured are those that:

- make objectives explicit;
- involve the learner in a process they see as relevant to their learning needs;
- involve the learners in making decisions and undertaking actions;
- can be monitored by a learning facilitator;
- allow intervention and interaction between participants.

Using a computer-managed learning system

Learning management systems, such as The Learning Manager, direct learners to learning resources, administer computer-scored tests, track students' progress, and determine the pace at which the learner progresses and the path he or she follows. As explained in Chapter 6, some integrated electronic learning environments provide facilities for learning management. These systems are potentially able to perform the full range of course delivery functions.

Computer-managed learning (CML) systems were developed in the mid-1970s. The original CML systems were not able to deliver courseware; they merely directed the learner to resources that were available in other media, such as print or video. This limitation existed because of the restricted capacity of computer storage media of the time. Now that storage capacity is cheap, most learning resources can be delivered in digital form (although copyright restrictions may preclude the electronic delivery of published material). Also, because many aspects of the administration of a course can be streamlined or automated, the efficiency with which a course is delivered can be considerably increased.

Using a learning management system increases the degree of flexibility that can be built into courses. Rather than requiring all learners to follow the same path through a programme, using a modular structure, learning management systems tailor the pathway the learner takes according to individual needs. Modules may direct learners to alternative resources such as print, video, courseware, and even appropriately scheduled face-to-face activities such as supervised practice.

Because courses delivered by means of a computer-managed learning system are constructed in a modular fashion, individual components of a programme can be added, modified or deleted without affecting the remainder of the programme. Courses are therefore more easily kept up to date than those based on self-contained courseware.

To manage the pace at which a learner progresses and the pathway they follow, learning management systems rely on the results of regular tests. Courses that are based on the use of learning management systems may therefore be seen as 'assessment driven'. Then, so is much formal education and training. This is not necessarily a problem if the assessment is appropriate to the learning needs and the learning outcomes sought.

If computer-scored tests are used, care needs to be taken with the design of test items. There is a risk that teachers and trainers who are not skilled in writing test items will limit the items they write to the easier-to-construct forms. These tend to test lower order learning outcomes such as recall of information. However, with careful design, computer-scored tests are capable of measuring higher order learning outcomes such as explanation, comparison, analysis, synthesis and hypothesis. Learning management systems can also accept the results of assessment that have not been administered by computer. Use of a learning management system is best suited to situations in which:

- time, place and pace flexibility are considered of prime importance;
- a variety of learning resources are employed;
- staff development in the appropriate use of the system and the design of test items and curricula can be provided.

Economies of scale can be obtained by extending use of the learning management system across several courses. Use of computer-managed learning is most suited to situations where:

- the potential market for a programme is large;
- there is a need to track the progress of learners who are progressing at their own pace and/or following different paths;
- it is particularly desirable that learners receive immediate feedback;
- assessment is to be conducted online at different times for different learners and security is a consideration;
- the teacher requires analysis of individual test items and feedback on their success.

Approaches and the role of the provider

In discussing the rationales for shifting to the knowledge media we pointed out that stand-alone materials maximize time, place and pace flexibility for learners. If, however, an organization produces nothing but fully stand-alone digital materials, with no assessment of students' work or other form of teacher/learner interaction, it acts as an electronic publishing house rather than as an educational institution. At the other extreme, to rely solely on direct teacher–learner interaction is to fail to utilize the potential and flexibility offered by digital media. It is a matter of striking an effective and efficient balance.

If we wish to play or retain a role as an educational or training provider, we need at least to retain the function of student accreditation. That is, we need to assess students' work and certify progress. Of course, we could decide to have it both ways by offering accreditation as an option and marketing materials on a fully stand-alone basis to individuals or to other education and training providers.

Should courseware be developed or acquired?

If you decide to adopt an approach involving courseware, you need to decide whether to engage in the design and development of courseware within your institution or whether to adopt or adapt existing courseware. The decision rests on a number of factors; key amongst them are:

- Is the market large or small?
- Is the market local or international?
- Is the subject matter specialized?
- What is the shelf life of the courseware?
- What are the costs of any copyright clearances necessary?

Size of market

If the size of the market or extent of the user group you are intending to tap is small, then you will not be able to obtain the maximum economies of scale that are potentially available (see Chapter 4). The costs of courseware development will be high in relation to the costs of delivery. You will find it much more economical in this case to use materials produced elsewhere than to develop your own, if suitable materials are available.

Nature of the market

If the market is international, course materials need to be internationally applicable. For example, references to local institutional titles need to be avoided and generic descriptors of such institutions employed, colloquialisms need to be avoided, examples need to be widely accessible or learners need to be encouraged to think of their own examples. Commercially available material should be assessed for its suitability. It may have been designed for the international market but some materials marketed internationally were designed for a local market.

Specialization

If the field of study you are targeting is popular, then there is likely to be a wealth of courseware already available for purchase or licensing. This would be the case, for example, in a field such as business statistics or basic topics in physics. In this case, you are likely to find that you can obtain access to suitable courseware at a lower cost than you would be able to develop courseware yourself. On the other hand, if the field of study is quite specialized, then there may be no alternative but to develop your own materials. However, even in a specialized field of study, it may be more economical to supplement existing material than to start from scratch. For example, a module in viticulture for local climate and soil conditions might not be readily obtainable on the market but a digital module on viticulture may be found and an electronic or print-based supplement to draw out consequences for local conditions might be prepared.

Shelf life

The frequency with which design and development will need to be undertaken affects how one should choose between developing materials, collaborating in development of materials, or purchasing or otherwise acquiring available products.

The concept of shelf life is most pertinent to largely stand-alone courseware. Traditionally, print-based distance education course materials, which are designed to be largely stand-alone, have been expected to have a shelf life of five years. There is usually some allowance for updating and minor modification in this period. In some fields of study, such as taxation law, substantial revisions are required each year. The rate of change in knowledge, the availability of constantly changing information, the rate of change in technologies, a climate of frequent upgrading of software, and the moves of competitors in an increasingly globalized education and training environment, suggest the shelf life should be reduced, perhaps to three years.

The shelf life can be maximized where the courseware, rather than containing current information, focuses on:

- appropriate approaches to learning in the area;
- types of learning activities that might be undertaken;
- types of resources that might be tapped;
- simulations and exercises.

The courseware might direct learners to appropriate use of library catalogues, to journal indexes, and to topics for Web searches.

While limited shelf life militates against making substantial investments in design and development of home-grown materials, it also suggests that substantial investment in commercially available courseware needs to be recouped in a three-year time span, unless the material contains timeless content.

Copyright clearance

In deciding whether to develop learning materials in-house rather than purchase available courseware, consideration needs to be given to the costs of any copyright materials incorporated. Copyright clearance, required where courseware incorporates materials subject to copyright, can constitute a significant cost. Providers engaging in significant amounts of courseware development may need to employ specialist staff to recognize copyright requirements and to identify and negotiate the necessary clearances.

Criteria for selection of courseware

Where the acquisition of courseware produced by another provider or by a commercial publisher is the preferred option, a number of considerations need to be taken into account when making a selection. The environment in which the materials will be used needs to be considered along with whether the materials are to be used as stand-alone or teacher-supported. The materials should be appropriate in terms of whom they are designed for and the prior skills and knowledge they presume. The content needs to be appropriate to the learners and organized to effectively facilitate their learning. Multimedia should be used to advantage without distracting from learning. There are advantages in learning packages that monitor usage, allow appropriate assessment of learner progress and interface with other approaches to learning. There are delivery matters to consider in terms of hardware requirements, costs and vendor support. These considerations can be organized into a checklist (see Table 8.2).

Considerations in design and development

Courseware design and development can be very expensive. It is frequently argued that educational consumers of the future will have high expectations of the sophistication of digital courseware. The commercial computer games industry indicates the potential to develop courseware that requires elaborate research, extensive programming and sophisticated graphics and audio. Design and development budgets for such software may run to millions of dollars. There is evidence, however, that students will readily accept courseware developed in-house that lacks aesthetic polish. What they will not accept is courseware that is difficult to operate or tedious.

How can the design of courses contribute to learning effectiveness?

In this book, we argue that learning is something that is individual. It is a process that builds on or modifies understandings, capacities, abilities, attitudes and propensities in the individual. This is not to say that people learn best when they learn on their own. On the contrary, learning is often best effected in interaction, whether that interaction is with teachers, mentors or peers, is synchronously or asynchronously, face-to-face or distant. It does, however, suggest that where the process involves courseware, the design and development of the courseware should anticipate variety in the circumstances, interests, needs and aptitudes of individual learners. This leads to a number of principles that should be applied in design and development of courseware. Courseware should:

Table 8.2   *A checklist for selecting pre-packaged multimedia courseware*

A. Pertinence

❏ Are the materials designed for the intended users?
❏ Are the materials designed for the appropriate instructional context?
  (For example: are they designed to be used as self-paced individually used materials
  or in conjunction with an instructor or together with fellow learners; are they
  designed to be used in the home, at a workstation, in a laboratory, in a training
  centre, in a classroom, or in a library or resource centre?)

B. Purpose

❏ Are the learning objectives clear and are the expectations of what the user is to do
  made clear?
❏ Is the program design systematically related to the learning objectives?

C. Prerequisites

❏ Are the prerequisite knowledge, skills and attitudes made clear and are they
  appropriate to the intended users?

D. Teaching and learning materials

❏ Are the knowledge, skills and attitudes facilitated appropriate to the intended
  learners?
❏ Can the key knowledge, skills and attitudes be readily identified?
❏ Does the program provide for increasing levels of complexity
  – for example from novice to expert?
❏ Do the materials provide for higher order learning skills such as problem solving,
  analysis, synthesis and creativity as against simple recall?
❏ Will the materials be motivating, interesting and challenging for the intended
  learners?
❏ Do the materials conform to accepted and current understandings in the content
  area?
❏ Are the materials free from error in expression and in use of terminology?
❏ Are the materials reasonably free from ethnic, gender and political bias?

E. Teaching and learning approach

❏ Is the underlying learning theory apparent and appropriate?
❏ Is there a clear relationship between the learning objectives, the learning activities
  and assessment tasks?
❏ Are the intended learning outcomes assessed?
❏ Does progress through the program depend on active/creative actions rather than
  reaction to set propositions or passive clicking forward?
❏ Are alternative strategies used to meet different learner needs?
❏ Can activities in the program be extended to face-to-face situations or through other
  learning materials?
❏ Is the learner able to interact with other learners and a teacher or tutor?

F.   Media and navigation

❏   Are media such as text, hypertext, graphics, animations, sound, photographs, video used to enhance learning? Is their presence likely to enhance or inhibit learning?

❏   Is the quality of media used satisfactory? Is its design appealing? Is text easily read?

❏   Are navigation tools clear, intuitive and consistent? Is the organizing logic of the material apparent to the user and the location of the user in the material apparent? Are tips on how best to use the courseware provided?

❏   Is material indexed? Is a glossary of technical terms and abbreviations provided? Is there a search facility? Is there a help facility?

❏   Has the material been trialed in relevant circumstances and user behaviours reasonably predicted and allowed for?

❏   Can the progress of learners be monitored and tracked and can records be saved and printed?

❏   Can the learner make, save and print notes?

G.   Performance

❏   Is the speed of the program satisfactory in the hardware and software situation in which it is to be used?

❏   Is the program crash-free?

❏   Is required hardware and software available?

❏   Is installation manageable?

❏   Can hardware or software settings be easily restored after use of the program?

H.   Support

❏   Are instructor guides available along with supporting teaching aids?

❏   Are student guides, activity sheets and the like available?

❏   Does the vendor provide training in the use of the materials?

❏   Does the vendor provide readily accessible support services?

❏   Is the vendor likely to continue in the field?

❏   Does the vendor provide upgrades?

I.   Cost-effectiveness

❏   Is the use of the courseware likely to be cost-effective against alternative approaches when hardware and software requirements are taken into account along with costs to the user? (See also Chapter 4.)

● Either be designed and developed to *anticipate the pre-conditions of the learners*, such as their existing range of skills and forms of understanding (including the various ways in which they currently conceptualize a topic), or it should *allow the teacher to assess the pre-conditions of the learners* and to respond appropriately.

● Have time, pace and place flexibility to allow for the various circumstances of the learners such as work and home commitments.

● Be designed and developed with the level of the learners' access to learning supports, including educational technology, in mind.

- Allow for learning style preferences amongst users – for instance that some may at times prefer a text-based form while other users, or the same users at other times, may prefer visuals and graphics or kinaesthetic activities.
- Provide for formative assessment, possibly through self-assessment tasks and, where courses are taken for credit, for summative assessment. The latter may require invigilated examinations. Experience in distance education indicates that it is usually possible to arrange for invigilated examinations to be taken at a distance. If this is to be done online, close supervision may be needed to ensure no access to unauthorized sources of information.
- Allow alternative entry points, alternative levels and depths of tuition, alternative topics and paths, alternative forms of assessment and alternative points of exit.
- Allow for partial completion at a session, preferably with a record of progress for each user.

How can the design of courses contribute to learning efficiency?

The general question of costs in the use of new knowledge media was taken up in Chapter 4. One of the conclusions from that chapter was that economies of scale, given the significance of the cost of labour in total cost, depend upon limiting teacher and learner interaction or at least limiting the teaching labour component of teacher and learner interactions.

Limiting teacher–learner interactions is problematic given the desirability from a learning effectiveness point of view of the teacher having an awareness of the circumstances, interests, needs and aptitudes of individual learners, not only initially but on an ongoing basis.

Whether we are focusing on understandings, skills, aptitudes or dispositions, the teaching task is to move the learner toward a desired outcome. Selecting the best means by which to move forward depends, at least in part, on having an understanding of the present location, interests and needs of the learner. The needs of learners, which must be divined through experience or determined through investigation and trialing, are influenced amongst other things by the likely:

- conditions of the place of study of the student;
- availability of the student;
- range and levels of existing knowledge and skills of students;
- alternative conceptualizations of a phenomenon entertained by students, both initially and as they progress.

Creating an appropriate learning environment may be assisted in the development of learning materials by calling upon instructional designers as well as expert teachers in the design of learning materials and careful trialing of materials during design and development phases.

Investigating and responding to learner needs and preferences has cost implications. As we explained in Chapter 4, attempting to contain teacher–learner interaction requires greater investment in design and development if quality is to be maintained. The point at which the investment in design and development of courseware is economical is discussed in Chapter 5. Suffice to say here it is easy to underestimate the complexity of *effective* design and development and thus to overestimate the efficiency that may be achieved through investing in the development of courseware.

Roles in design and development of courseware

If you determined that courseware will be designed and developed in-house, then decisions need to be made about design and development responsibilities. Individuals teaching in a face-to-face environment often complement their teaching with digital technologies and some will have the necessary expertise to design and develop their own materials. Even in the face-to-face environment, however, teachers typically need assistance with audio and video production and development of computer-based materials beyond basic presentation materials such as Power-Point slides. One approach is to provide in-service training to teachers to allow them to take a 'Do It Yourself' approach. Another is to provide support. In-service training, or recruiting teachers with knowledge and skills in the design and development of digital learning materials has advantages and limitations.

Adopting a multi-skilling approach

Some education and training institutions are putting considerable effort into enhancing the technical skills and knowledge of their teaching staff to allow them to engage directly in digital media design, development and production rather than relying upon the services of instructional designers, and media producers and technicians. The advantages of multi-skilling teachers include:

- The borderlines between the technological and the learning aspects of new learning technologies are difficult to define and it could be argued that their separation is theoretically unsound – the technologies constitute an integral part of the learners' experience; they are part of the learning plan and part of the educational precinct.
- Teachers remain central to and in control of teaching and learning transactions, which may enhance communication in the educational process.
- Teachers understand the education and training objectives for which they are designing.
- Many technological problems can be solved on the spot with suitable development of staff capabilities.

- The possibilities and capacity of technology to contribute to learning is best realized when those responsible for developing learning environments understand the capability of the technologies.
- The teachers are well placed to monitor and evaluate the application of the technology and to modify it to meet changing needs.
- Multi-skilling of the workforce allows greater flexibility in the allocation of time to various tasks and reduces down time where one skill is not required for a period.

Adopting a specialist approach

Specialists who might combine with subject matter experts to develop courseware and related products and services include:

- instructional designers who are experts in education and training approaches and formats that are effective in supporting independent learning;
- computer technicians;
- multimedia programmers, expert in programming computers to produce multimedia effects or in utilizing multimedia authoring software;
- computer technicians who have knowledge and skills in the operation and maintenance of information technology hardware and software;
- audio-visual media technicians who have knowledge and skills in the operation and maintenance of audio-visual equipment, though with the convergence of audio-visual and computing media the boundary between computer and audio-visual technicians is blurring;
- audio-visual media producers who assist in scripting audio-visual sequences and in directing and editing audio-visual productions;
- graphic designers who are experts in design of computer and visual graphics and in presentation of materials;
- photographers who are experts in image capture, digital manipulation and presentation;
- desktop publishers who are experts in design and production of print-based and screen-based presentation of materials.

The process that will be used to design courseware deserves to be given special attention. Designing courseware is often seen to be within the realm of the expertise of teachers. However, major distance education providers have found that engaging specialist instructional designers to work collaboratively with subject specialists generally leads to a better result. There is now a considerable body of knowledge on how to provide effective support for students learning at a distance. There is a growing body of knowledge on how best to support students studying online. Teachers in post-secondary education are usually employed for their understanding of the subject area rather than their knowledge of learning theory or their teaching ability. Instructional designers however bring to the task of courseware design an understanding of learning based on a consistent theoretical position. The processes that instructional designers employ can be applied in any teaching situation. However, their systematic approach to the design of courses is particularly applicable to the more flexible forms of delivery that involve the development of courseware that is costly to produce. Instructional designers orient their work towards designing courses that build student competence. Courseware designed by subject specialists working on their own is more likely to comprise mainly subject matter information. The advantages of a specialist approach are that:

- Technical problems are resolved effectively.
- Specialists appreciate the technical capabilities and application possibilities of the digital technologies.
- Specialists keep the organization abreast of the latest technological developments.
- Teachers may lack instructional design expertise for non-face-to-face educational interactions. Instructional design for courseware is an expert process.
- Courseware development can be a tedious business with a small element of a programme needing to be trialed many times before a product is released. The process may be more attenuated with lack of design and development expertise. The cost relativities of teachers, programmers, graphic artists, video producers and video technicians need to be considered.
- The professional life of teachers and trainers is often already multi-faceted including research and administrative responsibilities and other workplace requirements.

In general terms, it would be unreasonable to expect teaching staff to have a high level of understanding and skill in information systems and their operation and maintenance. Nor can they be expected to have expertise in programming for digital media, in the operation and maintenance of audio-visual equipment, in scripting audio-visual sequences and in directing and editing audio-visual productions, in design of computer and visual graphics and in presentation of materials, in image capture and manipulation, and in the design and production of print-based and screen-based presentation of materials.

In making a decision on whether to adopt a specialist approach, you need to take into account the size of your enterprise and the consequent scope for specialization. An organization engaging in digital delivery on a large scale may be able to support specialists in each of the technical areas. If a specialist approach is used, not only are the costs of initial training much reduced, but the costs of keeping skills up to date are also reduced. Furthermore, fewer software licences and less equipment are required. You need, however, to determine the range of specialists who will be engaged on an ongoing basis and where expertise will be brought in as required.

For smaller providers, a limited range of specialist technical services may be provided with other areas bought in on occasion, contracted out, incorporated in the roles of teachers or not provided at all. As indicated in Chapter 7 (see Figure 7.1) the zones of expertise of staff are nominal rather than discrete. Some areas of technical expertise are more aligned with usual teaching activities than others, and may be more readily taken up by teaching staff than is the case for other technical functions. Various specializations might be combined in one staff member and with the convergence of audio-visual and computing technologies this is more likely to apply in future.

When using specialists we advocate the use of a team approach to courseware design and development. The team approach was pioneered by the UK Open University and is now used widely within distance education.

Should courseware production staff be employed or contracted in?

Design and development in-house may involve buying in expertise on a consultancy or short-term employment basis. Buying in expertise has a 'just-in-time' logic that allows educational providers to acquire the quality and quantity of expertise required when needed without employing unnecessary labour. There can, however, be disadvantages:

- With the use of consultants, the ownership of intellectual property in courseware can be unclear. See Chapter 4.
- Courseware design and development is seldom a one-off process. Trialing is necessary, unexpected glitches occur over time, material requires updating or elaboration, and teaching staff and students continually desire improvements. If understanding of the programming of the courseware walks out the door with the consultant or short-term employee, amendments may be difficult or impractical.
- Corporate memory depends in part on retaining expertise in courseware design and development.

With regard to the last point, corporate memory can be enhanced by organized approaches to observing and documenting design and development processes and by evaluating during design and development phases of a courseware project as well as upon completion of the project. A systematic approach to the construction of corporate memory may help to offset the transitory nature of expertise obtained from consultants and short-term employees.

Courseware may be developed within a software development package or an integrated electronic learning environment obtainable on the market. Courseware development packages include Toolbook and MacroMedia Director, which automate elements of courseware programming. The software packages require some training to operate them. Teachers can use the packages but they may need the support of instructional designers, graphic artists, video producers and other technicians.

Project managing course design and development

The design and development of courseware involves multiple interests and often involves drawing upon resources from different organizational units. In a university for instance, it might require the expertise and time of:

● academics located in teaching departments;
● instructional designers located in a learning and teaching support service or a distance education unit;
● audio-visual producers and editors located in a media department;
● graphic artists and multimedia programmers located in a multimedia centre.

Other capital and equipment located in the units involved might be employed in the project.

There is a need then for the identification of the client or clients in the process; for clarity about roles and responsibilities, including responsibility for provision of resources; and for project management. There is logic to placing project management in the hands of the instructional designer. The instructional designer may be viewed as being in the centre of the activity, having some understanding of the needs of all the contributors, and having responsibility for the production of the courseware and therefore for the management of its production. Table 8.3 defines roles and responsibilities in the process of courseware design and development. Relationships between the parties involved are depicted in Figure 8.2

It is the responsibility of the project manager to:

● devise a project schedule, distinguishing key events – including needs analysis and evaluation – and setting timelines;
● determine resource requirements;
● clarify roles and expectations with participants;
● co-ordinate activities;
● monitor activities against the schedule and report progress to the project manager's supervisor.

The collaborative approach

If you are wanting to target a field of study that is also being targeted by other providers you may find it worthwhile to enter into collaboration with one or more of them as a way of reducing the level of your investment in design and development through sharing the costs. Diana Laurillard argues that the high cost of producing good quality multimedia material makes it impractical for most institutions to design and develop their own courseware (Laurillard, 1993).

Competitive considerations may discourage you from collaborating but collaboration can co-exist with competition. As the knowledge media breaks down barriers of distance, the number of competitors will increase. One may choose to

Table 8.3 *Roles in courseware design and development*

Activity	Role(s)	Responsibility	Resources Provided
Provision of subject expertise	Manager of subject expert Client of instructional design	Management of subject expertise resources	Time of subject expert Provision of specialist subject facilities
	Subject expert	Provision of subject expertise	
Instructional design	Manager of instructional design Client of digital media delivery	Management of instructional design processes	Instructional design and project management time Provision of specialist facilities
	Instructional designer Client of media design and production	Project management Instructional design advice	
Audio–visual and digital media design and production	Media design and production manager(s)	Management of audio–visual and digital media design and production processes	Time of media designers, producers and programmers Provision of media equipment and facilities
	Audio–visual producer	Audio–visual design and production	
	Audio–visual technician	Audio–visual labour including audio recording, video recording and still photography	
	Graphic designer	Graphic design for visual and digital media	
	Multimedia programmer	Programming of digital course materials	
Digital media delivery	Manager of digital media delivery (eg IT or ICT manager)	Delivery of information and communication technology	Provision of information and communication technology facilities

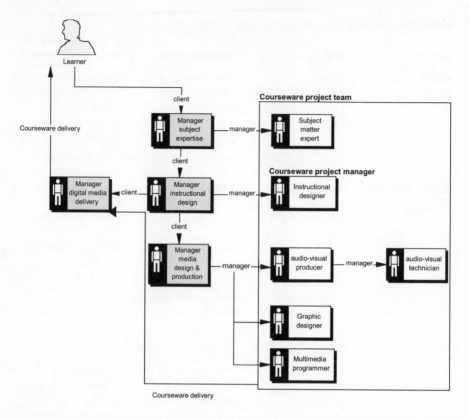

Figure 8.2   *Roles and relationships in courseware design and development*

collaborate with some providers while competing with others. Joint ventures are standard practice in the world of business and will become increasingly common in education and training.

Potential clients may be inclined to select professionally designed and developed courseware, which suggests that providers who have small-scale operations in a particular area may need to collaborate with at least some of their potential competitors to produce a high quality product.

Potential clients may choose courseware according to the reputation and prestige of the provider. Who will want to take a course from an obscure provider when digital technology allows them to take a course from a prestigious institution? Collaboration between providers may seek to address the marketability of courseware as much as the logistics and the costs of design and development.

The range of organizations with which you might collaborate need not be limited to other education or training providers. Potential collaborators also include marketing or financial organizations, or organizations that have a training need of their own in the area you are wanting to target.

Assessment issues

We know that assessment not only provides information on achievement but also affects the behaviour of learners. Assessment provides both a reflection on learning that has occurred and a stimulus and guide to future learning. Assessment procedures are therefore almost as important as the design of learning materials or the use of person-to-person communication. Several issues arise in making use of the knowledge media for assessment of student progress. These may include:

- educational issues;
- accreditation issues;
- pragmatic issues;
- social issues.

Assessment of student progress may be undertaken for educational purposes, such as providing feedback and guidance to students or an indicator to teachers on the success of their approach to teaching. On the other hand, assessment may be undertaken for accreditation purposes, to certify to interested parties the attainments of the student. The purpose of undertaking assessment raises different issues and may call for different solutions. It is important therefore to be clear about the primary intent of assessment. Whatever the intent, in delivering digitally there are also some pragmatic and social considerations that need to be borne in mind.

Assessment for educational purposes

Objective testing

Computer-assisted assessment is often identified with using simple quizzes – true or false, multiple choice, matching component or drag and drop items. The advantage of using these types of assessment tools is that responses may be coded as right or wrong and feedback can be automated and immediate. Providing immediate feedback is likely to be regarded as desirable if one has a behaviourist view of how people learn. It gives immediate positive or negative reinforcement, thus helping to shape behaviour in the manner desired. Such items are sometimes also termed 'objective', that is, they are regarded as not being open to the different interpretation by different assessors. This meets one of the requirements of assessment theory – reliability. Objective tests eliminate variation amongst assessors.

Objective assessment is suited to testing of lower order cognitive learning such as identification of correct responses, recall of information, and categorizing of items. It can also be suited to middle order cognitive learning such as analysis, comparison, and the solving of problems that have only one solution. Objective assessment can be used diagnostically to identify particular misconceptions and errors.

Case study 6: ANTA Toolbox Project

The initiative

The Australian National Training Authority (ANTA) recognized that technological advancements in communication systems were a catalyst for new forms of educational and training delivery systems that had the potential to increase the spread, the quality and efficiencies of education and training. The Toolbox Project was a strategy aimed at the development and delivery of more flexible learning materials. ANTA produced a smorgasbord of multi-media resources from which providers could pick and choose when designing online training products for their own use. It was ANTA's intention to use this project as a learning experience to inform and guide subsequent projects, an external evaluation team was established to monitor and evaluate the project.

Features

- national development of educational materials for the vocational education sector;
- development of scalable and sustainable online educational materials;
- development of generic yet customizable educational materials for widespread application.

Key concepts

Online learning resources, user customization, widespread application, economies of scale and efficiencies.

Stakeholders

Vocational education and training institutions in Australia; their distance education students.

The initiative at work

The toolboxes as defined by the project are a set of multimedia learning resources that provide a framework for the development of training programmes for online delivery. Each toolbox was required to utilize a range of 'building blocks' from which a teacher/designer could 'build' a multimedia package. Examples of building blocks include the following:

- packages of generic resources in a variety of media;
- developer's notes, guidelines, supporting documentation and technical guidance to facilitate online provision;
- learning materials 'translated' from existing curricula and combined with authoring software to facilitate the development of further customized materials;

- interactive tutorial packages on researching through the Internet, including directory services and simulated search tasks;
- generic case studies and interactive simulation exercises;
- guidelines for communication functions and student management systems;
- tips and hints for user-friendly instructional designs;
- Web sites with relevant and publicly accessible content information.

ANTA developed detailed specifications, which were put to tender for parties interested in the development of 'flexible toolboxes'. Over 100 applications were received in the first round – from which 12 were finally selected for funding. The toolboxes were developed over an eight-month period and were completed in the middle of 1999.

On completion of the project, nine toolboxes had been developed each representing approximately 40 hours of independent study. An online distribution system was established to enable institutions and training providers to view selections of available resources and to order them for their own use – and for the cost of the media and the distribution – a considerable cost saving compared to developing their own resources.

Technical requirements

The requirements for utility as defined in the project brief included multiple platform capability, modularity in structure and consistent file organization and directory structures. The large variation in approaches that were ultimately used created a number of challenges for determining how the products would eventually be used and distributed.

Key success factors

The success of the ANTA toolbox initiative is largely attributable to a centralized organization taking the initiative to provide seeding funding and develop projects that aimed at both content development and the development of a climate of cultural change towards an increase in the flexibility of programme delivery.

Further developments and applications

Feedback from the first project has been extensively used to guide and inform the second round of toolbox development. The second stage of the project has an increased budget and the benefit of the learning gained from stage one. The second stage of the project will increasingly focus on exploring ways to increase learners' knowledge and understanding.

Further information

The Web sites for the ANTA Toolbox Project are <http://flexiblelearning. net.au/toolbox/>

A couple of further cautions need to be raised about so-called 'objective' tests. We would maintain that while they are reliable (that is give consistent results) their objectivity is to a certain extent illusory. Somebody still has to determine what the right answer is. The selection of the right answer can depend upon assumptions that may not have been made explicit. Equally importantly, the range of possible responses is prescribed by the assessor – a subjective decision – which may preclude other feasible understandings, including other understandings held by those being assessed. Coming from a constructivist view of learning one would want a form of assessment that allowed learners to express their own understanding rather than having them select between possibilities determined by someone else.

Designing objective tests for diagnosis and for assessing middle order cognition requires time and skill. This has implications for staffing for digital delivery. Hurried construction of objective tests often leads to the design of assessment items that do no more than test the ability to recall information. If the learning task was more sophisticated, testing recall is not a valid form of assessment. To be valid, tests need to measure what they purport to measure, which is usually defined by learning objectives. Hurried construction can also lead to ambiguity in expression of items. The design of good objective test items then takes considerable time. There are a number of reasons for this:

- The items need to be reliable.
- Test items need to assess students' attainment of the actual learning objectives not simply test recall of information.
- The test should involve more than guesswork; true–false items are therefore not particularly effective.
- 'Distracters' – the alternative options to the right answer in multiple choice test items – must be feasible but incorrect, for instance by being framed around popular misconceptions.
- Test items should be pitched at a level that is appropriate to the stage of cognitive development of the student.
- For diagnostic testing purposes, test items need to be designed to determine the source of errors in understanding which requires determination of misconceptions likely to occur and of the possible causes of such misconceptions.

Open-ended approaches

If the learning objectives specify higher order cognitive skills – such as creativity, evaluation or open-ended problem solving in real life situations – objective tests will not do the job.

For higher order cognitive tasks, more open-ended approaches to testing, such as short answer or essay questions, give the opportunity for more valid responses, provided there is sufficient guidance to students about the criteria for assessment of their responses. They can also improve the chances of unearthing the learning of the individual student.

This limits the possibility for automated correction. For self-assessment purposes there are possibilities for automated responses such as providing a set of criteria for assessing the answer, model answers or key points, which should have been addressed in an answer. For responses that are to count toward a final accredited assessment, each needs to be assessed individually, in line with a constructivist approach, which expects individual differences in understanding. Integrated learning environments generally provide an online assignment submission facility. Essay marking software has been trialed searching for key expressions and using grammar and spell checking but it is difficult to come up with a foolproof automated assessment system for open-ended material.

Tests based on open-ended questions take less time to prepare than 'objective' tests. However, both for the sake of validity and reliability, the preparation of such tests should include setting out the criteria that will be used for test scoring. Nevertheless, the locus of the costs for open-ended tests then is the opposite of that for the 'objective test'. It comes at the marking end rather than at the design end of the process.

While possibilities for automated assessment are limited with an open-ended approach, there are still advantages in the digital approach to delivery. Learning environment software usually allows for assignment upload and various time-consuming aspects of assessment administration can be automated such as receipting of assignments, dating of assignment, imposition of due dates and penalties for late submission. Assignments can be marked online and returned with highlighted comments. Assessments can be hastened by use of online facilities. Both submission and return can be more dependable online in the sense of being less open to interception.

Online assessment opens up possibilities for learner collaboration in assessment tasks, not available to traditional distance education students. Listservs and discussion groups allow the formation of project teams that can work collaboratively on an assessment task. Some teachers encourage contribution to online discussion by making the discussion assessable. At its simplest, this may be assessed on number of contributions. A more sophisticated form requires students to submit for assessment what they rate as their best contributions to discussion during the course.

The assessment issues addressed above focus on student understandings. Learning objectives might also address skills, attitudes, values and propensities to act. They might involve the acquiring of complex competencies and the propensity to use them in real-world situations. Computerized simulations, while always a step from reality, can contribute to valid and reliable assessment. Because of the scarcity of *in situ* testing opportunities and for both cost and safety reasons computer-simulated assessment may be the most practical, economical and ethical option. The classic example is the flight simulator used in the training of pilots. There are many other situations in medical and industrial education in which simulation is appropriate. Simulation often requires considerable effort in expert and instructional design and in multimedia programming but may be economical.

Assessment for accreditation purposes

When assessment is being used to certify the learning of students, security is an issue. Traditionally, the way that security has been addressed in both on-campus and in distance education has been through a combination of simultaneous testing of students and invigilation. Learning and assessment software offers other possibilities. Objective tests can be made less subject to cheating by individualizing for each student the items that make up the test undertaken. Using 'objective' tests the questions issued to each individual can be of the same order of difficulty but varied in the questions asked or varied in their order, the value of variables, or in the distracters employed. This approach requires the construction of item banks from which the questions issued to an individual are drawn. For a 10-question test 50 to 100 questions or variations on questions might be developed for an item bank. This requires considerable design effort if the questions available are to be not only numerous but also valid. It also requires the licensing of testing software, which can be expensive.

Providing students with individualized tests by randomly selecting items from item banks can overcome the problem of students sharing what they know about the items on a test when they take the test at different times. There is no effective method of preventing cheating in this situation. For this reason, use of computer-scored tests for certification purposes is not recommended unless the tests can be taken under invigilated conditions.

Open-ended testing relies on individualized answers rather than individualized questions to combat cheating. Nevertheless, the problems of authentication remain. The copying of answers, especially where there are large numbers of students or multiple examiners involved is a problem. There is plagiarism software available, which can compare answers submitted in electronic format. It is confined to plagiarism from known sources – for example textbooks and other students' work – and is more useful in identifying possible cases of plagiarism than for making a final judgment.

A checklist for assessment considerations

Other considerations in assessment are the management of student progress through assessment, which is addressed below, and what might be classed as social issues. These include whether the form of assessment is ethical, whether the testing is reasonably accessible to all students and whether the testing involves a cultural bias where it is to be taken by students of different cultures. Amongst these issues, the accessibility of tests is an issue particularly pertinent to use of the knowledge media.

Table 8.4 provides a checklist for addressing some of the issues raised in this section. Note that it is not a matter of requiring a positive response to each item on the checklist. There are tensions between some of the items: high reliability can result in low validity; a choice must be made between criterion referencing

Table 8.4 *Assessment considerations*

Considerations		
From assessment theory	**Aspects**	**Checklist**
Is the assessment valid?	Face validity	Does it measure what is intended?
	Predictive validity	Does it predict future behaviour?
Is the assessment reliable?		Does it produce consistent results?
Is the assessment secure?		Is it insusceptible to cheating?
Is the referencing of the assessment appropriate?	Criterion referenced vs Norm referenced	Is it judged against criteria vs Is it judged against other students?
Does the assessment suit the purpose?	Formative assessment	Does it provide feedback on progress and guidance?
	Diagnostic assessment	Does it identify where errors are occurring?
	Summative assessment	Does it make judgements on final performance?
From learning theories	**Requirements**	**Checklist**
Behaviourist view of learning	Reinforces desired behaviours	Does it assist learning through timely provision of rewards/punishments?
Cognitivist view of learning	Appropriate to developmental level of the student	Is it pitched at the developmental level of the learner?
Constructivist view of learning	Relative to the student's understanding	Does it allow expression of the student's meaning/ understanding?
Situated view of learning	Integrated with the learning process in an authentic environment	Does it judge the student's response in an authentic context?
Pragmatic considerations	**Checklist**	
Practicality and costs	Is the item design and development effort required practicable/economical? Is the assessment judgement required practicable/ economical?	
Management and tracking	Are results retrieved and accessible for automated or manual management of learning and monitoring of assessment measures and items?	
Social considerations		
Ethics	Is the test ethical?	
Access	Is the test and testing format accessible to the student?	
Equity	Is the test culturally appropriate to the student?	

and norm referencing; the various learning theories are at odds with each other on some matters; and reducing marking costs can lead to increasing design costs. Decisions need to be made on the items on the checklist that are important from your perspective.

Summing up

Digital media can be used to provide self-contained learning packages, systems for communication between learners and those who can assist their learning, or some combination of these. A combination will usually be appropriate. While self-contained packages provide for time, pace and place flexibility, they have limited capacity to respond to individual needs and they are expensive to design and develop. Approaches based on computer-mediated communication, on the other hand, are expensive to operate and generally need to be supplemented by other learning resources.

Education and training providers wishing to employ new knowledge media have a choice between designing and developing their own courseware, utilizing available courseware or collaborating with others in the design and development or in the purchase of courseware. The appropriate line of action depends amongst other things upon the size of the market or user group, the peculiarity of the course and the shelf life of materials.

In choosing to use available software there are a number of considerations that might be taken into account. These include responsiveness to user requirements, the purpose for which the courseware is designed, prerequisite skills and knowledge required, the appropriateness of materials, the learning strategies employed, the user-friendliness of materials, support services available and cost-effectiveness.

Where the design path is taken, a choice needs to be made between buying in expert help and doing the job in-house.

An alternative to designing and developing your own courseware is to collaborate with other organizations. Collaboration may be between providers or with other enterprises. Such collaboration may include educational institutions, workplace training providers and enterprises that specialize in digital technology and/or marketing and financial institutions.

Digital delivery opens up possibilities for automated assessment, but judgement needs to be exercised in its use.

Chapter 9

Reorganizing learner support services

In this chapter we examine the ways in which the support services provided to students can be translated into an electronic environment. The support services we examine are:

- help desk services for handling academic and administrative inquiries;
- library services;
- counselling services.

Setting up help desk services

When, in Chapter 4, we examined the factors that influence the costs of electronic delivery, we pointed out that the costs of one-to-one communication with students is a variable cost and that as such it has the potential to escalate the average cost per student of delivering distance education programmes. We indicated that for delivery costs to be contained, this is where savings must be found.

One way in which savings can be achieved in supporting one-to-one communication is by making courseware as self-contained as possible. Trialing the use of courseware during development is always desirable. By using as diverse a sample of students as practicable in such trialing, the types of problem students are likely to encounter can be anticipated in advance. Nevertheless, even when there has been conscientious attention to detail in the development of learning packages, students will still discover that they are missing important information. They will still find that they have questions relating to administrative matters, the content of their courses and the delivery system.

A second strategy is to provide students with easy to use ways of obtaining information themselves. Frequently asked questions enable students to obtain answers to commonly asked questions quickly and easily. Bulletin boards, threaded discussions and chat groups enable students to seek assistance from other students.

Yet there will be some students who have a low tolerance for searching out their own answers and some problems that will require recourse to an academic or administrative adviser. Inability to obtain prompt satisfactory answers to queries is known to be one of the factors that leads to students dropping out of distance education programmes.

Major distance education providers generally find that the majority of student queries relate to administrative issues: for example, changes of address, course changes, examination arrangements and missing course material. It is possible to make considerable savings in labour costs by filtering student requests for assistance so that they are directed to those who are best placed to answer them. This approach can result in a considerable saving in labour costs while at the same time reducing the turnaround time for inquiries. By adopting this approach, teachers are left to deal only with student learning issues. Filtering messages requires a central point of contact to be set up for students who have queries.

Setting up a central communication node

The establishment of a central contact point for telephone and e-mail messages is a strategy that has commonly been used in distance education to ensure that students have their queries handled promptly. Yet, this type of service can be implemented even more efficiently and effectively in an online environment. One major advantage of routing all inquiries to a central point is that at reasonable cost the service can provide responses out of hours – at times when mature age students can be contacted and when they generally do most of their studying. Another advantage is that inquiries can be logged and tracked. This ensures that if a faculty member is attending a conference or is absent through illness, student inquiries will still be answered. Queries can be diverted to the next most suitable person to handle.

Filtering can also be used in relation to academic inquiries. Again, this can be facilitated by online communications. If learners are encouraged to dialogue with other learners through e-mail, threaded discussions and chat sessions in the first instance, the teacher need only step in when discussion is going off track or coming to a halt. A teacher may also, by noting when they have needed to intervene and noting what issues have been brought to them directly by students, make a list of frequently asked questions and distribute the responses to these through an electronic bulletin board or have them ready to provide on request.

Choosing software systems to support help desk functions

It is possible for a help desk service to be based on commercially available groupware software or to be integrated into the electronic learning environment. However, it is likely that a more efficient service can be provided by customizing the support software. Alternatively, the development of a dedicated system that operates in a way that recognizes the standard practices and divisions of responsibility within the organization may be considered.

Putting library services online

How important are library services to distance learners?

The needs of distance learners for library services will depend on the nature of their studies and also on the manner in which their programme is being delivered.

Technical and vocational education programmes generally do not make extensive use of primary sources. Learning packages produced for students studying at this level are typically designed to be fully self-contained. In programmes offered at this level, libraries serve the purpose of providing access to textbooks, journals in print and digital form, general reference materials and other resource materials such as video and audio tapes.

In undergraduate higher education, students are expected to learn to access the literature of their discipline. Most courses require students to draw on primary sources. However, in programmes offered by distance education, that does not necessarily entail provision of access to library collections. Because of the delays that occur in the turnaround of library materials, the limited availability of library resources and the limited time that students have to complete the requirements of most subjects, most distance education providers have steered away from heavy reliance on library collections. In the case of courses that have sufficiently large intakes, universities have sometimes found it practicable to publish readers, which students purchase in the same way as they purchase textbooks. The Open University has used this approach extensively.

However, the most common arrangement is for students to be provided with copies of original material under whatever provisions exist in the copyright legislation for educational use. Inclusion of copies of primary source material in learning packages has been a pragmatic response to the difficulty faced by the distance learner in obtaining timely access to such material. In the view of some educators, this expedient conflicts with the strongly espoused principle that a university education should challenge a student to become an autonomous learner.

Many distance educators fear that moving to electronic delivery will result in even more reliance being placed on pre-packaged materials. However, Stephens et al (1997) believe that collaboration between teachers and librarians will expand the boundaries of distance learning. The growing trend towards online distribution of scholarly journals together with the trend amongst academic libraries of subscribing for sets of online journals is making access to journal literature as convenient for students studying at a distance as it is for students studying on-campus.

Recently, the Association of College and Research Libraries, which is a division of the American Library Association, published *Information Literacy Competency Standards for Higher Education*. The Standards encourage an integrated curriculum approach to the development of the information-literate student. This will involve the librarian collaborating with the teacher to identify appropriate learning resources and develop assessment tasks designed to improve a student's information retrieval, evaluation and usage skills.

At the postgraduate level, access to primary sources is often considered an intrinsic part of a student's studies. In a survey of 1,000 postgraduate students across 19 disciplines in 23 universities in the UK, 78 per cent of respondents said that they felt the need for supplementary reading material. However, 51 per cent said that making use of library resources was not explicitly required of them (Stephens *et al*, 1997). So while students themselves appear to recognize the need for access to primary sources, the programmes they are studying may not expect this of them.

The Florida Institute of Public Postsecondary Distance Learning (1997) identified the minimum library services that should be available to distance learners as being:

- access to online resources including library catalogues, indexes to periodicals and full-text journal articles;
- reference and referral services providing guidance on how to use libraries, locate needed information and pursue research;
- library user instruction related to information retrieval skills;
- borrowing privileges at academic libraries belonging to institutions other than the one at which the student is studying;
- document delivery of physical objects including full-length books and non-print resources;
- course reserve services of materials that the teacher wants students to read in addition to the textbook;
- access to library equipment and facilities including microform readers, audio equipment, video equipment, computer workstations, copiers, printers and study space.

The Institute saw some of these services being provided through the introduction of reciprocal rights. However, many of the services, including access to catalogues, indexes and journals, reference and referral services and user education services, they saw being delivered online (see Case study 7).

How much scholarly literature is available online?

Major developments have occurred in the electronic delivery of indexes and published journals over the two years since *Delivering Digitally* was first published. A growing number of journals are now available in electronic form, libraries have developed more sophisticated digital services, and in some countries the copyright legislation has been amended to take account of development in digital publishing, making it less onerous for institutions wanting to distribute material electronically.

Because of the large number of journals to which academic libraries subscribe as well as the technical issues that arise in delivering documents online, it is not practicable for academic libraries to subscribe to electronic versions of journals on an individual basis. However, recognizing this fact, commercial publishers have begun aggregating journals in various fields of study and selling subscriptions to full-text databases. Examples of such subscription services include:

- Bell & Howell Information and Learning's Proquest;
- Gale Group's Infotrac;
- MCB University Press's Emerald.

By subscribing to these searchable collections of full-text journals, academic libraries are able to distribute periodical literature over their local area networks. However, distributing the same articles over the Internet has encountered some difficulties with publishers.

The issue that concerns commercial publishers of scholarly journals is limitation of access to those who are eligible to receive access under the terms of the subscription. Provision of access to full-text databases over the Web therefore requires the establishment of some suitable means of authentication of legitimate users. In some cases, this is managed by the distribution by libraries of generic passwords to patrons. However, this approach can lead to a range of difficulties with managing password distribution and advising of periodic changes to passwords. The development of authentication mechanisms allowing access to multiple vendors' products is a technical issue and easily solvable.

Non-commercial publishers of scholarly journals such as universities and professional associations are usually less interested in making a financial return than with increasing readership. They initially moved more quickly than commercial publishers to exploit electronic delivery of their publications. Because they were not motivated by profit, they have often been willing to make their journals available over the Internet without charging. Print versions of the same journals are in some cases also available for subscription.

In addition to the scholarly journals, there is a growing volume of authoritative information originating directly from government and semi-government organizations, research organizations and universities. It is becoming increasingly common to find academic staff using the Web to publicize the results of their work by placing their publications on the Web, when they are not precluded from doing so by copyright restrictions.

For undergraduate courses, the most convenient method of offering original source material online may be through an electronic reserve collection. Schiller and Cunningham (1998) provided detailed statistics on a pilot project in which an electronic reserve collection was operated across several campuses of the State University of New York. Documents were scanned, converted to either Adobe Acrobat Portable Document Format (PDF) or HTML and then linked to the

Case study 7: The Florida Distance Learning Library Initiative

The initiative

The US state of Florida has taken advantage of development in digital technology to establish one of the world's largest and most integrated shared library systems for supporting distance learners.

Over the past two decades, higher education institutions in Florida have been increasingly moving towards shared resource use. In 1984, the Universities in the State University System had established the Library User Information System (LUIS), one of the world's most extensive shared library catalogues with over 3,000 terminals and workstations spread across 10 universities. In 1989, the Florida Center for Library Automation (FCLA), was established as a parallel system for community colleges with over 1,000 terminals spread across 28 colleges.

The Florida Distance Learning Library Initiative, launched in 1997, sought to build a comprehensive set of services for distance learners on this existing foundation.

Features

The Initiative involved several components:
- electronic resources;
- establishment of a statewide Reference and Referral Center;
- library user training;
- document delivery;
- reciprocal borrowing privileges.

Stakeholders

The Florida State University System and Florida public libraries.

The initiative at work

While some of the new services proposed under the Initiative involved expanding access to physical resources, the majority of the services were designed to take advantage of opportunities being offered by the new technologies.

Electronic resources
A substantial portion of the funding provided for the Initiative was allocated to acquisition of a core set of reference and heavily used electronic resources. Open access was provided to the FirstSearch databases to higher education students and faculty via the Web with a valid borrower ID. A decision was made that these be available on the campuses of State University System and community colleges via LUIS and LINCC online directories, while off-campus access is provided via the Web.

Reference and Referral Center
Highest priority was given to establishment of an online student advising system. The Reference and Referral Center was established in 1997 on the Tampa Campus of the University of South Florida adjacent to the Reference Department of the University's library. The Center provides a central service for students and staff of any participating institution in the state accessible via e-mail, fax or phone. It provides a help desk and on-call reference librarian.

Library user training
A Web site hosted by the Reference and Referral Center provides training materials to enable students and staff to make more effective use of library resources.

Document delivery
A courier service provides inter-library delivery amongst nearly 300 libraries in the Florida Library Information Network. This service is particularly oriented to the provision of full-length books and non-print resources such as recordings and videos.

Reciprocal borrowing privileges
The Library borrowing privileges to any Florida public higher education institution were extended to the libraries of all 38 universities and community colleges. This enabled distance learners to borrow physical resources through their nearest academic library.

Key success factors

The success of the Florida Distance Learning Initiative is largely attributable to the high level of co-operation between Florida Libraries at the time the Initiative was launched. The new services constituted logical extensions to those that were already in existence.

Further developments

Since the Florida Distance Learning Library Initiative was launched, a further step has been taken towards integration of the infrastructure for supporting distance learning. A portal to the range of online offerings and online student support services provided by Florida's 38 higher education institutions has been established, called Florida Virtual Campus. Services introduced in the Florida Distance Learning Library Initiative have been made accessible via this portal.

Further information

The Web site for the Florida Reference and Referral Center may be reached at <http://www.rrc.usf.edu/>
  Documents relating to the Florida Distance Learning Library Initiative including planning reports may be found at <http://dlis.dos.state.fl.us/dlli/>
  The Web site for the Florida Virtual Campus is <http://www.flcampus.org>

library Web site. It was found in this project that it was possible to offer this kind of service more efficiently by encoding documents in PDF rather than HTML. PDF encoding offered several other advantages as well:

- PDF format retains the original layout – important when documents contain tables, yet documents can still be searched by keyword and be given hypertext links.
- PDF documents can be given individual passwords.
- High-speed scanners capable of encoding documents in PDF are now available.

Whereas physical libraries are restricted to the geographical locations of institutions, digital library services need not be based at a particular campus. Indeed they need not necessarily be located at a campus at all. The advent of digital library services opens the possibility of institutions sharing library services. By banding together, for the provision of digital library services, academic libraries can secure subscription services at more attractive rates and also achieve economies of scale in their use of infrastructure and staffing. A number of libraries are also offering Web access to locally digitized collections. Some examples include:

- State Library of Victoria's Multimedia Catalogues of Digital Images <http://www.slv.vic.gov.au/slv/mmcatalogue/>;
- The Library of Congress National Digital Library Program – American Memory <http://memory.loc.gov/ammem/amabout.html>;
- The Digital Library Program at Indiana University <http://www.dlib.indiana.edu/>.

How are online library services affected by copyright legislation?

If a library subscribes to a collection of full-text online journals, then the subscription contract will most probably permit teachers to link to individual journal articles from their course materials. If it does not, then the library may still have the right to distribute text materials electronically. The conditions under which this is permitted will be stipulated in copyright legislation of the particular country concerned.

Copyright legislation varies from country to country and therefore it is not possible in a book such as this to provide definitive information. In most countries, the advent of electronic document delivery has necessitated a redrafting of copyright legislation because the copyright legislation has been silent on copyright owners' rights.

Provision usually exists in copyright legislation for 'fair use' for a range of purposes including scholarship and research. The 'fair use' provisions may allow libraries to establish electronic reserve collections under similar arrangements to those which libraries must adhere to in photocopying material to hold in a physical reserve collection.

The provisions relating to audio–visual material are usually much more restrictive than those that apply to print material and so it is generally necessary to seek copyright clearance and perhaps pay a licence fee in order to distribute material of this kind, whether that be online, on CD or CD ROM, or in some other form.

Universities that have not hitherto had much experience in the large-scale provision of print-based distance education may consider the requirements for copyright clearance quite onerous. However, major distance education providers recognize this as one of the routine functions of distance education delivery. The key to managing this function efficiently is to develop a streamlined set of procedures for locating the owners of copyright material, requesting clearance, negotiating usage fees, and maintaining records of the clearances that have been obtained.

Inter-library loan agreements permit libraries to make copies of limited amounts of copyright material. The greatest difficulty here is that the library system is not set up to offer this type of service on a large scale. The inter-library loans services are generally set up to provide copies of journal articles and book chapters to the academic research community. They are neither equipped nor staffed to provide copies to the much larger student community. The advent of full-text online journals may well diminish the role of inter-library loans services although these services will still continue to be needed for providing access to monographs.

Another way of obtaining a document delivery service online is to subscribe to the Uncover service operated internationally by the Colorado Alliance of University Libraries (CARL). Articles are delivered by fax from a collection of over 17,000 journals. The response time is generally less than 24 hours and users can search the database of articles via the Web: <http://ucwb.carl.org>. UnCover takes care of copyright fees. The cost of retrieving an article via UnCover is made up of a standard document delivery charge plus a variable copyright charge.

The changing role of academic libraries

In considering how library services might best be provided to students studying online, it is important to take account of the impact on the role of academic libraries of changes in the way information is being located. Whereas traditionally the library has been seen as the repository of the documents to which reference is made in research and study, in an online environment it is possible to go directly to the original source of a document and bypass the library. Indeed, the form in which needed information exists may have changed completely. Instead of existing as tables in a reference work or journal article it may exist as records in a database accessed through a Web portal.

In this context, the strategies used by professionals to access authoritative information will also need to change. The professional of the future will increasingly turn to the Internet as the initial method of tracking down information. Students therefore need to be trained to be proficient users of Internet-based information retrieval tools and to discriminate between authoritative information and information of questionable value.

In this changing environment, the role of the library is changing too. Rather than serving as the custodians of information resources, librarians are increasingly taking on the roles of information skills educators and guides to the world of information.

There is in fact a large range of ways in which academic libraries can use the Internet to assist learners to obtain better access to information resources. These include:

1. online access to: catalogues, indexes, full-text subscription journals, electronic reserve collection, inter-library loan service;
2. library education services, including: online tutorials on accessing resources in the Internet, sets of online guides to information services and sources;
3. reference and referral services, including advice on: the way to access resources on the Internet and the availability of print and other resources at nearby academic libraries.

Offering counselling services online

Student counselling services generally conceive of their responsibilities as extending across three main areas:

- assisting students to develop their social networks;
- providing careers and learning skills advice;
- providing counselling in relation to personal issues.

Assisting students to develop social networks

Many students studying at a distance experience a sense of isolation. This has been one of the recurrent themes in the distance education literature. Asynchronous conferencing and chat systems offer a means of breaking down this sense of isolation. Providing the facilities for computer-mediated communication is an essential prerequisite to enabling students to meet in virtual venues. Equally as important as providing student lounges and cafés in an on-campus environment is provision for the incorporation of virtual meeting places into the design of online learning environments. However, consideration needs to be given to ways of encouraging students to use these facilities. Just as 'ice breaker' activities are often needed to enable some students to feel comfortable when interacting in face-to-face situations, structured activities may be needed to enable some students to feel comfortable with online interaction.

Providing career and learning skills counselling

Careers counselling includes the provision of advice on career options as well as on study pathways. Given the types of students who presently choose to study at a distance and the types of students who are most likely to be attracted to online learning, it is likely that the provision of advice on course choice will best meet students needs if information is organized by fields of study rather than by institution. National and international directories of courses, particularly if they are cross-referenced with occupational information, are likely to be more useful in locating suitable courses for study than catalogues of the offerings of individual providers.

May (1998) reviewed the range of sources of career information on the Internet to assist career counsellors and their students in investigating career choices. He identifies Richard Bolles' *What color is your parachute? The Net guide* <http://www.washingtonpost.com/parachute> and *The Riley Guide* <http://www.jobtrak.com/jobguide> as two of the most useful Web sites providing meta-listings of online career resources.

Most universities are now using the World Wide Web to make information on their range of courses available over the Internet, but as yet there is comparatively little consideration given to the way in which information needs to be structured and presented for accessibility.

Advising on personal issues

Traditional counselling services in learning organizations have a long history of making a real difference to their learning and in their lives. Traditionally too, administrators of these services are continually being challenged to provide cost-effective services that students will want to access before any of their issues reach a crisis stage.

It is usual for counselling services to provide a range of free literature on topics such as health and students' rights and responsibilities and basic self-help strategies. Most counselling services have recognized the potential that the Web offers for making this type of literature more readily available, even to students studying on-campus. Once this type of information has been placed on the Web it is accessible to students, irrespective of the mode in which they are studying.

Students who are able to access this type of information only online may need to be alerted to its availability. It will be advisable to provide pointers to the information from locations where students are given direction on course requirements.

The traditional role of student counsellors has been in the provision of face-to-face consultations with students who seek assistance with personal issues. Student Counselling Services are beginning to realize the benefits of offering e-mail advice services or full-scale Webcounselling as an adjunct to the provision of face-to-face counselling services to students. Here are the benefits of the provision of online advice services:

- It is cost-effective.
- Students can access services anonymously.
- Messages can be sent and received at any time of the day or night.

- The writer can take as long as necessary to explain the issue and there is opportunity to reflect on what should be said.
- An automatic record of communications is available for later reference.
- The writer is apt to feel less inhibited than in person.

Benefits accruing to the organization are the potential to store and measure student data, thereby improving the quality and effectiveness of support and intervention strategies.

As benefits are becoming apparent the provision of online counselling, and the potential for the development of large-scale student databases, raise concerns about student privacy and data security issues. The standard practice in counselling is that any interaction between a student and the counsellor must also remain confidential. Students need to be assured that any online interchange will remain confidential.

The development of standards in the provision of online counselling and guidance information

These issues have led many counselling and guidance associations to develop principles and standards to deal with a whole new set of ethical considerations brought on by the advent of this innovative use of technology.

One such organization is the National Board for Certified Counsellors at <http://www.nbcc.org>. By adopting a minimum set of technical and organizational policies, practices and procedures for online counselling, learning organizations will ensure that an appropriate balance is struck between access and the protection of client information.

The ethical practice of Webcounselling

The NBCC defines Webcounselling as 'the practice of counselling and information delivery that occurs when client(s) and counsellor are in separate or remote locations and utilize electronic means to communicate over the Internet'.

The following is a basic set of guidelines that could be adapted to an individual organization's requirements. While not being as detailed or as extensive as the NBCC standards they are compatible with them:

1. *Students should be informed of safeguards implemented to ensure the privacy of student/ counsellor communication.* Security concerns can make students reluctant to share information, undermining the quality of the service. Unless proper controls are in place, unauthorized users may be able to gain access to transmissions and/or records of online counselling sessions. Students should be advised of the risks of unsecured communication. Encryption should be used if it is available and other safeguards should be considered if a student being counselled is sharing a computer with family members, library patrons or other students.

2. *Students should be informed in what form and for how long session data will be preserved.* Many counsellors store data for research and administrative purposes. Students should be informed as to how long and for what purpose their personal electronic data will be stored.
3. *Informed consent should be obtained prior to any online counselling.* The student should be fully informed before he or she consents to receive counselling online. In particular, the student should be informed as to the process, the identity of the counsellor, the potential risks and benefits of those services and safeguards against those risks. The students should also be informed of the alternative to receiving counselling services online.
4. *The identity of the counsellor should be disclosed.* When a student–counsellor relationship is established in a virtual environment the student may be less well placed to make a decision on counsellor suitability than if the student can meet the counsellor face-to-face. Students accessing counselling online should have the same information available to them that they would have if they were receiving counselling face-to-face. The counsellor may also wish to provide supplemental information such as areas of special training or experience. Links should be provided to the Web sites of appropriate certification bodies and licensing boards.
5. *There should be adequate evaluation of students before provision of any counselling online.* Students with issues such as violence in relationships and sexual abuse that require specific expertise should be advised to pursue other more appropriate options than online counselling.
6. *Students should be informed of the vagaries of the technologies used in online communication.* Students need to be aware of the possibility that e-mail messages may be lost or delayed in transmission. Students should also be made aware that because of the lack of visual clues in online communication there is a greater risk of misunderstanding than is the case with face-to-face counselling.
7. *Standard operating procedures should be adopted in relation to turnaround time and emergency contact.* The student should be informed as to how soon after sending an e-mail message he or she may expect a response. The counsellor and the student should agree on the frequency and mode of communication and any responsibilities with regard to the interaction. Alternative contact arrangements should be in place for when the counsellor is offline or at a great distance from the student.

Summing up

Delivering courses online at a distance calls for reorganization of the ways in which support services are provided. This is important in order to ensure that the highest standard of support is provided for the resources available as well as to avoid the possibility of costs escalating. In most situations the most cost-effective arrangement will be achieved through the establishment of a centralized 'help desk' facility to track and manage students' requests for assistance, direct queries to staff best placed to answer them and ensure that requests for assistance receive timely replies.

The extent to which it is possible to provide library services online is presently constrained by copyright restrictions and the high cost of subscriptions to the electronic versions of commercially published journals. However, the use of electronic reserve collections and electronic delivery copies of articles through the inter-library loans arrangements allows considerable scope for development of online service. Moreover, the growth of electronic journals and other Internet-published literature will steadily reduce the reliance of academic programmes on print literature.

When designing library services, it is important to take into account the changing patterns of use of information retrieval resulting from growth of the Internet and the World Wide Web. The types of library services that students are likely to need most in future are those that direct them to available Internet resources and train them in the use of Internet-based information retrieval rather than simply the loan of monographs and the copying of articles.

Counselling services need to place their print literature on the Web. The major challenge facing counselling services will be to test the limits of the electronic media for one-to-one counselling.

Chapter 10

Developing an evaluation strategy

In this chapter we first identify the object of evaluation where knowledge media are employed and discuss some of the issues involved in evaluating. We focus particularly on teaching and learning innovations or projects utilizing knowledge media. We look at what you evaluate when you evaluate, how you evaluate, how you interpret the results of evaluation and who should evaluate. We then go to examine in more detail criteria for evaluating learning with knowledge media. We offer a frame of reference for selecting criteria and demonstrate how it might be employed.

Evaluation and the knowledge media

In striving to improve access, to reduce costs and to improve the quality of education and training, evaluation is vital. New educational technologies, along with new uses of existing ones, are being employed to improve both access and quality. Effort is being put into projects that use knowledge media to supplement or replace face-to-face classroom tuition and to facilitate distance learning. Are the anticipated benefits realized and are the benefits worth the effort? Systematic evaluation can help to answer this question.

Evaluation can not only assess and place value upon the outcomes of projects but, if applied to the early stages of projects, can help to shape them and improve the chances of producing worthwhile outcomes.

The use of knowledge media is often evaluated against objectives of projects involving new educational technologies or against alternative approaches. In either of these cases, the evaluation is of the use of media over a contained period. For this reason we will focus in this chapter on evaluating projects or initiatives employing the knowledge media; projects that have a beginning, development phase and an outcome. This raises a number of issues and challenges, some of which relate to the nature of learning using digital technology and some that derive from focusing on innovations.

Some issues arising from the nature of the knowledge media

The use of knowledge media for delivery of a course implies that something more than human resources of speech and action are used to facilitate learning. That something might be an interactive multimedia programme on CD ROM, Web resources, a computer-assisted learning programme or a computer-managed learning system. These media may be used with stand-alone delivery packages or may be used in conjunction with teacher–student interactions – whether face-to-face or at a distance. In evaluating the use of new learning technologies it is important to encompass both where those technologies are employed to deliver stand-alone resources and where they are used in teacher–student and student–student interaction.

Learning through knowledge media, then, is not a discretely definable process. There are many forms of media and many strategies for their use. This means that the knowledge media per se are not readily evaluated. All that can be evaluated are particular teaching and learning activities that involve the use of some form of digital technology.

The use of knowledge media to facilitate learning does not imply that the learning takes any particular form. The learning may involve acquiring information, understanding, skills, competencies and dispositions. Likewise, the learning acquired through digital technology may be assessed or evidenced through processes requiring recall, analysis, synthesizing, hypothesizing, competence or creative behaviours. What is being evaluated, then, is not a particular form of learning.

Neither does the use of knowledge media in itself imply a particular learning process informed by a particular learning theory. The process could involve simple teacher-led instruction. It may involve design catering for graded or alternative conceptualizations. The student may be largely passive or active and learning may take place through discovery or through direct instruction. The design of learning materials may be based on behaviourist, information processing, cognitive, humanistic or constructivist theories.

What is being evaluated then is not a particular approach to learning informed by a particular learning theory generic to the use of knowledge media. What are available for evaluation are particular education and training initiatives or innovations that employ new learning technologies.

Some issues arising from focusing on innovations

What constitutes an innovation? We need to decide how innovative an innovation has to be in order to serve as an indication of the value of adopting knowledge media for education or training purposes.

Use of new learning technologies can be more or less innovative. It can be innovative in some contexts while established in others. In trying to evaluate the impact of innovation using knowledge media do we include new uses of old technologies such as television or just new technologies; do we include innovations employing low-tech media, such as e-mail, as well as high-tech interactive multimedia? You need to define the boundaries of the types of innovation according to your own context and purposes.

How can we make evaluation of knowledge media effective?

The value that the knowledge media contributes to improved access, quality and efficiency is still being contested. Many innovations involving knowledge media have not yet been appropriately evaluated. Many have not been evaluated at all. Often evaluations of educational innovations involving digital technology originate from the innovators themselves. We can attend to the first point raised here – the want of systematic evaluation. We can also attend to the second point – evaluation by interested parties, in the sense that we can seek independent evaluation of knowledge media.

Evaluation is subjective. Evaluation involves placing a value upon findings. We may seek to make the process of data gathering as objective as possible. Yet the questions to be investigated, the choice of data to be gathered, the acceptance and rejection of data, and the interpretation and reporting of the findings are bound to reflect some subjectivity. Evaluation involves selection and judgement and the way these processes are carried out depends on the context of the evaluation, the interests of the evaluator and the frames of reference chosen by the evaluator in selecting evaluation criteria. As a consequence, one person's evaluation may not be suitable for another person's decision-making.

Some key issues in undertaking evaluation

It is obvious that the main value of evaluating projects that make use of the knowledge media is that it contributes to more effective decision-making. What are less obvious are:

- what to evaluate;
- when to evaluate;
- how to evaluate;
- who should evaluate.

Let us examine each of these aspects in turn.

What to evaluate

We cannot evaluate the knowledge media as such, any more than we could evaluate print, or evaluate the overhead projector. Evaluation of particular media is sometimes attempted. It produces results by media type; for example that overhead projectors are valuable for information presentation. However, with some creativity, we could also use an overhead projector to silhouette glove puppets in a role-play. We certainly cannot evaluate the computer as a medium, when it may be used in more ways than we could define. The value of a medium depends on how it is used. We can, therefore, evaluate media only in the context in which they are being used. For this reason we focus in this chapter on evaluating projects involving new learning technologies.

When to evaluate

It is traditional to distinguish between formative and summative evaluation. Summative evaluation is evaluation at the conclusion of a project. Formative evaluation is evaluation conducted during a project.

Formative evaluation is undertaken during a project in order to monitor progress and modify developments in the project as it proceeds. Formative evaluation might be undertaken at the end of discrete phases of the project. It might take the form of evaluating components of a project as they are developed or trialing a pilot version of a project.

Summative evaluation is suitable for reflecting upon the success of a project. It might be undertaken in order to satisfy accountability requirements established by sponsors of an innovation or project. Summative evaluation can be used to determine appropriate applications of the product and any support or supplementary materials or services that may be necessary. Summative evaluation can inform the conduct of similar projects in the future. As summative evaluation usually comes at the end of a project, it is not able to serve to inform developments during that particular project. Figure 10.1 shows the relationship between the timing of formative and summative evaluation.

Two further types of evaluation may also be employed – design evaluation and an evaluation of needs or a needs analysis. Design evaluation, like formative evaluation, is undertaken during a project to influence developments. However, whereas formative evaluation relates to phases or elements of a project as they are completed, design evaluation relates to stages or elements of a project yet to be commenced. Design evaluation can address minor points such as the way that people are likely to interpret an icon on a screen. On the other hand, it can address more fundamental matters.

For instance, suppose that it was proposed to design a sequence in an interactive multimedia programme in which students are required to distinguish between the graph of an exponential function and the graph of a simple curve. It would be worth checking first whether students who are typical of those likely to use the product are able to make this distinction. If they are not able to make this distinction and this is not discovered before the programming has been completed, a

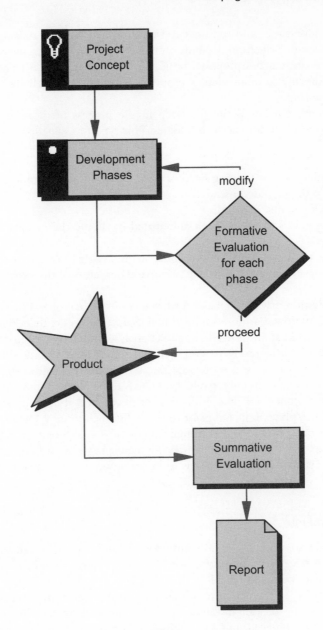

Figure 10.1 *A simple evaluation model*

considerable investment may be made in a product that subsequently has to be substantially redesigned. Design evaluation can be critical in major multimedia projects. It can uncover faulty assumptions about the capabilities, interests and predilections of users, which can lead to investment in design that needs later to be modified or even abandoned.

Whereas formative and summative evaluation may be undertaken as a matter of course, design evaluation depends on recognizing the need to check particular assumptions on which a proposed project is based. A project co-ordinator needs to be continually scanning design proposals to identify underlying assumptions that need testing.

Evaluation of needs is the first step in the process of mounting a project employing new educational technologies. This type of evaluation asks questions such as:

- What education or training need or needs is the project intended to serve?
- Who are the intended users?
- Is there a genuine demand?
- Are they needs that have been anticipated or should the original concept be modified?
- Are the proposed users, or someone on their behalf, prepared to meet the design, development, production and marketing costs of the project?

The last question may be seen as a further form of evaluation – a market analysis. Figure 10.2 illustrates a more sophisticated evaluation model than Figure 10.1. It incorporates evaluation of needs, a market analysis and design evaluation.

Whether we choose to use a simple model, which involves only formative and summative evaluation, or a more sophisticated model, evaluation should not be an add–on or an afterthought. Evaluation needs to be planned into a project from the time it is conceived. The evaluation of needs, and if appropriate, a market evaluation, must be conducted prior to the design of a project. Design evaluation needs to occur prior to the commencement of development of materials and may need to occur several times as development progresses from phase to phase. Formative evaluation likewise needs to occur at any stage a discrete element of the project is developed.

How to evaluate

What should we look for in instruments for conducting an evaluation? While evaluation is necessarily subjective, we can aim to make the means of gathering evaluation data valid and reliable.

Validity refers to the extent to which an evaluation instrument measures what is intended to be measured. Validity can be improved by carefully considering what is to be observed and by carefully crafting questions for checklists or interviews. For example, if we wish to discover whether potential students are likely to enrol in a course using knowledge media, then piloting the unit and asking whether students enjoyed using the particular medium does not ask the right question, at least not on its own. It is a question people typically include in evaluation of knowledge media but, in this case, it is not what you are setting out to test. It would be more pertinent to ask students whether, based on their experience with the pilot, they would enrol in such a unit in future.

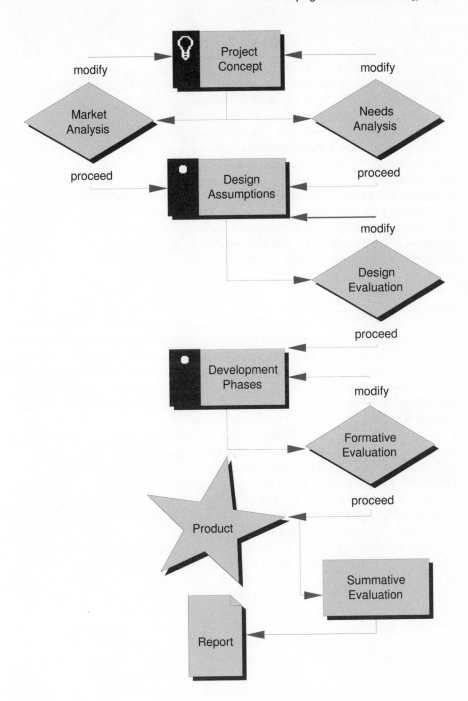

Figure 10.2 *A pre- and post-development evaluation model*

Reliability refers to the capacity of the instrument to return consistent results and ones that will be interpreted consistently. Reliability is indicated where the scope for argument about the meaning of questions asked or checklists employed and questions about the meaning of results are minimized. Reliability can be achieved, for example, by using several investigators who agree on guidelines to be used for interpreting data gathered from a questionnaire or by having the records of an interview and the interpretation of an interview confirmed by interviewees.

It is sometimes necessary to accept a trade-off between validity and reliability. You can increase reliability by asking yes/no questions on a questionnaire so that the responses to the questionnaire could be read by multiple investigators or by a computer and produce the same result. However, in switching to that approach you may impair the validity of the results. The evaluation instrument may give little scope for reporting of unexpected or complex responses to the educational initiative being investigated – that is, it may fail to produce a complete picture of responses and in that sense lack validity.

Who should evaluate

Applications for funding for innovative educational projects generally require a description of the evaluation strategy that will be used. This leaves open the possibility that evaluation is left in the hands of those undertaking the project. Is this the most appropriate approach? There are two questions you might consider: should evaluation be in the hands of an expert evaluator and should the evaluator be independent of the project team?

With regard to expertise, drafting an evaluation plan for a project requires some understanding of the nature of the process, of the phases and forms of evaluation, and of the design of instruments that optimize validity and reliability in data collection. You may have access to expert evaluators. On the other hand, you might acquire appropriate expertise through staff development using reference material such as this chapter or evaluation texts, or by having staff undertake professional development programmes in evaluation.

There are advantages to having an independent evaluator undertake some forms of evaluation, while having those involved in a project conduct other forms of evaluation. A market analysis might best be performed by a person independent of a proposed project to determine whether, from a sponsor's point of view, it is worth proceeding and the nature of what is demanded. Needs analysis, design evaluations and formative evaluations, on the other hand, are generally best carried out by those involved. These forms of evaluation inform design and development of the project. Various parties have an interest in summative evaluation: sponsors of projects, users of innovations as well those immediately involved in the project. As a result, there is an advantage in having someone independent of the project carry out summative evaluation.

The remainder of this chapter provides some guidance for the conduct of project evaluations. It is intended to inform and support both evaluation undertaken by members of a project team and independent evaluation conducted by people lacking evaluation expertise.

Some guidelines for carrying out evaluation

Evaluation instruments

There are many types of instruments or means of evaluation that can be applied to the use of courseware based on the knowledge media or to use of the knowledge media in delivery. The instruments most commonly used are:

- expert reviews;
- surveys;
- observations.

For an expert review of the product or service, a report is obtained from an appropriate expert. There are at least three forms of expertise that are pertinent to this type of evaluation: subject matter expertise, instructional design expertise and media expertise. It may be considered important in a particular situation to call on a variety of experts. When this approach is used, the sponsor of the evaluation usually hands over the responsibility for selecting the criteria for evaluation to the expert.

A survey instrument such as a questionnaire may be devised to evaluate an educational product or service. Decisions have to be made about criteria for selecting items to include. Decisions also have to be made about how open-ended the questions should be. (These points are discussed later.)

Observation may be made of the product or service in action, possibly against a checklist. The process might involve discussion with users as they employ the knowledge media. Videotaping use of the product or service can assist in making a detailed analysis of user behaviours. Again, criteria for establishing a checklist or items to be observed and for their interpretation have to be determined. (See the section on criteria below.)

Selecting an appropriate survey instrument

Questionnaires, interview schedules and checklists may be used as evaluation instruments in a number of approaches. Is there an appropriate format for such instruments? Should they adopt closed formats such as yes/no, Likert scales (eg strongly agree/agree/disagree/strongly disagree) or multiple-choice questions? Should they adopt open formats such as short answer questions, open-ended questions or loosely structured interview schedules? There are a number of considerations in determining whether to evaluate using open forms of evaluation such as loosely structured interviews or closed forms such as Likert scale questionnaires. These include:

- breadth of response versus ease of analysis;
- subjectivity;
- logistics;
- forms of analysis and representation of the data.

Breadth of response versus ease of analysis

Open-ended forms of investigation, such as loosely structured interviews with users or open-ended questions on a questionnaire, allow for unexpected responses and provide for depth of reporting. Closed formats like interviewing against a checklist or multiple choice questions on a questionnaire make data analysis simpler and more reliable.

Subjectivity

Open forms of data-gathering focus the subjectivity at the end of the evaluation; that is in the process of identifying or clustering like responses, in discriminating between responses and in interpreting the findings. Closed forms of investigation focus the subjectivity at the start of the process; that is in determining what questions to ask, in guessing the responses people may wish to make – as in selecting options for multiple-choice questions or bounding the responses people may make as in Likert scales or true/false questions. From this point of view, open forms have an advantage. The focus of the subjective element comes after you have heard what respondents have to say rather than before you have heard it.

Logistics

From a logistical point of view open-ended formats require less effort in construction but more in data manipulation and interpretation. Closed formats require more effort in construction, including trialing of questions. However, the responses are easier to handle. One consideration here is the scale of the investigation. Designing an elaborate questionnaire makes most sense where the number of people to be surveyed is large. Handling large amounts of qualitative data can be both complex and time-consuming. There are computer programs that assist qualitative data analysis, such as NUD•IST. However, to use these programs requires training. The process of getting the data into a form suitable for analysis by computer takes some time.

Forms of analysis and representation of the data

Closed questionnaires lend themselves to quantitative analysis and reporting. Responses may be presented in the form of graphs and it is possible to execute statistical correlations, for example between demographic elements of the data and successful use of the knowledge media – eg whether males or females, young or old, had most success in using the product. There are a couple of cautions here: the data must be valid in the first place and attaching meaning to the correlations depends on having a theoretical position from which to make an interpretation of any forces at work. It is possible to attach some quantitative elements to open-ended responses, and some qualitative data analysis packages provide this facility, but the quantitative results may well be nonsense. It would be inappropriate to report that 43.36 per cent of respondents said that navigation in the media being investigated was perplexing or confusing when sampling of the population was done on a convenience basis. The reporting implies a level of precision that was not built into the design. Suppose, on the other hand, that this response came from an open-ended question asking what was the most striking impression of the educational media. The fact that navigation was confusing came to mind for nearly half the respondents is much more powerful than 43 per cent of respondents to a closed questionnaire ticking a box that asked if they found the navigation confusing.

Conducting observations of a product or service in action

A product or service resulting from a project may be observed and evaluated against a set of criteria. As indicated in the following section, the criteria may or may not be designed to facilitate comparison with alternative products and services. Where it is designed to be comparative, a quasi-experimental situation can be established to observe the effects of applying the innovation. Comparison may be made with the condition of learners prior to application of the innovation or with a control group.

Some caution should be expressed here. Variables are likely to be very difficult to control or to otherwise account for and there are ethical considerations in experimenting with learners.

To take a quasi-experimental approach requires a theoretical expectation of outcomes and the establishment of an associated hypothesis that can be tested. The selection of a hypothesis often helps to indicate measures that are appropriate, such as observation schedules, pre- and post-tests of knowledge skills and attitudes, or artefacts produced by the users. It also indicates criteria for judging and interpreting data.

Criteria for evaluating innovations involving knowledge media

Whatever the evaluation instruments and methods we choose to use, we need criteria to select appropriate questions or matters to evaluate. The brainstorming approach – eg 'Why don't we ask them whether they found it easy to use?' – is sometimes employed. It is inappropriate; it lacks a rationale. There are alternative approaches we can use to establishing evaluation criteria. Four approaches are differentiated here:

Case study 8: The Flashlight Project

The initiative

The Flashlight Project assists institutions to evaluate the use of educational technologies for educational improvement and educational investment purposes. It was conceived in 1992. The Project aimed to develop a suite of evaluation tools that can be used to evaluate the usefulness of technology in implementing seven principles of good learning and teaching: interaction between the student and educator; student–student interaction; active learning; time on task; rich and rapid feedback; high expectations of the student's ability to learn; and respect for different talents, ways of learning. The Current Student Inventory contains about 500 items designed to assess the operation of these principles. The Flashlight Project offers three types of assistance: tool kits including Flashlight Online, a set of articles and case studies and a *Cost Analysis Handbook*; online and face-to-face training; and consulting services.

Features

- a Web-based system for evaluating the use of educational technologies;
- a Current Student Inventory (CSI) consisting of almost 500 indexed questions for constructing surveys and gathering and analysing information from currently enrolled students;
- focus on choices about learning and teaching with technology made by students and educators;
- stakeholders.

The Flashlight Project became a part of the non-profit TLT Group, the Teaching, Learning, and Technology Affiliate of the American Association for Higher Education. The TLT Group provides a range of services to help faculties, their institutions and their programmes make more sensible use of technology. Early stakeholders included the Fund for the Improvement of Post-secondary Education (FIPSE); the Annenberg/CPB Project; the Western Co-operative for Educational Telecommunications.

These stakeholders collaborated with the Education Network of Maine, Indiana University, Purdue University Indianapolis, Maricopa Community Colleges, the Rochester Institute of Technology and Washington State University. There are now many client colleges, universities, system offices, multi-institution projects and companies.

The initiative at work

To use Flashlight you need to obtain an account. You can then access the site and create your own surveys, which can be printed for administering in hard copy or the survey can be delivered directly online. The system allows you a detailed analysis of responses or gives you the option of obtaining summaries of student responses. Tailored forms of response reporting may be negotiated.

In 1997 Washington State University developed Flashlight Online, which is available to institutions subscribing to the Flashlight Tool Series Plus. Users can select items and add items of their own to produce a survey to which students may respond online.

Gary Brown of Washington State University used Flashlight to study a special seminar for at-risk students. He used Flashlight to explore the effectiveness of a multimedia initiative. He found that, in conjunction with a new approach to content and the organization of the programme, the multimedia initiative appeared to have a positive impact. The findings suggested that first-year students were making considerable use of the Internet to discuss programme subject matter. The findings suggested value in introducing more interaction and generative activities for learners.

At Indiana University Purdue University at Indianapolis (IUPUI) Susanmarie Harrington used Flashlight to survey similarities and differences in teaching practices and costs in networked classrooms compared to traditional classrooms. This stimulated a re-examination of how computer-networked classrooms were used. The findings are published in the Flashlight evaluation handbook.

A *Cost Analysis Handbook* has been developed which focuses attention on the way in which people utilize resources. Over 50 institutions are now members of the Flashlight Network and contribute to its development.

Requirements:

The Flashlight Tool Series includes institutional site licences for all Flashlight tool kits including the Current Student Inventory and the *Cost Analysis Handbook* in paper-based and disk form. An additional subscription is required for Flashlight Online. A Web-based service allows you to create, execute and analyse surveys online.

Institutions may also subscribe to the Flashlight Network receiving the Tools Series, Flashlight Online, plus a variety of consulting and training services.

Further information

<http://www.tltgroup.org/>

- using the objectives of the innovation;
- comparing effectiveness with a previous condition or approach;
- evaluating against the known potential of the technology;
- evaluating against a theoretical position.

A combination of two or more of these approaches is also a possibility. Let us look at each of these possibilities in turn.

Goals or objectives-based criteria

If the goals or objectives of the project can be identified, they are frequently used to provide the criteria for evaluation. This approach is satisfactory if the objectives of the particular innovation have been accepted as being worthwhile, if any unanticipated outcomes are seen as irrelevant and if costs are seen as given and acceptable. This is, at least prima facie, the case for some specially funded projects, such as projects funded by a university or by an outside agency, which calls for submissions for projects meeting certain criteria and provides support to a predetermined level. Even in these situations, evaluating a project against its own objectives is limiting. This method of evaluation will give no indication of unanticipated outcomes that may be as educationally or practically important as the intended outcomes. It does not allow for shifts in objectives. Focusing on project objectives can lead to costs being ignored or at least being taken as given – being those specified in a project submission. In fact, there are likely to be costs, both direct and indirect, that were not identified in project submissions. To ignore extraneous benefits, costs and other effects limits the understanding that could inform future actions.

Comparative criteria

An alternative method is to compare the outcomes of an initiative with an approach that does not employ the innovation. The learning outcomes using the initiative might be compared to learning outcomes using a previous approach, or the learning outcomes for a particular learner might be compared to the condition of the learner prior to using the innovation.

There are two sets of issues in attempting a comparison between teaching approaches: what to keep constant and what additional aspects of the situation need to be examined.

The learning environment is likely to change in multiple ways, so maintaining constants is difficult. If we cannot keep elements of the learning environment constant, we could try to run sufficiently extensive trials to use inferential statistics to make comparisons. However, this may not be practical either.

It would be unusual for educational and training initiatives using knowledge media simply to change the form of teaching without impact on other aspects of the educational transaction. The form of learning valued may change, the roles of learners and teachers usually change and even the boundaries of the subject may change. The intended learning outcomes therefore change as do appropriate forms of student assessment. It would not then be appropriate to measure the success of approaches using knowledge media against traditional approaches by using the same test or exam.

The comparative approach, as for other approaches to selecting evaluation criteria, has its limitations. Yet we are often obliged to attempt to answer the question 'Does the innovation make things better or worse?' In doing so, we need to acknowledge the limitations on our ability to provide a simple answer.

Criteria based on conventional wisdom

A further alternative in establishing criteria is to use benefits and costs anticipated from the literature or experience as a basis for evaluation. The result is to evaluate innovations employing digital technologies against benefits which could, on the basis of a conventional wisdom, be expected to flow from them and to likewise evaluate them on the basis of the costs that could be expected to be incurred. The rationale for this approach is that it can take into account a wider range of benefits and costs than those identified by the designers of a particular project.

Expectations arising from conventional wisdom may be that innovations will:

- provide new educational experiences;
- offer greater options for student selection of learning activities;
- extend information resources;
- extend opportunities for exchanges between students and between students and teachers;
- provide better opportunities for monitoring individual student progress;
- provide wider access to learning.

Theoretically based criteria

This approach to evaluation criteria requires not just a theoretical position on evaluation, but a theoretical position in relation to the realm being evaluated. For example, where learning outcomes are evaluated you need a theoretical under-standing of learning processes; where access to education is an issue, a position on equity is needed.

To take learning theories as an example, the criteria that one would use to evaluate an education or training innovation would differ according to the understanding of learning held by the evaluator. If you have a behaviourist understanding of learning you might look for a systematic, step-by-step approach, with frequent testing, which results in positive or negative reinforcement as appropriate to produce the prescribed learning outcome. An evaluator with a constructivist view of learning might be looking for the opportunity for the learner to engage with the material, bring personal experiences and needs, apply their own meaning and emerge with something applicable to their own situation.

As for any of the approaches to establishing criteria, the theoretical approach has its limitations. It may not address issues of the accountability of innovators to meet agreed objectives; in itself it says nothing about the comparative value of the innovation; and it will not be suitable for a decision-maker who holds different ideals or theoretical understandings to those of the evaluator.

Frames of reference for selecting evaluation criteria

A model for selection of evaluation criteria based on the alternative frames of reference outlined above is tabulated in Figure 10.3.

Combining approaches to establishing criteria

Each of the approaches to establishing evaluation criteria has its uses and its limitations. The approaches can be combined. For instance, for accountability purposes, one may be obliged to take an objectives-based approach to evaluating an innovation, yet still wish to report on unintended outcomes. For example, a training initiative may have been designed to create competency in basic keyboard skills. However, it may also have led to the development of other skills in the use of software or in the operation or assembly of hardware, which could be seen as valuable if criteria beyond the specified objectives were employed.

In combining criteria one has to be clear about the purpose of the evaluation; that is, those things on which we are putting a value. These purposes need to be consistent, or, if they are inconsistent, then the inconsistency needs at least to be highlighted when reporting. An evaluator coming from a constructivist view of learning who values the opportunity for the learner to engage with the material and to apply their own meaning may not regard a competency-based learning project as valuable even if it met its declared objectives. You could report on the project from both points of view but the difference in viewpoints needs to be made explicit.

Some good examples of combining criteria based on the educational potential of electronic media with criteria based on theories of learning may be found in the educational literature. Laurillard (1993) adopts expectations of educational media initiatives derived from an intersection of learning theory and an understanding of the potential of various forms of instructional technology. She argues that media should facilitate teaching approaches that are:

- discursive – allowing teachers and students to access each other's conceptions, allowing them to agree goals and allowing students to receive feedback on their actions;
- adaptive – responding to the relationships between teacher and student conceptions;

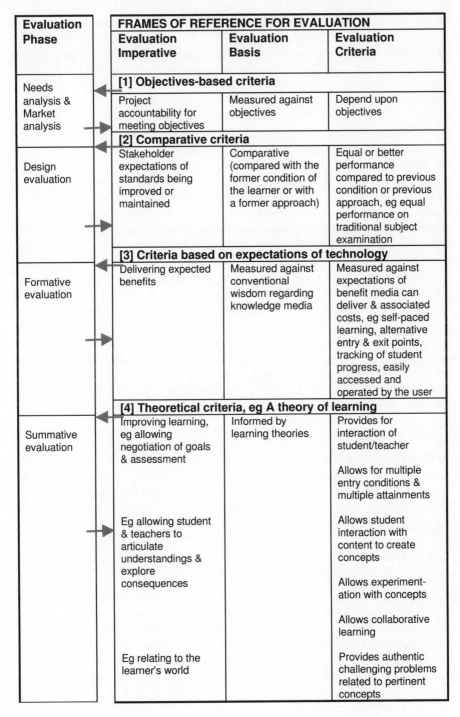

Evaluation Phase	FRAMES OF REFERENCE FOR EVALUATION		
	Evaluation Imperative	Evaluation Basis	Evaluation Criteria
Needs analysis & Market analysis	**[1] Objectives-based criteria**		
	Project accountability for meeting objectives	Measured against objectives	Depend upon objectives
Design evaluation	**[2] Comparative criteria**		
	Stakeholder expectations of standards being improved or maintained	Comparative (compared with the former condition of the learner or with a former approach)	Equal or better performance compared to previous condition or previous approach, eg equal performance on traditional subject examination
Formative evaluation	**[3] Criteria based on expectations of technology**		
	Delivering expected benefits	Measured against conventional wisdom regarding knowledge media	Measured against expectations of benefit media can deliver & associated costs, eg self-paced learning, alternative entry & exit points, tracking of student progress, easily accessed and operated by the user
Summative evaluation	**[4] Theoretical criteria, eg A theory of learning**		
	Improving learning, eg allowing negotiation of goals & assessment	Informed by learning theories	Provides for interaction of student/teacher Allows for multiple entry conditions & multiple attainments
	Eg allowing student & teachers to articulate understandings & explore consequences		Allows student interaction with content to create concepts Allows experimentation with concepts Allows collaborative learning
	Eg relating to the learner's world		Provides authentic challenging problems related to pertinent concepts

Figure 10.3 *A model for selecting criteria for evaluating media innovations*

- interactive – providing meaningful intrinsic feedback to student actions to achieve a task goal;
- reflective – allowing students to link feedback on their actions to the topic goal.

Educational media can then be evaluated against criteria that:

- emphasize the capacity to describe and redescribe conceptions;
- allow adaptations of task goals, which provide for feedback;
- allow subsequent adaptation of action.

Jones *et al* (1994), drawing on a wide range of writing on learning, established a 'technology effectiveness framework' (see Table 10.1) setting up quadrants about a learning axis ranging from passive learning (undesirable) to engaged and sustained (desirable) and a technology performance axis ranging from low to high. High performance of the technology is indicated by: connectivity to resources; inter-connectivity to other participants (teachers or students); inter-operability between systems (eg ability to transfer data between systems); distributed resources rather than one source of knowledge (for example, extending from stand-alone computers to LANs, WANs and the Web); the capacity to provide complex problems and complex links; functionality (access to sophisticated peripherals); and user-friendliness. In the lowest rated quadrant fall computer-aided learning programmes based on drill, while approaches that are networked, allow conferencing between participants, provide access to rich resources and include challenging tasks are at the other end of the scale.

Table 10.1 *Technology effectiveness framework (Jones* et al, *1994)*

	Engaged and Sustained Learning	Passive Learning
High technology	eg, challenging tasks with connectivity	
Low technology		eg, CAL based on drill

The framework of Jones *et al* (1994) shown in Table 10.1 is based on a conception of engaged learning as meaningful to the learner, collaborative, challenging, multidisciplinary and oriented around authentic tasks involving important real-world issues. The student is self-regulated and responsible, having optional routes and strategies. It would be inappropriate to evaluate innovations based on these principles by employing a test of traditional teaching designed on transfer of information concepts. In so far as evaluation includes assessment of student achievement, assessment working from this understanding of learning should be interwoven with the learning task, assessing the knowledge constructed by students, observing the processes they adopt and the artefacts they produce.

The models produced by Laurillard (1993) and Jones et al (1994) are not the only ways in which frames of reference can be combined. These examples are based on particular theories of learning and understandings of the possibilities offered by delivery technologies. Other models could have been produced by, for example, a set of criteria based on equity of access to education and training combined with a set of criteria based on the potentials of technology to contribute to learning. This would produce a model of the type shown in Table 10.2.

Table 10.2   *Equity/learning approach matrix*

	Interactive Learning Technologies	Information Transmission Learning Technologies
Readily accessible technology	eg, simulation on floppy disk	eg, videotape
Difficult to access technology	eg, professional flight simulator	eg, database material on a college server

Applying the frames of reference

Teaching and learning using knowledge media can be evaluated against a great range of possible questions. Sit a team of instructional designers down and they will come up with dozens of possible evaluation questions and criteria for assessing responses to them. A search of the Internet for criteria + evaluation + education + materials will turn up many possibilities. Yet you will need to generate questions appropriate to your situation. Which questions you choose to use depends, in part, on the frame or frames of reference that are appropriate to the evaluator. The frames of reference provide a rationale for selecting questions and criteria for evaluation. Table 10.3 provides examples of questions that could be used to evaluate teaching and learning using knowledge media and some possible criteria for judging whether responses to the questions are satisfactory. The rationale for including each is derived from the concern or focus of the evaluator indicated by the frame of reference.

Interpreting the results of an evaluation

Summative evaluation of a project involves placing a value upon the product of the project based on data collected about the project and against the criteria employed. As we determine the criteria we will employ to evaluate, we also determine the way in which the data is interpreted and reported.

Table 10.3 *Sample questions and criteria for various frames of reference*

Frame of reference: Objectives-based approach to evaluation

Question	Criteria
Are the objectives stated clearly?	The objectives are stated clearly.
What new skills, knowledge and/or attitudes will result from the application of the knowledge media?	The skills, knowledge and/or attitudes likely to be produced match learning objectives.
Is information appropriate?	Information is error-free, current, with balanced representations of cultural, ethnic and racial groups.
How will the skills, knowledge and attitudes gained during this learning be assessed?	Available assessment will test acquisition of the skills, knowledge and/or attitudes aimed for.
In what context will the skills, knowledge and attitudes gained from this learning be used?	The media simulates or approximates the context of users.
Does the material contain a tool to measure whether objectives have been met?	The media contains a student assessment instrument pertinent to the objectives.

Frame of reference: A focus on the conventional expectations of knowledge media

Question	Criteria
What are the hardware, applications, operating system and other requirements for operating the knowledge media?	Appropriate facilities are available to the learner, designer, teacher and staff responsible for technical delivery.
In what instructional setting will this material be used, eg, learner's workplace, a college laboratory, community library, learner's home?	Appropriate facilities are available in the instructional setting. There is sufficient access guidance and support for the user.
Does the knowledge media provide flexibility in location, time and pace of learning?	The media provides flexibility in location, time and pace of learning.
Are writing and instructions clear?	Writing and instructions are clear. There is correct use of grammar, spelling and sentence structure.
Are exercise instructions easy to follow?	Exercise instructions are easy to follow.
Will the material be enjoyable to use?	Learners will probably enjoy using the knowledge media. The media stimulates imagination and curiosity.

Frame of reference: A focus on the conventional expectations of knowledge media

Question	Criteria
Is the design of materials of high quality?	Supportive feedback is provided. There are options for help. Screen displays are uncluttered. There are captions, labels or legends for visuals. The typeface is easy to read. The layout is attractive. The overall look is professional. Icons and graphics are used appropriately. There is a clear index. There is a useful glossary. Sound and music are relevant to screen displays. The digital technology is bug-free.
Is navigation efficient?	The knowledge media offers rapid retrieval of information and screen transitions. It uses intuitive icons, menus and directional symbols that foster independent use. It is controllable in pace, including options for stop/pause/exit. It offers controllable sound.
Does the knowledge media offer save and record-keeping features?	The educational innovation has options for: printing/downloading text; save option for games or activities in progress; note-taking feature, when appropriate; record-keeping feature to monitor student progress.
Is there a teacher's guide for knowledge media materials?	There is a teacher's guide, which offers: a description of target audience; summary of the contents of the application; instructional and/or behavioural objectives; suggestions for classroom use, lesson plans, related activities; ancillary materials for student use, such as camera-ready worksheets and activity pages.

Frame of reference: Teaching/learning process oriented evaluation

Question	Criteria
What prerequisite knowledge or skills are required before utilizing this knowledge media?	Prerequisites are made known. Learners are likely to have the prerequisites.
Are the materials educationally appropriate?	The materials are appropriate to the desired learning outcomes and to the learners' skills, understandings and learning interests.
Does the material flow logically with key concepts presented first or introduced appropriately?	The learner can identify key concepts within the learning materials. There is a logical progression of topics with options for increasing complexity.
Does the knowledge media engender appropriate learner behaviours?	The materials focus on learner behaviour rather than information presentation. The educational media offers a variety of activities, which require the learner to engage skills, knowledge and attitudes appropriate to the intended learning outcomes, eg, the educational innovation provides for creative problem solving.
Who will be using the knowledge media, eg, students directly, students with the intervention of teachers?	The knowledge media used directly by students is easy to use and has built-in flexibility to cater for varying student needs and responses. The knowledge media used in conjunction with teachers is pertinent to the desired learning outcomes and complements other elements of teaching.
Does the material adequately cover the subject or the elements of the subject it is intended to cover?	The material covers the area intended or students are directed to other appropriate learning resources. Information is of sufficient scope to adequately cover the topic for the intended audience.
What educational resources would be needed or could be used to supplement these knowledge media materials?	Lectures, tutorials, seminars, tutor assistance, handouts, bibliographies, videos, etc, that complement or supplement the knowledge media can be identified and made available.

When evaluation is undertaken against the objectives of the particular project, the interpretative task is to determine whether the data collected indicates that the objectives have been met. Likewise, if the evaluation is a comparative one then the task is to determine whether the data collected indicates that the outcomes obtained are as satisfactory or more satisfactory than those that would have been obtained by using alternative approaches. The answers may often be partial rather than definitive.

Where evaluation is informed by a theoretical understanding about learning, such as constructivism, criteria such as scope for the learner to express his or her own understanding would have been adopted. Evaluation instruments that allow determination of whether such opportunity exists would have been employed. The interpretative task is to place the data collected against the theoretical framework. One might report that a particular knowledge media innovation provided the opportunity for learners to express their own understandings or to demonstrate skills and that this complies with one of the requirements for effective learning situations coming from a constructivist approach. If, on the other hand, one held a behaviourist theoretical understanding of learning, one would use criteria such as: the learning task is divided into clear steps, correct responses are rewarded and incorrect responses punished or negatively reinforced. The task of the interpretation would then be to determine whether data collected indicated that clear steps and appropriate rewards and punishments were present. If so, the evaluation report would indicate that the educational innovation establishes an appropriate environment for learning. Different theoretical positions, then, lead to placing value upon different attributes.

Evaluation and cause

Evaluation may indicate the success of the approach used in a project compared to alternative approaches. This leaves open the question of causality. Beyond the evaluation of innovations, you might want to know what factors are associated with the success of projects and what factors with failure. You might wish to be able to make pronouncements on the steps one needs to take to ensure success in using the knowledge media. To do so, you need more than an evaluation. You would need to be comfortable with adopting a positivist approach; you would need to conduct an investigation within a theoretical framework; and you would need a way of treating multiple variables in complex educational contexts.

Summing up

Evaluation is an aspect of courseware development that needs to be conducted from the outset of a media project to inform and modify development. Evaluation also needs to be conducted at the end of a project to reflect upon the process and outcomes, to determine appropriate applications of the product and any support or supplementary materials or services that may be necessary, and to inform decision-making around similar activities in the future.

The design of evaluation instruments should be appropriate to the type of data that need to be collected. Criteria that relate to the rationale underlying the evaluation need to be employed. Evaluation is a matter of attributing value and requires a frame of reference for selecting criteria. Examples of such criteria have been provided in this chapter.

Innovations based on the knowledge media often occur in a context of multiple obligations requiring more than one form of evaluation and implying more than one frame of reference. Data will be interpreted against the premise of the evaluation, such as a theoretical position, and according to the criteria chosen to guide the collection of data.

Finally, it should be noted that evaluation is generally not designed to determine cause and effect. That would requite a research study rather than an evaluative one.

Chapter 11

Managing the transition

In this chapter we draw from the implementation strategies discussed in this section of the book. We discuss the phases of the change process. We provide a timetable for sequencing the phases of transition and we conclude by identifying a range of principles by means of which it is possible to execute the transition to digital media without escalating costs.

Organizational responsibility

For most organizations, the transition to electronic delivery will represent a significant shift. It will involve major changes to the organization: changes in staffing, procedures, infrastructure, and most of all to the culture of the organization. For some organizations, which approach the task in a more tentative or exploratory fashion, the transition may be less momentous. The significance of the changes to the organization will depend on how critical the transition is to the organization's future and perhaps even to its long-term survival. However, the impact of the transition depends not only on outcomes but also on the efficiency of the transition process itself.

Negotiating the transition successfully depends upon senior management accepting a high degree of responsibility for it. Change management on a large scale cannot succeed without the support of senior management. This does not imply that the vision of the project and the planning of its implementation needs to be a top-down process. On the contrary, there needs to be ownership, vision and enthusiasm at all levels of the organization. It does, however, mean endorsement of change strategies at the top and support for change agents. It means putting in place project managers for the change strategy as a whole and for particular initiatives within it. In a small organization, the top management may take on this project management function. In large organizations or large departments in organizations, it is more appropriate for someone to be given operational responsibility for management of the project.

Project management and evaluation

Existing distance education providers will already be very aware of the crucial importance of project management to the successful conduct of distance education programmes. Institutions and organizations coming into this field for the first time are likely not to be as alert to the importance of this role. However, the types of skills needed for management of electronic delivery of courses are somewhat different from those needed for the management of print-based delivery, and the skills required for management of the transition to electronic delivery of courses are different again.

One of the most important requirements is familiarity with the characteristics of the range of computer and communications technologies that are used in electronic delivery. Particularly important is awareness of the factors that are likely to impact the learner's experience in learning by this mode – factors such as response times, times taken to download Web pages and failure characteristics of networks.

The role of the project manager

If the transition is to be made smoothly, it will be important for one person to be delegated responsibility for overall operational management of the project. Without this provision, important issues are likely to be missed. If one person holds ultimate responsibility for the success of the project, then that person's duties can be defined in terms of successful completion of the project rather than in terms of particular functions. The person responsible for operational management of the project will require well-developed skills in the areas of:

- team leadership;
- interpersonal communication;
- time management;
- budget preparation;
- project scheduling;
- report writing;
- evaluation procedures;
- group presentation skills.

The person responsible should also possess a good understanding of the educational issues at stake as well as a good technical knowledge of computer and communications systems.

One of the most important roles that this person will play will be to ensure that the technical infrastructure meets the educational requirements of the project.

Phases of the change process

Most descriptions of innovation involving the new learning technologies examine what is involved in terms of the aspects of the innovation rather than in terms of aspects of the change process. For example, Mitchell and Bluer (1996) describe a detailed planning model that is broken up into four stages: an initial planning stage, a production stage, a delivery and support stage and an evaluation stage.

However, making the transition to digital modes of delivery may be better described in terms of the phases of the organizational change process. We consider that there are three major phases to this process: initial planning; start-up; and changeover phase.

An important aspect of the process of making the transition will be to put in place new organizational structures, policies and procedures for operating in the digital mode.

The complexity of the processes and the preparation needed make it imperative for them to be initiated and undertaken in parallel if they are to be completed over a reasonable time span. We see the major activity areas as being:

- planning and project management;
- infrastructure re-engineering;
- staff development;
- courseware development or procurement;
- evaluation;
- support systems.

Phase 1: Developing a proposal

It is standard practice for grant-providing authorities to require applicants for research and innovation funding to set out detailed plans of what they propose. How much more important is it for an organization that may be spending many times the amount offered in a typical research or innovation grant to formulate a detailed proposal? The purpose is the same in each case: to produce a document that ensures that the proponents are clear about the goals, methodology, costs and other requirements of the project and to enable those who are accountable for the resources to discharge their responsibility for ensuring that the funds are well used. With regard to the latter it is essential that estimates of costs are realistic if goals are to be attained (see Chapter 4).

In this initial phase of development it is more appropriate to think of this document as a proposal rather than as a plan. What is put forward initially will need the approval of the relevant stakeholders before it can form the basis for action. In the course of gaining stakeholder approval, the details of what is proposed are likely to undergo some change. The major components that should be incorporated into the proposal include:

- a detailed analysis of what is wanted and why with supporting evidence;
- a breakdown of the tasks involved;
- a month-by-month schedule for implementation;
- an estimate of staffing requirements;
- infrastructure implications;
- a projected budget.

What is wanted and why?
You need to define the purpose or purposes of the transition to digital delivery:

- Is it an attempt to reduce costs?
- Is it to enhance reputation?
- Is it to improve student learning?
- Is it to promote educational offerings?
- Is it to generate additional income through the marketing of software?

The answers to these questions will determine the nature of the changes that are needed and the best strategy to follow in making those changes. Specifying purposes makes explicit the expectations of the benefits expected to arise from the project. This can help not only in drafting goals, but in stimulating a review of the expectations of adopting digital delivery.

An opportunities analysis
As indicated in Chapter 10, an early step is to undertake an opportunity or market analysis to determine:

- nature of market opportunities;
- size of the market;
- needs of learners.

If it is proposed to make the transition with an existing cohort of students then it will be necessary to establish that the students have the requisite equipment or are willing to acquire it, and whether they are comfortable with the idea of changing their method of delivery.

It is not uncommon for institutions to overestimate the preparedness of students to change their mode of study. If this is found to be the case then it may be better to initiate the transition with a new cohort of students who arrive with the expectation of studying with digital media. Many institutions have started out by launching new full-fee courses on line.

Detailed planning and task prioritization

Detailed planning requires the identification and the scheduling of the critical tasks over the important tasks required to effect the transition. A broad schema is provided in Figure 11.1 and the quality improvement framework (see Chapter 12) can be used to identify which areas need to be tackled first.

A more detailed month-by-month schedule, including specification of who is responsible for the actions, will also be needed. A detailed schedule might be drafted at the beginning of each phase.

A specification of staff requirements

This concerns the profile and quantity of staff required for the project. If the staffing plan is adopted it may mean some staff redundancies, some staff re-skilling and some recruitment. It is unlikely that the full staffing requirements can be anticipated in advance. However, staffing requirements are the most critical element of the proposal from the point of view of expenditure, often accounting for 70–80 per cent of costs, and some indicative estimate is required.

Infrastructure implications

Infrastructure requirements depend upon the education and training strategies proposed and the administrative and support arrangements envisaged as well as the size of the exercise. At the proposal stage an indication of the infrastructure implications of the proposal, including a costing, is critical to decision-making. Next to staffing, technological infrastructure may be the largest cost item.

A projected budget

The project plan will need to make an attempt to estimate the likely costs and returns of the change programme. Costs need to be assessed realistically. They also need to be viewed as one side of the investment equation. The aim is not to minimize costs, but to strike a balance between costs and returns appropriate to the organization's objectives (see Chapters 4 and 5). Under-funded projects can generate worthless outcomes.

Gaining organizational commitment to change

A proposal, when endorsed, earns the organization's commitment to the project. The plan, however, needs to be seen as an evolving document that will be revised in the light of events as the project proceeds. The general thrust of the plan may stay in place but information and communication technologies are continually changing, with the possibility that infrastructure, delivery equipment and software requirements may change. This may have consequences for organizational arrangements and for resource requirements, including staffing.

Depending on the scale and complexity of the task of adopting digital delivery of programmes, detailed planning may be undertaken at the level of minor projects contributing to the overall plan.

Phase 2: Start-up

Re-engineering infrastructure

The extent of technological infrastructure requirements depends upon educational strategies, administrative and support demands and the quality and extent of the existing infrastructure.

It is important that the systems chosen are appropriate for the purposes for which they are required. It is therefore important that the education and training strategies and the administrative and support requirements have been fully worked out before a review of infrastructure requirements commences. These may need to include new arrangements for infrastructure responsibility, in particular arrangements for the allocation of responsibilities between central services and local services. Policies for technical standards and for software and hardware compatibility may also need to be revised. An audit of the computers, communications and software requirements against the new requirements will determine the extent of re-engineering required.

While the educational and administrative requirements should drive infrastructure re-engineering, technical and supply considerations and costs need to be taken into account. There may need to be some negotiation in the process of determining infrastructure capabilities to ensure that the educational and administrative strategies intended are technically and economically feasible. There may be technical reasons, such as software and hardware compatibility and supply reasons, such as service agreements, which suggest the acquisition of particular brands of hardware or software. Those responsible for technological infrastructure may also wish to build in a capacity beyond that immediately required in order to meet anticipated requirements. There is a balance in this process between obtaining an infrastructure result that meets present and future requirements and having the infrastructure limit or prescribe the functions available and thus drive educational and administrative strategies.

Acquisition of major items of hardware such as servers and the installation of new communications facilities will almost certainly introduce some delay. It is therefore important that decisions on these items be made as early as possible in order to allow sufficient lead-time for installation and commissioning of new systems and the rectification of any faults that are found.

Staff development

The types of activities considered under this heading are the specifically planned staff development programmes. Development of the skills of staff will, of course, result from participation in the process, especially in cases where staff are working in teams. However, the management of these opportunities is more subtle.

It is important to get the timing of staff development programmes right. They need to be scheduled for when they will be most effective. Premature development of skills and knowledge can be ineffective because the newly acquired skills cannot be consolidated and extended. On the other hand, delays in the provision of staff development can cause frustration and also erode the commitment of staff to the proposed developments. A 'just-in-time' approach is required. However, the adoption of a just-in-time approach may have logistical implications for a large organization.

There are three stages at which the conduct of formal staff development activities is likely to prove particularly beneficial. The first stage needs to occur when the programme is being launched. Gaining the commitment of staff is important for the success of organizational change of this magnitude and providing an occasion that both symbolizes the beginning of a new era for the organization and informs staff what is planned and what to expect of the process. An appropriate form for a launch event to take might be a forum or series of forums at which visiting speakers who have already been involved in such a process outline their own experiences and demonstrate products on which they have worked.

The second stage is when the development of new courseware is being initiated. During this phase of the transition, teaching staff will require training in the procedures and processes that will be followed in the design and development stages of preparing courseware. If it has been determined that a team approach to development will be followed, then it will be important that all the members of each development team understand the contributions that they are being expected to make and the contributions that other members of the team will be making. Development of staff skills can be undertaken as part of the collaborative work of the team. The choice of team leaders will be important in ensuring that team members are supported.

The third stage during which staff development will be important will be when new course delivery modes are being implemented, particularly during the initial trials. For many teaching staff the use of computer-mediated communication to support online tutorials will be a new experience. The accent in training will need to be on the pedagogical aspects of using this form of interaction with students. However, staff can be familiarized with communication elements – such as e-mail, document transfer, bulletin boards and discussion sites – by using these systems for communication between them.

Courseware development or acquisition

Decisions need to be made about the extent to which digital resources will be developed in-house or involve bringing in expertise, contracting out assignments or procuring existing materials. Decisions in this area need to be made following market and needs analysis and concurrently with the early stages of a staff development programme. Opportunities to procure and adapt available materials need to be reviewed from time to time as needs become clearer some way into a project and as new materials come on the market.

In so far as it is decided to design and develop materials in-house or through collaboration, decisions need to be made about the extent to which this will be achieved through specialization of functions and the extent to which it will be in the hands of teachers and trainers. Staff development will need to be tailored accordingly.

Implementation of new support systems

A separate implementation programme will need to be set out for each of the new support systems. The time frame for implementation will differ according to the system. Implementation of each support system will include infrastructure and staff development components. The task of managing the introduction of each support system may be seen as a complete sub-project, with all the attributes of the larger project.

Evaluation

Market and needs analysis will have been undertaken in developing a proposal as indicated above. Design evaluation and formative evaluation are required during courseware design and development to avoid the need to redesign media products and to ensure their applicability to the anticipated clientele.

Courseware available on the market also needs to be evaluated at an early stage for its suitability to the project's purposes (see Chapter 10).

Phase 3: Changeover

The changeover phase is likely to extend over a long period, perhaps years. It will be characterized by successive mainstreaming of electronic delivery functions and involvement of an increasing proportion of teaching staff. The changeover process will amount to a repetition of the processes adopted in the start-up phase, modified in the light of information provided by the evaluation of these processes. It would be reasonable to expect the transitional processes to proceed more smoothly, more rapidly, and with greater confidence on the part of staff.

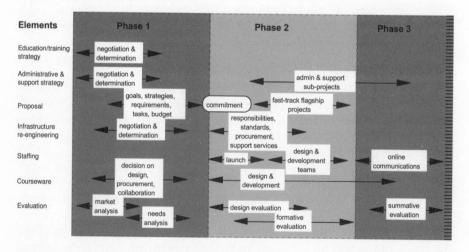

Figure 11.1 *Managing the transition schedule*

Strategies for managing costs

One of the important management functions in making the transition to the knowledge media is managing costs. If you are aware that there is a risk of the costs of electronic delivery rising above those of print-based or face-to-face delivery, then it is important to have strategies for containing costs that don't adversely affect the quality of teaching or return on investment. The following strategies are some that are suggested by what we already know about the cost-effectiveness of using the various digital media in the delivery of education and training programmes.

Deliver courses in parallel forms

The same design and development costs apply to print and online delivery. Yet costs of translation of textual materials into HTML is small, especially when using current generation Web authoring tools. This allows you to obtain maximum economies of scale while still enabling you to start making the transition to online delivery. Delivery via alternative media enables you to tap both traditional distance education and online markets while the demand for online delivery grows. The major disadvantage to this approach is that it limits the extent to which you can take advantage of the unique possibilities of the World Wide Web.

Be selective in the development of interactive multimedia courseware

Producing interactive multimedia courseware is much more costly than producing textual materials. The use of interactive multimedia should be targeted at applications for which video, animation or interactive elements offer specific advantages. Interactive multimedia projects should be carefully planned and their cost justified in terms of the contribution they will make to improving the quality of student learning or decreasing the time taken to reach specified outcomes. Look for opportunities to procure suitable interactive multimedia, together with rights to modify or supplement it if necessary.

Look for opportunities for collaboration in expensive courseware development projects

The high costs of development of interactive multimedia courseware can be partly accommodated by entering into collaborative ventures with other providers that have similar needs and interests.

Give responsibility for multimedia programming and Web page design to production staff

The cost of training teaching staff in multimedia programming and Web page design can never be recouped from the small number of projects on which such staff will be able to use these skills. Furthermore, without a significant investment in ongoing training, the skills will soon become out of date. Over the medium and longer term, the cost of employing or hiring multimedia programmers and Web page designers will be amply repaid as a result of shorter lead-in and production times and higher production values.

Seek multiple uses for expensively produced multimedia courseware

Economies of scale apply just as much to the development of small segments of instruction as they do to developing whole subjects. Interactive multimedia projects with high fixed costs require more students to bring down the cost per student to that of media forms with lower fixed costs. One way of accommodating the higher costs of interactive multimedia products is therefore to find multiple uses for them. The smaller the size of a courseware module, the more likely it is that it can find a use somewhere else in a teaching programme.

Provide a clear structure for computer conferencing sessions

Experience with the use of computer conferencing for promoting interaction amongst students shows that effective student participation depends on providing a clear structure, with specific tasks, and tutors being actively involved in promoting interaction amongst participants. Once group members feel that they know each other and the tutor they will be much more ready to take the lead in promoting discussion. This suggests initial face-to-face contact if practicable. Computer conferencing is most economical where a group is involved. It can be oriented to group work.

Encourage the establishment of peer support groups

If the staffing costs of tutoring online are high, there is scope for achieving significant savings by enabling students to support each other. One of the benefits of computer-mediated communication is that it allows students to communicate with each other in groups. Students can form study groups in a virtual study centre. Teachers can monitor the operation of study groups and offer support where needed rather than being the centre of communication.

However, be careful not to take students' capacity to use this new medium too much for granted. If they are to use the medium effectively they will need to be given some initial training in its use. The time involved in these activities will not be negligible. It needs to be included in the overall budget.

Summing up

The transition process may be conceived of as taking place in three phases:

- planning;
- start-up;
- changeover.

The planning stage is concerned with 'thinking through' the change process, development of a change programme and gaining the commitment of all parts of the organization to the proposed programme.

The start-up phase is focused on implementing and testing new systems, processes and procedures and piloting new methods of development and delivery.

The changeover phase is concerned with extending the tested systems, processes and procedures across the whole organization. This phase may last several years.

The purpose of organizational change is generally to increase efficiency and thereby save costs. However, there is a cost attached to the change process itself. Whether a process does in the end yield the expected savings can only be gauged much later.

Part 3

Quality improvement

Chapter 12

Improving the quality of online learning programmes

In this chapter we define the concept of 'quality' in relation to teaching and learning and describe the benefits of implementing a quality improvement methodology for online learning. We provide a comprehensive 'best practice' framework, which can be used by managers as a tool for the implementation and evaluation of digital technologies in education and training and show, by means of a practical example, how the framework can be applied in practice.

The demand for quality

Developments in the new learning technologies are providing opportunities for education and training organizations to reconsider the ways they deliver their programmes. High-quality, interactive learning materials exemplify potentially new and exciting ways of approaching the provision of education and training and addressing the increasing demands of learners for access to training. There is now widespread agreement that these new technologies have the potential to serve a greater and more diverse student body and make significant improvements in the quality of student learning while at the same time containing the expensive infrastructure costs and the labour-intensive lecture of the campus-bound classroom.

The demand for 'quality' in education and training programmes has never been greater. Students, governments, funding bodies and the community expect an education system that delivers quality products, services and graduates and makes the best use of their money. At the same time, education and training providers are also operating in a new, competitive market where student demands cannot be taken for granted. Rather, students and employees will be attracted to education and training organizations that offer products and services that come closest to meeting their needs as they perceive them. In this competitive environment, education and training organizations must therefore:

● be flexible and responsive;
● develop quality systems and management processes;
● meet the needs and expectations of their customers and clients.

With the new technologies driving the changes from traditional delivery methodologies to a more open and client-centred approach, the effective use of new learning technologies is often seen by writers in the field as a key factor in meeting the triple challenge faced by education and training organizations: providing a high-quality education to all students who need and can benefit from it in the most cost-effective way.

Many education and training organizations have already adapted their delivery strategies to take advantage of new developments in the information and communications field and are making considerable investments in the development of their technological infrastructure. Education and training organizations must therefore assure themselves that the perceived benefits, especially in tight fiscal environments, justify the costs. In order to reap the benefits for which they are hoping, and to ensure that the quality of programmes is not compromised, management needs to develop comprehensive quality assurance processes to evaluate and improve the impact of these new learning technologies.

There is a growing recognition amongst education and training providers that an increased focus on concepts and strategies borrowed from the corporate sector and directed at achieving 'world best practice' are critical in addressing this problematic relationship between quality and competitiveness in education and training organizations.

The quality agenda in education and training

Quality as a discipline has its roots after war-torn Japan was helped by Edward Deming, a US consultant, to restructure and revitalize the Japanese manufacturing industry. Edward Deming is considered today to be the father of the Quality Movement. He introduced the concepts of quality control and continuous improvement to the Japanese manufacturing industry, thereby transforming the image of Japanese products on the world market. Gradually, other industries across the world, including non-manufacturing industries, and even service industries like the education sector, recognized the necessity of applying 'quality principles' to the daily business of work. Applying these 'quality principles' in organizations has generally contributed to improved capability, be it in terms of productivity, more satisfied customers, or – in education and training – the provision of better courses.

While it is not possible to define quality in education in the same way that manufacturing organizations might define the quality of their products, it is possible to identify practices that are effective in producing quality learning outcomes.

The concept of best practice

Best practice is a comprehensive, integrated and co-operative approach to the continuous improvement of all facets of an organization's operations. It is the way leading-edge organizations manage their operations to deliver world-class standards of performance. In general, the features of best practice companies are those that simultaneously improve the quality, cost and delivery of their products or services, use technology to advantage and maintain close links with their customers and stakeholders.

An Australian study of international best practice (Department of Industrial Relations and Australian Manufacturing Council, 1992) identified the following attributes as being characteristic of companies engaging in best practice:

- strong leadership from top management in developing a vision and implementing a strategy for world-class performance;
- extensive consultation and communication with employees to develop a shared understanding and commitment to corporate goals and strategies;
- a focus on simultaneous improvement in cost, quality and delivery;
- better utilization of existing technology and the adoption of the most appropriate advanced technology;
- implementation of training and education programmes to enhance and broaden the skills of employees;
- commitment from employees through increasing the breadth of their decision-making and involvement in traditional management responsibilities;
- closer links with suppliers and customers;
- a culture in which everybody is encouraged to make ongoing improvements in the way they work;
- integrated approaches and less hierarchical structures for greater flexibility;
- human resource policies that promote continuous learning, teamwork, participation and flexibility.

A definition of best practice in education

In Australia, the Committee for Quality Assurance in Higher Education (CQAHE) was established in 1993 to review and rank Australian universities against a set of teaching and learning criteria. These included course design, delivery and assessment and staff recruitment processes. The CQAHE defined quality assurance in the area of teaching and learning as:

the totality of the arrangements by which an organization discharges its responsibility for the quality of the teaching it offers, satisfying itself that the mechanisms for quality control are effective and promote improvement.

In its report, the CQAHE (1995: 3–8) identified the following characteristics of good teaching and learning:

- an institution-wide approach to planning and management;
- integrated university-wide processes for evaluating, monitoring and review;
- use of national and international benchmarking;
- course approval procedures;
- use of external stakeholders in course design and review;
- matching of delivery style to learning needs of particular groups of students;
- monitoring of examination standards and mark scaling;
- rigour of staff appointment procedures;
- weight given to teaching skills in promotion;
- staff appraisal systems;
- opportunities and programmes for improvement of teaching skills;
- innovation in the area of teaching and learning;
- alignment of student services to institutional mission including the targeting of support;
- access to and availability of effective student services especially library and information technology;
- provision for effective student participation on university committees;
- practical implementation of student grievance procedures;
- feedback on changes resulting from student surveys.

While the focus of the two investigations is different, there is a remarkable degree of similarity between the two findings. Globally, too, there is recognition of the convergence of a set of universal 'best practice' principles and quality concepts that have emerged from the experience of 'best practice' organizations. This convergence can best be evidenced in the development of very similar and internationally recognized Quality Awards. In the USA, we have the Baldridge Award, which recognizes those organizations that score highly on the criteria of:

1. leadership;
2. strategic planning;
3. customer and market focus;
4. information and analysis of data;
5. human resource focus;
6. process management;
7. business results.

Similar awards with similar criteria are presented to best practice organizations in the European Quality Awards, the Deming Prize in Japan and the 'Australian Business Excellence' Award in Australia.

Essentially these seven criteria embody the same quality principles originally espoused by Deming and indicate the importance of:

- a commitment to change throughout the organization driven by the full and public support of the leadership of the organization;
- a strategic plan, developed in consultation with the workforce, which encompasses all aspects of an organization's operations and which sets out short, medium and long-term goals;
- flatter organizational structures supported by the devolution of responsibility, the empowerment of the workers and improved communication – often involving a team-based work structure;
- a commitment to continuous improvement and learning, with a highly skilled and flexible workforce and a recognition of the value of all people in the organization;
- focusing on data and evidence to reach decisions and the use of performance measurement systems and benchmarking;
- quality as defined by the customer.

The similarity between the quality criteria of the various Quality Awards can therefore be considered to be the critical elements that define a 'best practice' organization. The Baldridge Model can be accessed on the World Wide Web on <http://www.quality.nist.gov/>

Many organizations now recognize the potential that exists for improving their competitiveness by assessing themselves against these models of business excellence. As a consequence, the models are increasingly being used in both private and public sector enterprises to drive quality improvement initiatives.

When combined with a self-assessment approach, these models identify opportunities for improvement and provide measures of the organization's quality journey.

Applying models of best practice to education and training

Many enterprises have been convinced that an application of quality and 'best practice' principles contributes to productivity; that it is possible to do more with less and to do it better, while at the same time containing costs. Education and training providers confront the same issues as other organizations in other industries. They must satisfy their students (customers), manage change, manage people within a changing environment, allocate resources and plan for long-term viability. Funding cuts, pressures to increase provision and the need to develop greater accountability have made it imperative that education and training organizations follow a 'best practice' approach.

Quality is not a new concept in education. However, it is only relatively recently that educational institutions began considering the formal application of quality principles to their practices.

It is taken for granted that education and training providers should be accountable for the quality of their activities. The pace of technological change and the necessity of public accountability and competitive pressures have increased to the point where a fundamental requirement for education and training organizations is a capacity to manage change and improvement. Organizations need to assure their customers that the services they offer are carried out as intended.

In 1995, the National Institute of Standards and Technology in the United States piloted programmes to adapt the Malcolm Baldridge best practice model to educational organizations. They concluded that the model was as applicable to educational organizations as it was to the manufacturing sector.

In 1996 in Australia, the Australian National Training Authority conducted a similar exercise. They too concluded that the model was a suitable and practical tool for evaluating and describing key improvement strategies for educational organizations.

The quality concepts and principles embodied in these international 'best practice' models have provided the basis for a quality improvement framework for the provision of online learning and new learning technologies.

A quality improvement framework for best practice in new learning technologies

The intention of the framework is to provide a systematic tool that enables managers to assess the implementation of new learning technologies against a model that defines 'best practice'. The framework provides an approach to assessing the quality provision of new learning technologies in education and training organizations.

The primary purpose of the framework is to provide a set of principles and best practice indicators that address the essential areas in the quality provision of online learning and new learning technologies and against which managers can assess the extent to which they have achieved 'best practice'.

Both technology and innovative teaching and learning practices are developing so rapidly that any description of 'best practice' is likely to be out of date by the time it is published, and this framework is no exception. We therefore take the view that the notion of 'best practice' is not one that can be packaged and defined for the long term. Before we explain the framework, we propose that you complete the following 10-second quiz (Figure 12.1).

Are you keeping up with best practice in online learning? Try this quiz.

☐ An improvement plan identifying responsibilities, performance indicators and critical processes has been developed and is monitored to evaluate online programmes.

☐ Strategies have been implemented to provide a level of complex technical and online support required to run efficient, reliable and 'user-friendly' systems.

☐ Delivery media are selected on the basis of 'best fit' between learner effectiveness, accessibility and cost.

☐ A process for assessing student requirements and satisfaction is developed and implemented.

☐ Criteria for evaluating student performance are clearly established, stated in course guidelines and are generally understood by students and staff.

☐ Formal or informal professional development for online delivery activities (inc subject, technical and instructional design expertise) are identified and systematically implemented.

☐ Staff work plans incorporate staff's professional development needs for the development, delivery and support of online course delivery.

☐ Information technology standards are in place and members of online projects are aware of these so that they can make an informed choice when making technology purchases and designing learning materials.

☐ Qualitative and quantitative performance indicators for online learning have been identified.

☐ Copyright and intellectual property implications of buying, licensing or developing materials have been explored and processes are in place to ensure policy compliance.

☐ Online delivery has an organized system for admission, assessment, orientation, support and student follow-up compatible with the circumstances of students.

☐ Educational programmes address differing skill levels of users, and strategies are implemented to provide online help and support.

If you checked about half of the boxes, you are well on the way to developing a quality online course.

Figure 12.1 *Ten-second quiz*

Components of the framework

The framework comprises principles, indicators and checklists with evidence guides, as shown in Figure 12.2. There are 10 essential principles for implementing or assessing best practice for online learning. For each principle there is a set of indicators that identify when best practice has been achieved. Strategies to achieve best practice can then be developed by course teams using checklists and evidence guides.

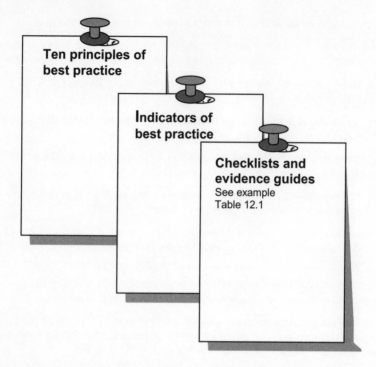

The framework is nested and identifies 10 essential principles to consider when implementing good practice. Each principle lists four to five indicators, which identify when good practice has been achieved. Strategies to achieve good practice are developed by each team. Checklists can be developed by course teams as evidence that they have achieved good practice.

Figure 12.2 *Structure of the framework*

Principles

The 10 principles related to the development of 'best practice' for the provision of quality new learning technologies are:

1. informed planning and management of resources;
2. sustained committed leadership;
3. improving access for all clients, incorporates equity and promotes cultural diversity;
4. understanding the requirements of the learner and reflects stakeholder requirements;
5. the design, development and implementation of programmes for effective and active learning;
6. creating confident and committed staff with new competencies;
7. managing and maintaining the technical infrastructure;

8. evaluating for continuous improvement;
9. providing effective and efficient administrative systems and services;
10. supporting the needs of learners.

These principles, while being broad enough to be applicable to any organization, are sufficiently explicit to enable education and training organizations to develop quality processes for the delivery of online learning and new learning technology programmes.

Indicators of best practice

Each principle is linked with statements that indicate recognized and acknowledged best practice. The best practice indicators have been derived from research, case studies and interviews with successful practitioners in the field. The indicators define areas of best practice, thereby providing a basis for comparison. While these best practice indicators do not specify clearly defined strategies for the achievement of best practice, they do provide managers with best practice targets against which they can identify their own strategies as they journey towards best practice.

Checklists and evidence guides

Checklists and evidence guides can then be developed by course teams as evidence that they have achieved good practice. See the sample checklist and evidence guide for principle 7 in Table 12.1.

A best practice framework for the delivery of online learning and new learning technology programmes

PRINCIPLE 1. BEST PRACTICE FOR ONLINE LEARNING AND NEW LEARNING TECHNOLOGIES
INVOLVES INFORMED PLANNING AND MANAGEMENT OF RESOURCES

Corporate policies and mission statements adopted by the organization must include reference to new learning technologies as a component of its teaching and learning strategies. The training organization ensures that suitably trained people, facilities and infrastructure are adequate and available for the provision of online learning.

Indicators of best practice

- There is evidence that online learning and new learning technology programmes are being integrated across all planning levels within the institution, including financial, human resource and support service planning.
- Corporate policies and mission statements (or equivalent) identify the broad-based educational objective of new learning technology programmes.
- Organizational structures are flexible and responsive and assist the implementation of new learning technologies across all departments and faculties.
- The institution employs communication processes, which lead to a clear sense of purpose and direction in the development and delivery of new learning technologies.
- A management plan for the provision and implementation of new learning technologies has been developed, with a time schedule including identification of critical events.
- Organizational strategies include the development of mainstream new learning technology programmes as well as the piloting of innovations.
- Performance indicators for new learning technology programmes have been identified.
- Efficient and equitable resource allocation models are developed and adopted.
- Collaborative arrangements with other educational institutions and with the corporate sector are in place to ensure effective access to and use of resources.
- A realistic costing of all aspects of development, trial and (as far as is measurable) implementation of new learning technology activities has been made.
- Resources (financial, material, human) are available to support all aspects of development, trial and implementation of new learning technologies.
- The institution has a process in place to ensure that the equipment and materials are sufficient for the provision of new learning technologies for students with special needs/disabilities.
- The organization has defined the constituencies it intends to serve as well as the parameters under which new learning technologies programmes can be offered and resources allocated.
- A human resources development plan has been formed based on an analysis of the tasks required for development, delivery and support of new learning technologies.

Leadership style and behaviour is critical in ensuring that the organization's goals for new learning technologies are achieved. Institutional support for the development and use of new learning technologies is a critical prerequisite to widespread adoption and integration into mainstream programmes.

Indicators of best practice

- Appropriate performance indicators have been developed for the monitoring and evaluation of new learning technologies.
- Leadership behaviour demonstrates commitment to the provision and maintenance of new learning technologies and ongoing improvement processes.
- Policies and practices are developed to support the provision of new learning technologies.
- There is a commitment to provide the level of complex technical and online support required to run efficient, reliable and 'user-friendly' systems.
- Communication systems are open and multi-directional.
- A realistic costing of all aspects of new learning technologies developments, pilots and implementation phases have been made.
- The impact of new learning technologies on existing physical facilities has been assessed.
- Leadership behaviour demonstrates commitment to an organization-wide approach to improving teaching and learning through the use of new learning technologies.
- The impact of new learning technologies and its outcomes on existing managerial, administrative and physical facilities has been assessed.

PRINCIPLE 3. BEST PRACTICE FOR ONLINE LEARNING AND NEW LEARNING TECHNOLOGIES INVOLVES IMPROVING ACCESS FOR ALL CLIENTS, INCORPORATES EQUITY AND PROMOTES CULTURAL DIVERSITY

The provision of new learning technologies improves the access, participation and success rates of under-represented groups. Learning opportunities ensure that learners are not limited in their engagement due to physical location, disability, race, ethnicity, level of technological skills or level of access to physical resources and that their level of language and literacy skills are taken into account. New learning technology programmes are accessible to all students irrespective of income and location. The organization actively seeks diversity.

Indicators of best practice

- Indicators to establish access, participation and success rates for equity groups are collected, reviewed and acted upon.
- Barriers that prevent current and potential students accessing new learning technology products and services are identified and strategies to improve access and participation are implemented.
- The training organization conducts research and monitors the emergence of new equity groups (eg those lacking in information competence).
- The institution fosters an affirmative environment in which diversity is embraced and every person is treated with respect.
- New learning technology performance indicators have been established for each equity group.
- Courseware development for new learning technologies accommodates the background skills and interests of equity groups.
- Delivery media are selected on the basis of 'best fit' between learner effectiveness, accessibility and cost.
- Programmes do not impose prohibitive attendance requirements, or unnecessarily control the pace of learning, or restrict entry and exit options.
- Technologies used enable improved access for disadvantaged groups and work-based learners.

PRINCIPLE 4. BEST PRACTICE FOR ONLINE LEARNING AND NEW LEARNING TECHNOLOGIES INVOLVES UNDERSTANDING THE REQUIREMENTS OF THE LEARNER AND REFLECTS STAKEHOLDER REQUIREMENTS

The main focus of developments in new learning technologies is the needs of learners, clients and stakeholders. The organization has a student-centred approach to new learning technologies that is soundly based in an understanding of learners' characteristics and needs. Stakeholder requirements are reflected in the provision of new learning technologies.

Indicators of best practice

- Planning stages of new learning technology provision take into account the intended learners' objectives, cognitive level, learning styles, access requirements, and the demands of the curriculum.
- New learning technology policies and practices make clear the training organization's obligations to its learners and the learner's obligations to the institution.
- An appropriate range of resources is available to accommodate student learning.
- A process for assessing customer requirements and satisfaction is developed and implemented.
- External and internal clients and stakeholders have been identified (eg government agencies, community groups etc) and their needs and expectations are reflected in new learning technology policy and processes.

PRINCIPLE 5. BEST PRACTICE FOR ONLINE LEARNING AND NEW LEARNING TECHNOLOGIES
INVOLVES THE DESIGN, DEVELOPMENT AND IMPLEMENTATION OF PROGRAMMES FOR
EFFECTIVE AND ACTIVE LEARNING

Course design, development and implementation processes are sufficiently rigorous to ensure that courses meet the requirements of learners, industry and the professions and are effective in achieving learning outcomes.

Indicators of best practice

Course design

- Design of new learning technology programmes is informed by research on learning.
- The responsibility for design, approval, implementation and revision of new learning technology courses is vested in designated bodies with clearly established channels of communication, control and review.
- Course design, development and implementation processes are sufficiently flexible to adapt to the prior experiences of learners, their learning needs and situations.
- Course design is structured and incorporates interactive instruction techniques mediated by human intervention and a supportive learning environment.
- Programme design encourages a realistic progression towards self-direction and recognizes varied starting points in levels of confidence and motivation.
- Courseware is designed to suit the characteristics of learners, provide a clear learning pathway, reinforce important concepts and promote active learning.
- Programme and course objectives clearly specify the subject matter to be covered, the intellectual skills to be acquired and the learning methods used.
- Course assessment is related to intended learning outcomes and to students' learning needs and situations.
- Learning-to-learn strategies are incorporated into all course units.
- Course design processes reflect desired graduate attributes.

Course development

- Policies and procedures for additions and deletions from programmes and courses are carefully planned, implemented and are consistent with the resources of the organization, staff capabilities and the needs of stakeholders.
- Programme design, development and accreditation processes are systematically reviewed and opportunities for improvement identified to ensure the continued relevance of programmes.

Assessment

- Criteria for evaluating student performance are clearly established, stated in course guidelines and easily understood by students and staff.
- Assessment practices are fair, valid and reliable and allow for a variety of circumstances.
- Assessment practices reward competence in the process of learning as well as knowledge of content.

PRINCIPLE 6. BEST PRACTICE FOR ONLINE LEARNING AND NEW LEARNING TECHNOLOGIES INVOLVES CREATING CONFIDENT AND COMMITTED STAFF WITH NEW COMPETENCIES

The organization recruits, manages and provides development opportunities for its staff to ensure that they have the skills to meet client-focused new learning technology programmes.

Indicators of best practice

- Subject expertise and technical and instructional design expertise are available to develop and support quality new learning technology programmes.
- Professional development for the provision of new learning technologies, for all categories of staff, are identified and suitable arrangements made.
- Best practice in new learning technologies is effectively disseminated to staff; for formal or informal training.
- Staff development provision meets organizational and individual development needs for the effective provision of new learning technologies.
- Appropriate cross-functional project teams address specific requirements of new learning technology projects.
- Staff development processes for new learning technology activities are equitable, well resourced and systematically implemented.
- Changes to staff roles and work practices as a result of changes to teaching and learning are recognized, and there is a well-resourced consultative process undertaken to address industrial relations issues.
- Procedures and incentives are in place to encourage staff to make appropriate and innovative use of electronic information resources to improve the academic programme, publish scholarly information, and to encourage equitable student use.

PRINCIPLE 7. *BEST PRACTICE INVOLVES MANAGING AND MAINTAINING THE TECHNICAL INFRASTRUCTURE TO SUPPORT ONLINE LEARNING AND NEW LEARNING TECHNOLOGIES*

Decisions about the choice of technology are driven by consideration of learners' needs, the ability of teachers and other staff to provide support for learners, and the curriculum content of the programme. Resource materials are of sound quality, suitable for the purpose, and well matched with technologies and with staffing requirements.

Indicators of best practice

- Information technology strategies support the implementation of new learning technologies.
- The choice of technology, including the delivery method, reflects learners' needs, the curriculum content of the programme and human resource availability.
- The technology is supported by a technology plan that includes:
  - how the technology is to be used for learning;
  - how people are to be trained to use the technology;
  - how the technology is to be managed and maintained.
- Stand-alone and networked computing systems are used as a tool to support individualized learning and to enhance access to resources.
- The relevance of different technologies to different learning approaches is understood.
- A decision has been made about the support mechanisms that should be associated with technology and resource materials, and the way in which these components interrelate.
- There is an institution-wide co-ordination of the process for evaluating and acquiring emerging technologies.
- Information technology standards are in place and members of the institution are aware of these so that they can make an informed choice when making technology purchases.
- Software, hardware and network resources are appropriate in quantity and quality to meet academic programme needs.
- Decisions have been made about the extent to which equipment will be provided to learners (eg on loan or by access in a library).
- Funding, staff time and skills are available to operate the technology and provide technical support for teachers and learners.
- Decisions have been made whether to buy in or adapt existing learning materials or to develop new materials.
- Copyright and intellectual property implications of buying, licensing or developing materials have been explored, and processes are in place conforming with policy.

PRINCIPLE 8. BEST PRACTICE FOR ONLINE LEARNING AND NEW LEARNING TECHNOLOGIES
INVOLVES EVALUATING FOR CONTINUOUS IMPROVEMENT

The organization evaluates and continuously improves its provision of new learning technologies. New learning technology initiatives are continuously informed by the evaluation of learning outcomes, equity considerations, cost-effectiveness and stakeholder satisfaction.

Indicators of best practice

- The organization continuously monitors and measures the effectiveness and efficiency of new learning technology programmes as part of its continuous improvement process.
- Courses are systematically reviewed to assess their effectiveness.
- Design assumptions about student use of courseware are tested before a prototype is developed.
- A prototype of courseware is tested before an innovation is introduced.
- Qualitative and quantitative data regarding student outcomes are used to measure the effectiveness and efficiency of key new learning technology processes.
- Performance indicators have been identified, eg increased participation, faster student throughput, higher student retention, higher enrolments/re-enrolments, improved graduate attributes, improved access for workers and disadvantaged groups.
- The organization regularly benchmarks its new learning technology processes and outcomes against other organizations.
- New learning technology outcomes are regularly benchmarked against learning outcomes in mainstream courses.

PRINCIPLE 9. BEST PRACTICE FOR ONLINE LEARNING AND NEW LEARNING TECHNOLOGIES
INVOLVES THE PROVISION OF EFFECTIVE AND EFFICIENT ADMINISTRATIVE SERVICES

The organization provides administrative services that support and complement the provision of new learning technologies.

Indicators of best practice

- The impact of new learning technologies and their outcomes on existing managerial, administrative and other procedures is taken into account.
- Management information systems are flexible and take into account all aspects of new learning technology activities, including student enrolment, production scheduling, delivery processes, planning and costing mechanisms and meet the demands of stakeholders in terms of time frames, reliability and accessibility.
- Administrative processes facilitate learner progress while allowing maximum flexibility in programme choice.
- Administrative information resources are provided electronically so as to increase the effectiveness and efficiency of the institution.
- There is ready electronic access to information resources such as bulletin boards, etc with sufficient capacity to supply high-volume data when appropriate.
- The organization provides for formal investigations and specific action to deal with student complaints.

The needs for student learning, technical and personal support for new learning technology programmes are identified, provided for and regularly reviewed. Decisions relating to the comprehensiveness of services depend on the purposes of the institution and the diversity of its student body.

Indicators of best practice

- Constraints and opportunities for learner support have been analysed and support structures, including interaction with teachers, trainers or facilitators are in place.
- A decision has been made about the extent to which equipment will be provided to learners (eg on loan or by access in a library), and the extent to which equipment must be provided for staff use.
- The training organization systematically studies the characteristics of its student cohort and identifies the support needs of the student population.
- The institution has an organized system for admission, assessment, orientation, support and student follow-up compatible with the circumstances of students.
- Student publications describe relevant new learning technology policies and procedures.
- Institute staff working in new learning technology programmes co-ordinate their efforts and work in collaboration with library and other student learning support staff.
- The total costs of new learning technology programmes are made explicit to students.
- Support services are provided to enable all students to participate effectively in courses and to enhance their success in achieving their educational outcomes.
- Precise, accurate and current information is provided in information to students concerning (a) educational purposes; (b) degrees, curricular offerings; (c) student fees and other financial obligations, student financial aid and fee refund policies; (d) requirements for admission and for achievement of degrees; and (e) assessment processes.
- Policies on student rights and responsibilities, including the rights of due process and redress of grievances and rules defining inappropriate student conduct, are clearly stated, well publicized and readily available and they are implemented in a fair and consistent manner.
- The institution makes provision for the security of student records of admission and progress. Student records, including transcripts, are private, accurate, complete and permanent. They are protected by fireproof and otherwise safe storage and backed by duplicate files. Data and records maintained in computing systems have adequate security and provision for recovery from disasters.
- Educational programmes address differing skill levels of users, and strategies provide online help and support facilities.
- The organization's computing, telecommunications centres, library, technological infrastructure and computing laboratories are appropriate for the academic programmes and the nature of the institution.

Implementing the framework – a user guide for managers

The framework is intended to foster the development and implementation of quality arrangements tailored to the needs and circumstances of individual education and training organizations.

While it is unlikely that any single prescriptive best practice framework can be applied to all situations, the framework provides a broad platform to underpin the quality arrangements adopted by each organization.

The framework offers a systematic means of reviewing, measuring and improving the delivery of online learning. By using the framework either in team discussions or through a more rigorous self-assessment approach, managers can begin to identify and improve the processes that are critical to implementing and developing quality new learning technology programmes and online operations.

Advantages of using the framework

The framework has the potential to:

- identify and prioritize improvement targets to ensure resources are allocated effectively (for example, see Figure 12.3);
- provide a structured approach for the assessment of an organization's progress towards its goals;
- integrate improvement activities into normal operations;
- encourage staff to share successful approaches and to embrace continual improvement practices;
- generate opportunities to recognize progress and reward the achievement of results;
- provide an indication how far and how successfully planned activities have been adopted throughout the organization;
- provide hard data and evidence with which to reach conclusions rather than reliance on individual perception or anecdotal data;
- enhance team spirit and enthusiasm through staff involvement;
- provide a common basis for reporting performance;
- provide a tool to benchmark performance with other organizations.

Best practice statements – finding the answers

We do not believe that anyone outside the organization can come up with the most appropriate way to implement best practice. We expect that organizations will make informed choices about ways to proceed that are most suited to themselves and their learners at a particular time.

Managers may find that there are no easy strategies to best practice solutions in their organization. For example, it can be difficult to find really good solutions to some of the aspects of industrial relations that arise from implementing online learning throughout the organization. In this case, we suggest that you use the statements as the basis of discussion in your organization and to help you think through your approach.

There are many helpful resources in the system, which can lead you to the solution of any particular problem; and many of these are on the World Wide Web. We have listed some of these in the book.

The framework has been structured for a range of uses. Primarily it is a tool for managers in organizations that are developing or implementing the delivery of online learning and new learning technologies.

1. Using the framework as a planning tool

Managers or practitioners who are considering using new learning technologies to deliver or support learning can use the framework as a planning tool. Individuals or teams can use the framework to guide them in making good planning decisions. For example, prior to implementing a new learning technology programme, managers should develop comprehensive implementation plans. The indicators will help in the development of these plans and consideration of those areas critical to its success. The framework may also indicate priority areas for the allocation of resources and quality initiatives.

2. Using the framework as a self-assessment tool for continuous improvement

Using the framework as an evaluation or self-assessment tool was initially promoted through the various international models of best practice. Organizations using such models, are able to measure systematically their progress and determine whether their product, services and management processes meet the quality criteria of the model. The results of this self-assessment process are then used to identify and prioritize improvement opportunities. This framework can be used in a similar way to evaluate completed projects against the best practice principles and indicators.

Using checklists to report to external organizations

Table 12.1 is an example of a self-assessment checklist relating to principle 7. This checklist could be adapted to your own organization, and can be used by an organization for reporting performance to external agencies or for benchmarking activities.

3. Using the framework as a basis for professional development activities

The framework can also be used as a foundation for staff development programmes. A staff development programme could be designed to develop an understanding

Table 12.1 *Sample self-assessment checklist for principle 7*

Managers should decide that the focus of their improvement would be those that rate below 3.

Principle 7 Managing and maintaining the technical infrastructure

Decisions about the choice of technology are driven by consideration of learners' needs, the ability of teachers and other staff to provide support for learners and the curriculum content of the programme. Resource materials are of sound quality suitable for the purpose and well matched with technologies and with staffing requirements.

Indicators that demonstrate best practice Rating 1–5 (key to rating below)	The following documentation and processes can provide examples of evidence that demonstrate that best practice has been implemented (these will need to be contextualized).
• Information technology strategies support the implementation of electronically mediated learning.	☐ Consultative forums
• The choice of technology, including the delivery method, reflects learners' needs, the curriculum content of the programme and human resource availability.	☐ Minutes from meetings ☐ Professional development records ☐ Documented and communicated strategic planning process, which enables the organization to reach its goal
• The technology is supported by a technology plan.	☐ Technology plans linked to strategic outcomes of the organization
– How the technology is to be used for learning.	☐ Systematic and collaborative approaches that address the needs and expectations of the university's customers, staff and other key clients
– How the people are to be trained to use the technology.	☐ Survey information
– How the technology is to be managed and maintained.	☐ Brochures, advertising and other marketing information
• Stand-alone and networked computing systems are used as a tool to support individualized learning and to enhance access to resources.	☐ Action taken to improve products and services based on feedback from students and other stakeholders
• The relevance of different technologies to different learning approaches is understood.	☐ Key performance indicators have been developed to measure the effectiveness of the products, services, facilities and processes
• A decision has been made about the support mechanisms that should be associated with technology and resource materials, and the way in which these components interrelate.	☐ Systematic continuous improvement strategies have been implemented ☐ Documented quality policies and processes are followed
• Copyright and intellectual property implications of buying, licensing or developing materials have been explored, and processes are in place conforming to university policy.	☐ Position descriptions and other statements, which identify roles and responsibilities

- Appropriate performance indicators have been developed for the monitoring and evaluation of new learning technologies.
- There is an institution-wide coordination of the process for evaluating and acquiring emerging technologies.
- Information technology standards are in place managers are aware of these so that they can make an informed choice when making technology purchases.
- Software, hardware and network resources are appropriate in quantity and quality to meet academic programme needs.
- Decisions have been made about the extent to which equipment will be provided to learners (eg on loan or by access in a library).
- Decisions have been made whether any technology is required for the programme, and the preferred technology or mix of technologies to satisfy requirements has been identified and prioritized.
- Funding, staff time and skills are available to operate the technology and provide technical support for teachers and learners.
- Decisions have been made whether to buy in or adapt existing learning materials or to develop new materials.

☐ Reports and performance plans
☐ Business plans and resource allocations
☐ Computer data and other data from management information systems
☐ Departmental project action plans
☐ Newsletters and institute correspondence
☐ Range of services and facilities provided for staff and students
☐ Course evaluations
☐ Institute statistics
☐ Complaint processes
☐ Induction procedures
☐ Number of changed practices
☐ Enterprise agreements
☐ Financial strength statements

Ratings against best practice statements

1=**Not met** There is no evidence that this statement describes the programme.
2=**Partially met** There is some evidence that this statement describes the programme.
3=**Mostly met** There is sufficient evidence that this statement describes the programme, but improvements could be made.
4=**Fully met** There is a great deal of evidence that this statement accurately describes the programme.
5=**Exceeds expectation** There is overwhelming evidence that this statement describes the programme, and evidence exceeds expectations.

of concepts related to the use of new learning technologies and the identification and solution of real-life problems. Managers might choose to set up one or two project teams, which would identify problems or decisions that need to be made, and use the framework both as a source of information and as a guide for discussion of the learning.

Implementing the framework – a practical example

The following practical example shows how the framework can be implemented at a post-secondary institution.

Step 1. Gaining acceptance and integration into policy

In order for the framework to gain acceptance across the organization, it was presented to several key committees for adoption into policy. An implementation committee was formed, which recommended that the framework be shortened, contextualized and piloted.

Step 2. Steps to contextualizing the framework to a specific training organization

In this case, the committee decided to use the framework as a staff development tool. The implementation committee felt that the framework was too long for practical use by course teams. They identified the most important four or five indicators from the framework and contextualized these to the organization's procedures. The committee also eliminated those indicators over which course team leaders did not have direct control.

For example, in principle 7, the following indicator was eliminated as it applied across the whole organization: 'There is an institution-wide co-ordination of the process for evaluating and acquiring emerging technologies.'

The committee also felt uncomfortable with the idea of developing 'best practice', they believed that best practice was really a moving target and preferred to rename the framework as a 'good practice' framework.

Step 3. Prioritizing improvement activities

Course teams using the 'good practice' indicators as a guide identified and prioritized improvement activities for their online course delivery (see the worked example of the improvement matrix in Figure 12.3).

For example, one course team, who had received funding to develop a new online course for 'Accounting 1', failed to convince management of the need for ongoing funding for their online course. They had not gathered enough evidence of the ongoing viability of their online trial.

Priority Improvement Matrix – 10 principles of good practice

Best practice indicator	1	2	3	4	5
1. Planning	✓				
2. Leadership					
3. Equity	✓				
4. Learner		✓	✓		
5. Design					
6. Staff					
7. Technical					
8. Improvement					
9. Administration	✓				
10. Support					

✓ indicates improvement priority

This matrix is included to assist course teams to identify and prioritize improvement opportunities. Improvement teams can identify improvement activities by checking each of the 4—5 indicators in each of the 10 categories.

Improvement Priorities – Business Studies Department

1. Develop a realistic costing of the development costs for the online delivery of Accounting 1
2. Survey both mainstream and online delivery of Accounting 1 students and compare the extent of student satisfaction with their course.

Figure 12.3 *A worked example of the use of the Improvement Matrix in developing a good practice framework for online delivery*

This course team identified one of their improvement activities as being the development and comparison of client satisfaction and enrolment data for both their online and lecture-based courses. Lecturers were convinced that client satisfaction data and improved enrolment figures would indicate that students were much happier with the flexibility offered by the online accounting subject than the lecture-based subject.

Step 4. Developing an action plan for improvement activities

Once improvement activities were identified, an action plan was developed to ensure improvement activities were carried out.

(See worked example in Table 12.2.)

Table 12.2 *Example of a departmental action plan*

Good Practice Indicator	Strategy/Activity	Performance/Indicator	Due Date	Accountability
The objective.	How?	How will we know when we have achieved the objective?		Who?
A realistic costing of all aspects of online delivery has been made including the efficient and equitable allocation of all departmental resources.	1. All costs are identified and allocated to an online account. 2. Costs are analysed and efficiency measures implemented. 3. Partnership activities explored.	The department can establish the exact cost of delivering an online programme to 200 students.	Oct	Head of Department
Qualitative and quantitative performance indicators have been identified.	Client satisfaction surveys developed and implemented for both online and mainstream courses.	Client satisfaction surveys indicate positive trend to satisfaction with online courses.	June–Oct	Course Team

Below we present the good practice framework for online delivery.

PRINCIPLE 1. GOOD PRACTICE FOR ONLINE DELIVERY INVOLVES INFORMED PLANNING AND MANAGEMENT OF RESOURCES

Policies and mission statements adopted by online projects must include reference to teaching and learning strategies. Online delivery ensures that trained people, infrastructure, and facilities are available and adequate for each project.

Indicators of good practice

1. Planning for online delivery is integrated with all planning activities within the faculty/department, including financial, human resource and support service planning.
2. An improvement plan identifying responsibilities, performance indicators and critical processes has been developed and is monitored to evaluate online programmes.
3. A realistic costing of all aspects of online delivery has been made including the efficient and equitable allocation of all departmental resources.
4. Online policies and processes have been incorporated into the organization's quality system.
5. Projects are regularly reviewed and opportunities identified are acted upon.

PRINCIPLE 2. GOOD PRACTICE FOR ONLINE DELIVERY INVOLVES SUSTAINED COMMITTED LEADERSHIP

Leadership style and behaviour is critical in ensuring that the organization's goals for online delivery are achieved. Institutional support for the development and use of online activities is a critical prerequisite for widespread adoption and integration into mainstream programmes.

Indicators of good practice

1. Staff in leadership roles demonstrate commitment to the provision and maintenance of online activities and ongoing improvement processes.
2. Strategies have been implemented to provide a level of complex technical and online support required to run efficient, reliable and 'user-friendly' systems.
3. Collaborative arrangements with other faculties and departments and/or with other educational institutions and/or with industry have been explored to ensure effective access to and use of resources.
4. The impact of online projects and their outcomes on existing managerial, administrative and physical facilities has been assessed.

PRINCIPLE 3. GOOD PRACTICE FOR ONLINE DELIVERY INVOLVES IMPROVING ACCESS FOR ALL
CLIENTS, INCORPORATES EQUITY AND PROMOTES CULTURAL DIVERSITY

The provision of online projects improves the access, participation and success rates of under-represented groups. Learning opportunities ensure that learners are not limited in their engagement due to physical location, disability, race, ethnicity, level of technological skills or level of access to physical resources and that their level of language and literacy skills are taken into account. Appropriate access to the outcomes of online delivery is available to all students irrespective of income and location. Online delivery actively encourages the diversity of student groups.

Indicators of good practice

1. Barriers that prevent current and potential students accessing online delivery products and services are identified and strategies to improve access and participation are implemented.
2. Existing data from the statistics office is used to identify and develop specific strategies for targeted equity groups.
3. Courseware development for online delivery accommodates the background skills and interests of equity groups.
4. Delivery media are selected on the basis of 'best fit' between learner effectiveness, accessibility and cost.
5. Programmes avoid prohibitive attendance requirements, unnecessary control of the pace of learning or restriction of entry and exit options.

PRINCIPLE 4. GOOD PRACTICE FOR ONLINE DELIVERY INVOLVES UNDERSTANDING THE
REQUIREMENTS OF THE LEARNER AND REFLECTS STAKEHOLDER REQUIREMENTS

The main focus of online developments is the needs of learners, clients and stakeholders. Online delivery has a student-centred approach that is soundly based on an understanding of learners' characteristics and needs. Stakeholder requirements are reflected in the provision of online projects.

Indicators of good practice

1. External and internal clients and stakeholders have been identified (eg government agencies, community groups, etc) and their needs and expectations are reflected in online delivery processes.
2. Online delivery policies and practices make clear the organization's obligations to its learners and the learner's obligations to the institution.
3. An appropriate range of resources is available to accommodate student learning.
4. A process for assessing customer requirements and satisfaction is developed and implemented.

PRINCIPLE 5. GOOD PRACTICE IN ONLINE DELIVERY INVOLVES THE DESIGN, DEVELOPMENT
AND IMPLEMENTATION OF PROGRAMMES FOR EFFECTIVE AND ACTIVE LEARNING

Course design, development and implementation processes are sufficiently rigorous to ensure that courses meet the requirements of learners, industry and the professions and are effective in achieving learning outcomes.

Indicators of good practice

Course design, development and assessment

1. Course design incorporates interactive instruction techniques mediated by human intervention and a supportive learning environment.
2. Programme and course objectives clearly specify the subject matter to be covered, the intellectual skills to be acquired and the learning methods used.
3. Course design processes reflect desired graduate attributes, promote active learning and recognize varied starting points in levels of confidence, learning styles and motivation.
4. Criteria for evaluating student performance are clearly established, stated in course guidelines and easily understood by students and staff.
5. Online project outcomes are regularly benchmarked against learning outcomes in mainstream courses to ensure consistency.

PRINCIPLE 6. GOOD PRACTICE IN ONLINE DELIVERY INVOLVES CREATING CONFIDENT AND
COMMITTED STAFF WITH NEW COMPETENCIES

Recruitment and management processes provide development opportunities for all staff to ensure that they have the skills to meet client-focused and equitable outcomes.

Indicators of good practice

1. Formal or informal professional development for online delivery activities (including subject, technical and instructional design expertise) are identified and systematically implemented.
2. Changes to staff roles and work practices as a result of changes to teaching and learning are recognized, processes are in place to inform the human resources department and to address potential industrial relations issues.
3. Good practice of online delivery is both rewarded and effectively disseminated to all staff across the organization.
4. Procedures and incentives are in place to encourage staff to make appropriate and innovative use of electronic information resources to improve the academic programme, publish scholarly information, and to encourage equitable student use.

5. Where relevant, staff work plans incorporate staff's professional development needs for the development, delivery and support of online course delivery.

PRINCIPLE 7. GOOD PRACTICE IN ONLINE DELIVERY INVOLVES MANAGING AND MAINTAINING THE TECHNICAL INFRASTRUCTURE

Decisions about the choice of technology are driven by consideration of learners' needs, the ability of teachers and other staff to provide support for learners, and the curriculum content of the programme. Resource materials are of sound quality, suitable for the purpose, and well matched with technologies and with staffing requirements.

Indicators of good practice

1. The choice of technology, including the delivery method, reflects learners' needs, the curriculum content of the programme and human resource availability.
2. The technology is supported by a faculty technology plan that includes:
   - how the technology is to be used for learning;
   - how people are to be trained to use the technology;
   - how the technology is to be managed and maintained.
3. Information technology standards are in place and members of online projects are aware of these so that they can make an informed choice when making technology purchases.
4. Decisions have been made as to whether any technology is required for the programme, and the preferred technology or mix of technologies to satisfy requirements has been identified and prioritized.
5. Decisions have been made as to whether to buy in or adapt existing learning materials or to develop new materials.

Principle 8. Good practice for online delivery involves evaluating for continuous improvement

---

Online delivery evaluates and continuously improves its provision of flexible delivery. Online initiatives are continuously informed by the evaluation of learning outcomes, equity considerations, cost–effectiveness and stakeholder satisfaction.

Indicators of good practice

1. Qualitative and quantitative performance indicators relating to learning outcomes have been identified.
2. Improved access for workers and disadvantaged groups.
3. Online delivery processes and outcomes are regularly benchmarked against other departments or institutions.
4. Online delivery provides for formal investigations and specific action to deal with student complaints (see student complaint policy).

PRINCIPLE *9. GOOD PRACTICE FOR ONLINE DELIVERY INVOLVES THE PROVISION OF EFFECTIVE AND EFFICIENT ADMINISTRATIVE SYSTEMS AND SERVICES*

The institution provides administrative systems and services that support and complement the provision of online delivery.

Indicators of good practice

1. Management information systems are flexible and take into account all aspects of online delivery including student enrolment, production scheduling, delivery processes, planning and costing mechanisms and meet the demands of online delivery in terms of time frames, reliability and accessibility.
2. Administrative processes facilitate learner progress while allowing maximum flexibility in programme choice.
3. There is ready electronic access to information resources such as bulletin boards, etc with sufficient capacity to supply high-volume data when appropriate.
4. Copyright and intellectual property implications of buying, licensing or developing materials have been explored and processes are in place conforming with organization policy.

PRINCIPLE *10. GOOD PRACTICE IN ONLINE DELIVERY INVOLVES SUPPORTING THE NEEDS OF LEARNERS*

The needs for student learning, technical and personal support for online delivery are identified, provided for and regularly reviewed. Decisions on the comprehensiveness of services depend on the purposes of online delivery and the diversity of its student body.

Indicators of good practice

1. Online delivery systematically studies the characteristics of its student cohort and identifies the learning and support needs of the student population.
2. Online delivery has an organized system for admission, assessment, orientation, support and student follow-up compatible with the circumstances of students.
3. Support services are provided to enable all students to participate effectively and to enhance their success in achieving their educational outcomes.
4. Educational programmes address differing skill levels of users, and strategies are implemented to provide online help and support.
5. A decision has been made about the extent to which equipment will be provided to learners (eg on loan or by access in a library), and the extent to which equipment must be provided for staff use.
6. Precise, accurate and current information is readily available and well publicized to students concerning:
   - educational outcomes;
   - degrees, curricular offerings;
   - the total costs of online delivery modules;

- other financial obligations;
- student financial aid;
- fee refund policies;
- requirements for admission;
- and for achievement of degrees;
- assessment processes;
- rules defining inappropriate student conduct and the redress of grievances.

The example will help managers develop their own checklists when developing an evidence-based self-assessment process. The evidence listed is provided as an example only. Each manager will need to adapt the checklists to their own organization.

Part 4

The future

Chapter 13

Anticipating tomorrow's innovations

In this concluding chapter, we shift our attention from the present to the future. We try to anticipate the directions of change. We consider, first, the changes that we are likely to see in the field of education and training. We then consider the development that we are likely to see in the area of technology. We conclude by underscoring the importance of maintaining a focus on learning and all that implies.

Trends in education and training

There can be no doubt that the shift to digital delivery of courses represents one of the most profound changes we have seen in education and training in recent times. It is also apparent that the possibilities offered by online delivery have captured the interest of teachers and trainers. As the technologies employed in online delivery of courses become simpler to use and more powerful, it is likely that the interest amongst teachers and trainers in using these technologies will grow. However, it is one thing to say that online delivery can be expected to become more popular and quite another to say that traditional modes of delivery will become obsolete.

As the country that is still responsible for most of the advances in digital technology, the United States is also the country that sees the greatest potential in the development of information technology for education. However, most of this increase is accounted for by an increasing emphasis on lifelong learning. Most will be tied to the workplace requirements. The learners who are expected to be the main beneficiaries of the shift to digital delivery are therefore people who are working and mature part-time learners. These already represent the majority of the students in post-secondary education.

We need to be particularly cautious in predicting the impact that the shift to digital delivery will have at the technical and vocational level. The greatest threats to traditional technical colleges and like institutions are in the fields of workplace training and continuing professional development. Around the world, the vocational education and training sector has been moving towards a competency-based model. Initially, attention was focused on the specification of required competencies. However, more recently, attention has shifted towards the methods used to assess the attainment of competencies. This shift in attention has in turn resulted in a shift in focus from teaching to assessment.

Concurrent with the introduction of competency-based training, the training market has been opening up to a wider range of private providers than in the past. The effect of this could be to strip courseware development out of the institutional providers and to concentrate resources on assessment.

This overlooks a factor that is often not taken into account by educational innovators but which is well understood by educational policy-makers – that programmes in the vocational training sector are frequently a substitute for having people on unemployment benefits. By convincing or obliging those who are unemployed to take up training, governments can lower unemployment statistics, thereby bolstering their reputations for economic management. For people who undertake training as an alternative to unemployment, the social interaction that is available in on-campus settings is likely to make this a more attractive option than studying in isolation. Distance education is favoured by those who are already employed and who therefore require a mode of study that fits with their work as well as their family commitments.

It has become a cliché to say that we live in an age of rapid change. Nevertheless, both the environment of education and the means of educating are indeed changing rapidly and significantly. Rapid change generates the need for retraining and lifelong learning. This in turn leads to a changing clientele for post-compulsory education – a clientele who demand more flexible forms of delivery responsive to their economic and social circumstances. It leads to a 'just-in-time' approach to educational delivery: the delivery of small segments or modules of learning mixed and matched when and where the need arises.

In the case of higher education for full-time students, changes to educational delivery may continue to be on the margins, particularly in relation to programmes populated by secondary school leavers. The use of instructional technology will continue to be complementary and supplementary to traditional forms of delivery. However, the new clientele will demand a flexibility in delivery for which the knowledge media has the potential to provide better solutions. One of the challenges for educational leadership in the on-campus higher education sector in this context is being clear about how far the institution wishes to pursue these changes and the market that the institution wishes to address. There is a risk, as a result of the incremental employment of digital technologies in teaching, of slipping into provision of distance education with all that implies for administration of distance programmes, markets and competition.

The largest distance education providers have refined their production processes to the point of achieving maximum efficiency with the media they are using. They are able to do that by employing delivery methods that are appropriate for the size of market they are serving. As we have pointed out, the shift to online delivery is not likely to enable providers to become more efficient. What this shift will enable providers to do is to gain access to more dispersed and more distant markets.

While interactive multimedia offers the possibility of improving the quality of education and training it does so at greatly increased cost. To recoup the additional costs, the use of the interactive multimedia products must be spread over larger numbers of users. The way in which distance education providers will be most likely to exploit the potential of interactive multimedia in the changing marketplace will not be in the creation of whole courses based on interactive multimedia but in the development of small segments of courses. In tackling the task of creating such materials they will need to put greater effort into design and development than they may have in the past in order to ensure that the much greater investment generates the expected return. They will need to invest in gaining a better understanding of the teaching–learning processes that are involved in online delivery.

It would not be reasonable to expect that the principles that have been shown to apply to print-based distance education and to face-to-face teaching will all be equally applicable to teaching via the knowledge media. Tapping the full potential of these media is likely to involve the application of principles of which we are not yet aware. If a full understanding of the potential of these media can only be gained through research or a process of trial and error then we should not expect that this understanding will be arrived at overnight.

The advance of digital technology

Throughout this book, we have expressed the view that digital technologies should be seen as playing roles in the service of education and training. Education and training should not be seen as providing a stage on which the capabilities of digital technologies can be displayed. We nevertheless consider that the dramatic changes in the ways education and training are delivered can best be explained by the new possibilities that recent developments in digital technologies have brought.

It is a rash person indeed who is prepared to forecast what is going to happen in the field of information and communications technology more than three years ahead. Nevertheless, if you are about to embark on re-equipping your institution or training organization as part of the first stage of making the transition to the knowledge media, then it would be comforting to have some foreknowledge of the areas where the most far-reaching changes are likely to occur. While we may not be able to anticipate individual developments we can, with a considerable degree of confidence, anticipate a number of general trends. To do this we need to identify the main factors that are responsible for change. Some of the changes are software-oriented and some hardware-oriented. Learning environment software issues are taken up later. On the hardware side, the factors that are contributing to the continuing increase in the power of microcomputers include:

- the falling cost and therefore increasing capacity of computer memory;
- the falling cost and increasing capacity of disk storage media;'
- the increasing speed of microprocessors;
- developments in compression technology;
- the trend towards digitization of all forms of information.

Let us first examine how each of these factors has so far contributed to the way digital technology has advanced.

Increasing memory capacity

A very widely accepted rule of thumb in the computer industry says that the number of devices that can be packed on to a microchip doubles approximately every 18 months. This is known as Moore's Law after its discoverer, Gordon Moore, co-founder of the Intel Corporation. In 1965, Moore observed that the number of transistors per square inch on integrated circuits had doubled every year since integrated circuits had been invented and he predicted that this would continue for the foreseeable future (Moore, 1965). The pace of development slowed sometime later and Moore revised the doubling time to 18 months 10 years later, which it has remained ever since. Moore's Law has become so much part of the folklore of the IT industry that players in the industry make their forward projections based on the anticipation that Moore's Law will continue to apply. Consequently, the continued upholding of Moore's Law has become something of a self-fulfilling prophecy. It is therefore likely that Moore's Law will continue to apply until the limits of semiconductor technology are reached, expected to be towards the end of the 2001–2010 decade.

As the cost of memory chips varies inversely with the packing density of transistors on the chips, the cost of computer memory also halves every 18 months. While the downward trend in the cost of memory may not have tracked a straight-line path year by year, over time the relationship has held. We can confirm this by comparing the present cost of memory with the cost some years ago.

The cost of computer memory has been falling ever since computers were first invented. In 1975, in Australia, RAM chips cost approximately $1 per byte. By 2000, they cost approximately $1 per megabyte. The continuous falling cost of memory has allowed the memory capacity of personal computers to be steadily increased over time. This in turn has allowed the size and therefore the sophistication of computer programs also to be increased.

Increasing disk storage capacity

The cost of disk storage is about one-hundredth the cost of memory storage. The cost of disk storage has been falling at approximately the same rate as the cost of memory. In 1985, hard drive storage cost approximately $500 per megabyte. By 2000, the cost of a megabyte of hard drive storage had fallen to less than a cent.

The development of the CD ROM was the event that opened up the world of interactive multimedia. When the CD ROM drive first appeared, most desktop computers were sold with drives of 100 Mb capacity – one-sixth of the capacity of a CD ROM. Now the standard drive is 10 or 20 Gb – up to 30 times the capacity of a CD ROM. The additional capacity of the CD ROM was needed in order to add video and audio segments to computer-mediated instruction. However, no sooner had the CD ROM been released than the capacity limits of this medium were reached.

The limits of hard drive and memory capacity are set by manufacturing tolerances, which are a function of the precision of manufacturing processes. That is the reason manufacturers have been able to increase the capacity of hard drives and memory so rapidly. All that has been needed has been an improvement in chip fabrication technologies. However, replacement of the CD ROM required the establishment of a new set of standards and achieving agreement on standards takes much longer than reducing the manufacturing tolerances on a production line.

Advances in removable storage media technology have also occurred at regular intervals. The original eight-inch floppy diskettes gave way to five-and-half-inch floppy diskettes, which in turn gave way to three-and-a-half-inch micro diskettes. Now the ZIP disk has carved out a niche as an alternative portable storage medium for those who are dealing with large amounts of data. Here again, the need for standards has been the factor that has most governed the pace of change.

Increasing processor speed

The increasing sophistication of software has placed ever-increasing demands on the microprocessors that provide the processing capabilities of personal computers. This has in turn resulted in demands for microprocessors offering higher and higher processing speeds. Replaying digital video is particularly demanding because the generation of images and sound normally involves decompression of the video. The higher the frame rate (the number of times the image is 'redrawn' each second) the greater the processing speed. The increase in the speeds of microprocessors has led to a rapid and very obvious improvement in the quality of video reproduction over recent years.

Improvements in compression technology

The single function that defines the field of interactive multimedia is the capability that computers have now acquired to replay digital video. All the other functions that go to make up interactive multimedia presentations have been possible for many years – graphics, animation, audio, branching presentation, and the capacity to respond to a user's input. However, it is only as a result of recent developments that computers have acquired the ability to reproduce full-screen, full-motion video.

The amount of data that is needed to reproduce full-screen, full-motion video is immense. It was impractical until recently to store this volume of data on disk. Compression of the video data enabled the size of a video file to be to be reduced to as little as a tenth of its original size. A compressed video file for a full-colour, full-motion, full-screen video of more than a minute or two's duration is still quite large. However, increases in the capacity of storage media have enabled these large-size files to be accommodated.

Video compression technology was originally developed to enable video-conferences to be conducted over narrow bandwidth communication links. (When we speak of 'narrow' in this context, the term is being used in a comparative sense. Broadcast video requires 30 megabits per second. Video conferencing can be supported over links of only 56 kilobits per second.) Once video compression became available it was recognized that this technology offered a solution to the problem of storing digitized video as well.

In recent years, video compression has found much wider use in the field of interactive multimedia. The same type of technology is now being used also in transmitting audio and video over the Internet.

However, compressing video involved a prodigious amount of computation. Initially the microprocessors used in desktop computers did not have the processing power to perform this function. This problem was solved originally by equipping computers with plug-in video cards. As the speed of microprocessors increased, it became increasingly practicable for the main processor of a computer to take over the role of video-processor and for decompression to be done in software.

Increasing trend to digitization of all forms of information

The invention of the laser printer enabled digitized type to be reproduced at a cost that was affordable to business and to individuals. Before the invention of the laser printer digitized type could only be reproduced by very expensive digitizing phototypesetters. The development of this technology led to the creation of the entirely new field of desktop publishing.

The growth in desktop publishing created a demand for methods of digital image production, which led soon after to the development of software for the creation and manipulation of line art and photographic images.

The development of the CD heralded the transition from analogue to digital audio recording – a transition that in a matter of a few years made the vinyl disk obsolete.

The net effect of advances in digital technology

What has been the combined effect of these five key factors and what will their effect be over the next five years? The most important effect has been to increase enormously the amount of information that can be stored and processed. This has allowed the size and therefore the sophistication of applications software to be greatly increased.

The second major effect has been to enable an increasing variety of information to be processed concurrently. As has been pointed out, the growth of desktop publishing relied on development of products that would allow concurrent processing of text, line and half-tone images. Similarly, development of the field of interactive multimedia has relied on development of products that in addition allowed the processing of audio, video and animations.

The third major effect has been to put the tools needed to work with digitally encoded information into the hands of more and more people. As software developers have been increasing the sophistication of their products they have also sought to take advantage of the increasing power of personal computers to make them easier to use (although admittedly not all software developers have been equally successful in achieving this result).

There is every reason to expect that these trends will continue. Future advances in information technology will be driven by the removal of restrictions on storage and the speeding up of even quite complex processing tasks. The area where changes will be occurring most rapidly in the immediate future will be in digital video recording. As the restrictions on processing and storage are removed, computers will quickly eclipse the capabilities of analogue technology and in doing so will replace the corresponding analogue technologies.

What's on the horizon?

DVD technology

In Chapter 1 we described the replacement of VCRs with DVD players in the home entertainment industry and pointed out that DVD technology is starting to replace CD technology. Over the next three years, we can expect to see this transition progress to completion as the manufacturing cost of DVD mechanisms is not significantly higher than the manufacturing cost of CD mechanisms.

Most computers are presently supplied with CD drives. As the R & D cost of the development of DVD drive technology is amortized we can expect DVD drives to replace CD drives throughout each manufacturer's range of personal computers. In higher end machines the DVD drives will have read–write capability. Indeed, Apple's top-of-the-line Macintosh comes equipped with a DVD read–write drive.

In looking ahead to the replacement of CD technology by DVD technology, it makes sense for education and training providers to think in terms of using a computer equipped with a DVD ROM drive as a standard replay unit for digitally delivered courseware. The integration and standardization of media and replay technology will make it relatively simple to present learners with a standard interface.

ADSL (Asymmetric Digital Subscriber Line)

In the first edition of *Delivering Digitally* we commented on the communication log-jam caused by the slow speeds of dial-up connections and commented that this situation was not likely to change quickly. Since we wrote the first edition the situation has changed significantly. A new communications technology called 'asymmetric digital subscriber line' or 'ADSL', for short, has emerged. This provides connections up to 100 times faster than via dial-up modems. ADSL has started to compete with cable for high-speed communications.

The major advantage of ADSL is that it doesn't require fibre optic cable. It can be carried over existing copper cable. This makes it less expensive to install.

ADSL is a packet switching technology that provides a continuous connection to the Internet. In this respect, being connected to the Internet through an ADSL service is similar to being connected to an Ethernet Intranet.

An ADSL service is more secure and more reliable than a cable service and the speed of transmission is not affected by the number of other users who are nearby as is the case for cable.

Connecting to an ADSL service requires an ADSL modem. This costs about the same as a cable modem. The tariffs for ADSL services are comparable to tariffs for cable services. However, the costs of these services are determined more by marketing strategies than the underlying costs of the technologies and are likely to change with time and differ from country to country.

The main factor that affects the speed that can be supported is the length of the line. So, speeds that can be supported in remote locations are much lower than the speeds that can be supported in major cities.

As competing technologies, cable and ADSL are reaching somewhat different markets. Cable is being chosen by homeowners who install cable TV and choose to take a cable data service as well to obtain high-speed Internet access. ADSL is being chosen by business users and users outside cabled municipalities who want or need high-speed Internet access.

As the Internet becomes increasingly a broadcast medium the boundary between the cable TV and Internet markets is likely to blur. This will give ADSL a relative advantage.

Streaming video

Streaming video takes advantage of certain features of data communications and video technologies to enable video to be displayed more or less as soon as it is received. Streaming video overcomes the limits placed on the use of video as a remote presentation medium by the speeds of data communication links.

Streaming video relies on a streaming server to deliver video over the Internet. Video replay software needs to be installed on the user's workstation to display the video stream as it is received.

Streaming video technology has been available since the mid-1990s. However, the quality of the images that could be produced with streaming video was relatively poor. Recent improvements in the technology have allowed the quality of video imaging to be greatly improved. This has opened the door to Internet broadcasting.

Streaming video may be considered by many educators to be a particularly attractive technology because it allows students studying at a distance to view the same lectures that students studying on-campus are receiving. However, specialists in distance education would see this as a retrograde development and a case of misuse of technology. Distance educators have sought to have students involved much more actively in their learning and restoring the lecture to its earlier role of the principle means of instruction would undermine this goal. On the other hand, the presentation of educationally rich video material as a basis for discussion and other learning activities offers opportunities for the enhancement of education and training at a distance. The developments in streaming video may therefore present both a threat and an opportunity for distance education.

Integrated electronic learning environments

We have already drawn attention to the growing popularity of integrated electronic learning environments as delivery platforms for online courses. However, this type of delivery platform is still at an early stage of development. Over the next 2–3 years we can expect to see significant developments in the features offered by these systems:

- The customizability of products will be enhanced to accommodate a wide range of teaching models and to allow readier 'badging' of courseware by education and training providers.
- The interoperability between the integrated electronic learning environments and productivity software such as word-processors, spreadsheets and databases will be improved for both teachers and students.
- Individual products will become more modular, allowing third-party components to be incorporated into the integrated environment.
- Gateways will be created for interfacing the electronic learning environments with institutional student records systems.

With these developments we can expect, as has been the case for personal and office software and for Internet browsers, further sophistication in commercially available learning environments, which will make the inadequacies of home-grown products apparent and drive some of the less popular products out of the market. Associated with this is the development of meta-data tagging and technical standards for learning objects facilitating deployment and exchange of object using learning environment software.

It is possible that the suppliers of integrated electronic learning environments will begin to offer fully hosted services where courseware and student progress information resides on servers belonging to the hosting service rather than on servers belonging to the institution. In that scenario, the servers will increasingly be located outside the country in which the provider is located.

The growth in use of integrated electronic learning environments is over-shadowing the use of authoring systems such as Director, Authorware, Toolbook and Supercard. Education and training providers are understandably favouring the more economical textual forms of presentation for major institution-wide initiatives. In the immediate future, development of interactive multimedia authoring tools is likely to be driven more by the needs of the advertising and entertainment industries than by the needs of education and training. However, such tools will nevertheless continue to play very important roles in courseware development.

Learning objects

Learning objects are small, reusable chunks of courseware. The concept of a learning object owes its origins to object-oriented programming in computer science. The term 'learning object' was coined by the Learning Technology Standards Committee of the Institute of Electrical and Electronic Engineers (IEEE), which was formed to develop and promote instructional technology standards (Learning Technology Standards Committee – IEEE, 2000).

While there are a number of pilot attempts at operationalizing the concept of learning objects there are as yet relatively few examples of attempts to operationalize the concept on a large scale (see Wiley, 2000). The reason for this is the standards and even many of the underpinning principles of operation are still being developed.

Instructional design theories for guiding the development of courseware have also to be developed. Nevertheless, considerable work is presently going on in resolving the practical issues concerned with incorporation of learning objects into courseware. This is being driven mainly through the IMS Project, discussed below. Wiley (2000) describes one of the first attempts to develop instructional design theory for learning objects.

XML (Extensible Mark-up Language)

XML is a mark-up language that has been developed by the World Wide Web Consortium. It is a greatly simplified dialect of SGML or, in other words, comprises a subset of SGML commands. It is intended to make SGML usable for distribution of materials on the Web.

As was explained in Chapter 1, HTML is an instance of SGML. HTML uses a fixed set of commands to format Web pages. While successive version of HTML have increased the number of commands available, the command set has never-theless remained fully defined.

XML differs from HTML insofar as it allows users to create their own sets of commands. This allows versions of XML to be created for particular uses and already versions of XML have been created for formatting mathematical text documents, and showing chemical reactions.

The success of XML depends on the availability of browsers that will understand how to display documents marked up in it. XML is unlikely to replace HTML for many years because of the large number of documents that are already formatted using the HTML standard. However, the use of HTML and XML is likely to become somewhat differentiated, with HTML being used more for machine-generated documents and XML for authored documents.

The promise of expert systems

Two decades ago a great deal of interest was being shown in the development of expert systems that could monitor a learner's progress and present instruction according to the learner's readiness to receive it. These were known as 'intelligent tutoring systems'. They were based in part on artificial intelligence technology.

However, this type of courseware authoring system did not yield the results that had earlier been expected of it. The problem lay largely in the development of suitable user interfaces.

Over time, interest in intelligent tutoring systems waned, although it did not die completely. In recent times, there has been a renewal of interest in this area. It is possible that with the much greater computing power now available in microcomputers we could see some breakthroughs in this area.

Overcoming the inherent limitations of the Web

When Tim Berners-Lee implemented the Web version of hypertext, he left out a number of the features that Ted Nelson had considered essential to effective implementation of the concept. The effects of these omissions are now being felt.

Andrew Pam (1995) has examined the differences between Xanadu and the Web. He identifies the following as the most crucial:

- Each document is served from a single location with the result that the reliability of the Web is degraded.
- Documents are identified by location (URL) rather than by a unique identifier so that there is no assurance that a document will be available at the location to which a hyperlink is pointing.
- Hyperlinks are embedded within documents rather than within the metadata of the document so that it is only feasible for hyperlinks to point one way.
- Support is not provided for multiple versions of the same document to be publishable as such.
- Support for transclusion (the inclusion of another document by reference to it rather than by copying it) is only provided for images.

Pam considers that solutions to these problems are likely to be provided by the development of more advanced Web servers that provide additional features. One such server is Hyperwave, the commercial implementation of the Hyper-G that was originally developed at the University of Graz.

Hyperwave is the Web server that currently offers the most faithful implementation of Nelson's concept of hypertext. It is able to run on machines using the Microsoft NT or Unix operating systems.

Development of standards for interactive multimedia delivery

One of the most enticing prospects that recent advances in interactive multimedia holds out to us is that of being able to customize the delivery of education and training to the needs of the learner. The possibility exists of providing learners with learning opportunities that take into account their learning styles and which are matched with their rate of learning.

Yet, the attainment of this ideal is being thwarted by the proliferation of incompatible learning systems and the proliferation of learning materials that can only be used in specific environments.

How does one ensure that courseware developed for one platform and one authoring package can be supported by an interactive learning environment provided by a different supplier and running on a different platform? Should the choice of learning management system limit the range of courseware upon which one can draw? Clearly, this is not desirable. What are needed if this situation is to be avoided are sets of standards that guarantee the interoperability of systems that adhere to the standards.

The work by the Learning Standards Technology Committee (LSTC) of the Institute of Electrical and Electronic Engineers (IEEE) in the US on development of the concept of learning objects resulted in some of the first attempts to develop standards in this area. It was recognized that to translate the notion of building courseware from a collection of learning objects required a standard method for describing such courseware components.

However, separately from the LSTC IEEE, the consortium of education institutions then known as EDUCOM, but now called Educause, had launched a National Learning Infrastructure Initiative (Twigg, 1994). The work by being undertaken by Educause is subsumed under the Instructional Management Systems (IMS) Project. The goal of the IMS Project is to enable an open learning architecture for learning with digital media. The way the project has set out to achieve this goal is through the promulgation of a technical specification for learning materials and systems and the implementation of a proof of concept (EDUCOM, 1998).

A number of other bodies have also initiated attempts to develop standards for interoperability. These include the US Department of Defense, which has developed the Shareable Object Model under its Advanced Distributed Learning Initiative, and the Aviation Industry CBT Committee, which has developed the Computer-managed Instruction Model. Over time, efforts have been made to bring these initiatives into alignment. However, the IMS Project has taken the leading role in this area.

Development of the IMS specification has been preceded by the development of a set of core assumptions and requirements related to online learning systems and online courseware. The assumptions have been refined through focus groups, conferences and other interactions with prospective end-users as well as through discussions with the technical developer community.

The IMS Project is focused on providing a standard way of delivering and managing information common in learning interchanges. The vision of those responsible for guiding the project is to create a standard for developers of high-quality materials for an interactive learning environment. Learning materials that are easy to use, interoperable and customizable will be able to be developed. A developer of learning materials will be able to create learning materials that can be highly customized to an individual learner's needs. A learner will be able to track a personalized pathway through a learning programme.

Educause argues that development of the IMS standard will advance the field of educational multimedia development by bringing about:

● lower-cost development and deployment of learning materials;
● improved quality of online learning materials and environments;
● greater access to learning opportunities;
● more customized learning experiences.

The promulgation of the IMS specification is not intended to stifle innovation in the development of interactive multimedia systems. It is not expected to lead to a situation in which all multimedia systems offer the same set of features.

While the IMS Project began by addressing the needs of the education and training community in the United States, involvement with the project has spread worldwide through the Educause consortium. There are four main aspects of courseware delivery for which standards are evolving:

● description of course structures;
● listing and describing the files belonging to a course for the purpose of moving and re-installing the files in a different system;
● description of the attributes of learning objects for the purpose of finding and retrieving individual learning objects or learning objects with particular characteristics;
● maintenance of the records for tracking student progress within a course.

There is considerable overlap in what different standards attempt to specify with greatest overlap occurring, as one might expect, in the area of the description of course structure.

Work on the development of interoperability standards is in its early stages and it is likely that over time, the range of areas for which standards are developed will be extended. Once standards do gain widespread acceptance, it is likely that increasing competition in the market will result in their rapid adoption by suppliers of integrated electronic learning environment systems and other delivery systems.

Putting the developments together

The options available to education and training providers will depend upon the nature of technological developments. The immediate developments in technology will be centred on the convergence of computer and communications technologies. Advances will be most evident and most rapid in the area of migration of video into the online and multimedia environment. The adoption of DVD, improvements in compression technologies, improvements in streaming technologies and increases in processing speeds will all make contributions here. Advances in the area of data communication will centre on the uptake of high-speed services in place of dial-up connections. Developments in software will greatly increase the ease with which the capabilities of digital technologies can be exploited, particularly by those who are less technically inclined. Together, these technological developments will offer distance education providers greatly increased flexibility in meeting the education and training demands of tomorrow's world.

In the end, teaching is about facilitating learning

Fifty years ago, distance education (or 'correspondence education' as it was then known) was regarded as very much a second-best mode of delivery: failure rates were high; non-completion rates were even higher; and the reputation of this mode of delivery was poor.

The success of the UK Open University changed educators' perceptions of what was possible in distance education. The reputation of distance education rose to the point where, if it was not always seen as the equal of face-to-face teaching, it was certainly considered a respectable alternative mode of delivery.

Twenty years ago, distance education providers began exploring the potential of technology to support the delivery of programmes. They started simply with e-mail; moved on to computer-managed learning; and recently began entering the field of online learning. Today, distance education, far from being regarded as a second-best mode of delivery, is held up as the way of the future.

Nevertheless, there is a risk that in rushing to embrace the possibilities that the digital technologies offer, advocates of the new learning technologies may lose sight of the primary goal – improving student learning.

The message we have tried to convey throughout this book is that the true potential of the knowledge media lies not so much in lowering the costs of the delivery of programmes and courses but in enhancing the quality of the student's learning experience.

Taking advantage of economies of scale to increase the rate of recovery of the investment in courseware development, forming consortia of providers to lower the costs of development and make electronic delivery more affordable are worthwhile undertakings. However, the primary reason for choosing to use technology ought to be to better facilitate learning.

Communications technology offers the potential to deliver programmes more economically, to deliver programmes to a wider market, to increase interaction, to increase the range of ways in which we teach, and even to make learning more fun. The convergence of technologies offers the possibility of achieving advances that go beyond the wildest dreams of those who first conceived of the concepts of hypertext, annotation systems, computer-assisted instruction and computer-managed learning. However, technology is seductive. Without realizing it we can allow the application of technology to become the end rather then the means of delivering digitally.

In trying to assess the importance of what advances in digital technology have to offer distance education we need to keep to the forefront that at the core of the educational experience there are teachers and there are learners. Without the committed participation of both teachers and learners whatever contributions technology may have to offer will count for nothing. The value of the advances we are seeing in digital technology lies in the extent to which they enable teachers to do more effectively and efficiently those things that enable students to learn.

Glossary

In this glossary, *italics* are used for terms that have their own entry.

ADSL   See *Asymmetric Digital Subscriber Line.*

Anonymous FTP   A form of *FTP* service that allows users to log on to a file server without providing a password to gain access. It is used to make collections of files such as collections of shareware software generally available to *Internet* users.

Applet   Literally 'little applications'; small programs written in Java programming language that are downloaded from a *Web server* and run inside a *Web client*. Applets are generally written to provide functions that cannot readily be provided using *HTML*.

Asymmetric Digital Subscriber Line (ADSL)   A broadband communication standard capable of being implemented over existing copper cable.

Asynchronous   Occurring at different times; in relation to communication, interaction in which the parties each participate at different times.

Asynchronous conferencing   A form of computer conferencing in which participants need not interact at the same time. Contributions to the conference are generally posted to a conferencing system that arranges the contributions by topic or by time of receipt and makes them available to other participants.

Asynchronous Transfer Mode (ATM)   A communication standard for broadband-*ISDN* transmission capable of supporting data rates of up to 600 Mbits/s.

ATM   See *Asynchronous Transfer Mode.*

Australian Quality Awards   A programme designed to support business excellence in Australian organizations to increase international competitiveness using self-assessment as a tool. Many nations around the world have similar programmes, eg the Baldridge Award in the United States.

Bandwidth The transmission capacity of a telecommunications link. In the case of digital communications, bandwidth is measured in terms of bits per second. The greater the bandwidth the greater the volume of information that can be transmitted over the link in a given period.

Benchmarking The concept of benchmarking that has been adopted in this book is: the ongoing systematic process of measuring and comparing the work processes of one organization with those of another. The purpose of benchmarking is to provide a point of reference for evaluating the improvement in a process.

Best practice The adoption of work practices which, when effectively linked together, can be expected to lead to sustainable world-class outcomes in quality customer satisfaction, flexibility, timeliness, innovation and cost-competitiveness.

Browser See *Web client*.

Cable modem A modem that connects to metropolitan cable services. Installing a cable modem may require taking out a subscription to a cable television service. This provides a high-speed connection from homes and businesses. However, the cost of installation and use is high and the service is only available in districts that have been cabled for television.

CAL See *computer-assisted learning*.

CERN The European Laboratory for Particle Physics, a collective of high-energy physics researchers. This was where the idea for the World Wide Web was conceived. It was originally developed as a way of transporting research information throughout the organization.

Chat See *synchronous conferencing*.

CML See *computer-managed learning*.

Collaborative tools See *e-mail, asynchronous conferencing, synchronous conferencing*.

Computer-assisted assessment (CAA) A collective term that refers to various types of applications of computers in assessment from use of computers to administer tests to use of computers to check for plagiarism in students' essays.

Computer-assisted learning (CAL) Learning facilitated via computer. In the past this would have been referred to as 'computer-assisted instruction'.

Computer-managed learning (CML) A form of computer-assisted learning in which the computer is used to manage the pace and sequence in which a learner proceeds through a course. The concept of CML originated from early attempts at obtaining the benefits of computers without incurring high costs. CML systems delivered computer-scored tests and directed a student's learning but the learning materials were delivered via other media, usually print.

Computer-mediated communication (CMC) Any form of communication that relies on computers and networks. The term is most commonly used to refer to *asynchronous* and *synchronous conferencing*, but also includes use of *e-mail* and *listservs*, and *desktop video conferencing*.

Courseware The digital material designed to facilitate learning of behaviours, understandings, attitudes and/or propensities. It usually refers to materials that cover a topic, module or unit.

CQAHE The Committee for Quality Assurance in Higher Education (Australia).

Desktop videoconferencing   Videoconferencing by means of digital cameras attached to desktop computers that has been made possible by the development of real-time video compression technology.

Digital delivery   Delivery of courses via World Wide Web, interactive multimedia and any other medium in which the information is carried in digital form.

Distance education   A mode of study in which students rarely, if ever, participate in face-to-face interaction and both instruction and support are provided via learning packages or synchronous forms of delivery mediated by technology.

DVD ROM   Successor to the CD ROM. It uses the same optical technology but can record at a much higher density owing to use of a higher frequency laser and a dual layer, double-sided platter. Like CD ROMs, DVD ROMs will be available in both read-only and write-once versions.

Economies of scale   Economies that arise from increasing the size of an operation; in the case of distance education, economies that arise from increasing the numbers of students entering an institution or entering a subject.

Effectiveness   When used in relation to courseware, the term 'effectiveness' refers to the ability to effect changes in the learner's understanding, skills, competencies, attitudes and dispositions.

Efficiency   The minimization of resource consumption (or possibly the maximization of return on investment). When used in relation to education, the term 'efficiency' implies having the desired effect but it does not imply maximizing effectiveness. Where efficiency is the goal, a balance must be struck between costs and benefits.

E-mail   Contraction of 'electronic mail'. The facility that enables messages to be sent from person to person electronically via the Internet.

Ethernet   A local area network system originally developed at Xerox Palo Alto Research Center and later made a standard. The original Ethernets operated at 10 Mbps over coaxial cable and linked computers and servers in 'daisy-chain' fashion. Now Ethernets can operate at 100 Mbps and more commonly use twisted pair cable and link computers and servers in a 'star' configuration.

Expert system   Computer-based systems in which the knowledge of a field is captured as a knowledge base. An inference engine allows conclusions to be drawn based on a given set of assumptions.

Extensible Mark-up Language (XML)   The adaptation of *SGML* that is expected to replace *HTML* as the mark-up language for authored text on the Web. Unlike *HTML*, it has the capacity to support the definition of new formats and is therefore much more versatile than *HTML*.

File Transfer Protocol   A widely used protocol for transferring files across networks.

Flexible delivery   The provision of learning experiences in a variety of ways (eg face-to-face, workplace, print, interactive multimedia), which are responsive to learners' needs and/or preferences.

Flexible learning   The offering of learning experiences using media or combinations of media, which provide time, place and pace flexibility for learners.
Formative evaluation   Evaluation undertaken for the purpose of monitoring the progress of a project. It may involve either gathering information on components of a project as they are developed or tracking a project through its pilot stage.
FTP   See *File Transfer Protocol*.

Hyperlink   Connections between *hypertext* documents.
Hypermedia   Hypertext that includes other media.
Hypertext   Text that, when selected, results in the retrieval of other documents.
HyperText Mark-up Language (HTML)   The formatting language used to create documents for the World Wide Web.

Integrated electronic learning environment   A system that provides a comprehensive range of learning support services such as courseware delivery, e-mail, conferencing, computer-scored testing and learning management. Examples of commercially available electronic learning environments include Blackboard, FirstClass, LearningSpace, The Learning Manager, WebCT.
Integrated Services Digital Network (ISDN)   A high-speed public network that is able to carry voice, data and video. In its basic configuration it offers two transmission speeds: 56 Kbps and 1Mbps. However, two or more 56 Kbps channels can be coupled to provide intermediate speeds.
Internet   A collection of networks and computers that has evolved from a couple of computers 30 years ago into a loosely connected global network comprising thousands of smaller regional networks. It allows users to exchange information in a wide variety of forms.
Intranet   A network internal to an organization.
ISDN   See *Integrated Services Digital Network*.

Knowledge media   A collective term referring to the World Wide Web and interactive multimedia.

Learning object   A small reusable chunk of instructional courseware. The development of banks of learning objects has been seen as the way to take advantage of the power of computers in assisting learning without bringing about an escalation in costs.
Listserv   A computer program that maintains mailing lists, automatically receiving and sending messages to members on the list. A person who has subscribed to a listserv can mail to the other members of the list by sending an e-mail message to the listserv. A listserv can also place new members on the list and remove members from a list automatically upon request.

MIME   See *Multipurpose Internet Mail Extensions*.
MOO   See *Multi-user dimension Object-Oriented*.

Mosaic   The first publicly available *Web client*. Mosaic was commercialized as Netscape Navigator.

Moving Pictures Experts Group (MPEG)   The term generally refers to the standards for digital video and audio compression that the group is responsible for developing and promulgating.

MPEG   See *Moving Pictures Experts Group*.

MUD   See *Multi-User Dimension*.

Multipurpose Internet Mail Extensions   A standard for specifying an action that is to take place when a file that has certain characteristics is transferred.

Multi-User Dimension *or* **Multi-User Dungeon (MUD)**   A type of *networked virtual environment* in which the objects are defined by the developer of the environment.

Multi-user dimension Object-Oriented (MOO)   A type of *networked virtual environment* that is able to be extended by the user.

Network   A collection of digital devices such as servers, computers and printers, connected together for the purpose of allowing people to share, store, retrieve and print information.

Networked virtual environment   Virtual environments created on the *Internet*.

NVE   See *Networked virtual environment*.

Open learning   A mode of study that offers admission to programmes irrespective of students' previous educational achievements and which offers a measure of flexibility in relation to the time, place, pace and method of study.

PDF   See *Portable Document Format*.

Performance indicators   Quantitative and qualitative descriptors used for assessing performance, eg percentage of students who complete a course, the number of times course inquiries are recorded, or a description of the condition that applies when a particular task is completed.

POP   See *Post Office Protocol*.

Portable Document Format (PDF)   A standard for formatting documents developed by Adobe Corporation. Documents that have been stored in PDF format require Adobe Acrobat Viewer for viewing and printing.

Post Office Protocol (POP)   A protocol used by mail client programs for receiving mail from mail servers.

Quality assurance   The totality of the arrangements by which an organization discharges its responsibility for the quality of the teaching it offers; satisfying itself that the mechanisms for quality control are effective and promote improvement.

Quality improvement   All of the actions taken throughout the organization to increase the effectiveness and efficiency of activities and processes in order to provide added benefits to both the organization and its clients.

Scalable systems   Systems that are capable of being greatly expanded to support much larger numbers of users.

Self-assessment   An internal review by which an organization assesses its own processes and performance against given criteria such as those described in best-practice documents, for example the Australian Business Excellence Framework.

SGML   See *Standard Generalized Mark-up Language*.

Simple Mail Transfer Protocol (SMTP)   The protocol used by mail servers to exchange mail with other mail servers and by some client mail software to send mail to a mail server.

SMTP   See *Simple Mail Transfer Protocol*.

Standard Generalized Mark-up Language (SGML)   A generic language for formatting documents.

Summative evaluation   Evaluation that is undertaken for the purpose of providing information in relation to the success of a project. A summative evaluation may be undertaken in order to satisfy the requirements of a funding authority, or to provide information that may be useful in later projects.

Synchronous   Occurring at the same time; in relation to communication, interaction involving participation at the same time.

Synchronous conferencing (chat)   A form of computer conferencing in which participants interact at the same time. Contributions to the conference are posted to a conferencing server, which re-transmits them to other participants in the conference. Participants may be located in any part of the world. The most widely used form of chat system is Internet relay chat (IRC).

Threaded discussions   A method of sequencing the contributions to computer conferences by topic. This permits the contributions on a single topic to be reviewed. The alternative method of sequencing contributions is in order of their receipt.

Uniform Resource Locator (URL)   The method of representing hypertext addresses on the World Wide Web. A URL comprises an initial part specifying the method of action, a second part specifying the address of the computer on which a document or service is located and perhaps further parts specifying the names of files, the port to connect to or the text to search for in a database.

Usenet   A global network of news servers.

Web client   The piece of software that runs on a user's machine to provide an interface to the World Wide Web. The most widely used Web clients are Netscape Navigator and Microsoft Internet Explorer.

Web page   The contents of a single *HTML* file.

Web server   The software that delivers *Web pages* (*HTML* files) over the World Wide Web.

Web site   A collection of HTML files (ie W*eb pages*) made available from a *Web server*.

Xanadu Project   The project initiated by Ted Nelson to create a worldwide *hypertext* system. The Xanadu Project was supported by Autodesk Corporation for a period.

XML   See *Extensible Mark-up Language*.

References

Argyris, C and Schön, D (1974) *Theory in Practice*, Jossey-Bass, San Francisco

Ashenden, D (1987) Costs and Cost Structure in External Studies: A discussion of issues and possibilities in Australian higher education, EIP, Australian Government Publishing Service, Canberra

Australian Vice-Chancellors' Committee (1996) Exploiting Information Technology in Higher Education: An issues paper, AV-CC, Canberra <http://www.avcc.edu.au/avcc/pubs/eithe.htm>

Ausubel, D (1963) *The Psychology of Meaningful Verbal Learning*, Grune and Stratton, New York

Bacsich, P, Ash, C, Boniwell, K, Kaplan, L, Mardell, J and Carvon-Atch, A (1999) *The Costs of Networked Learning*, Sheffield Hallam University, Sheffield

Bloniarz, P A and Larsen, K R (1997) A Cost/Performance Model for Assessing WWW Service Investments, Centre for Technology in Government, University at Albany, Albany, New York <http://www.ctg.albany.edu>

Boud, D and Feletti, G (1991) (eds), *The Challenge of Problem Based Learning*, Kogan Page, London

Bush, V (1945) As we may think, *Atlantic Monthly*, **176** (1), 101–08 <http://www.ps.uni-sb.de/~duchier/pub/vbush/>

Committee on Open University (1975) *Open Tertiary Education in Australia: Final report of the Committee on Open University to the Universities Commission*, Australian Government Publishing Service, Canberra

Committee for Quality Assurance in Higher Education (1995) Report on 1994 Quality Review, Vol 1 & 2, Australian Government Publishing Service, Canberra

Cross, J (2001) A Fresh Look at ROI: Learning circuits <http://www.learningcircuits.org/2001/jan2001/>

Cunningham, S, Tapsall, S, Ryan, Y, Stedmar, L, Beyton, K and Flew, T (1998) New Media and Borderless Education: A review of the convergence between global media networks and higher education, DEETYA, Canberra

Department of Industrial Relations and Australian Manufacturing Council (1992) International Best Practice: Report on the overseas study mission, Australian Government Publishing Service, Canberra

Drucker, P F (1993) *Post-capitalist Society*, Butterworth-Heinemann, Oxford

EDUCOM (1998) EDUCOM/NLII Instructional management systems specification document,Version 0.5 <http://educause.edu/program/nlii/nliihome.html>

Evans,T and Nation, D (1989) Dialogue in practice, research and theory in distance education, *Open Learning*, **4** (2), pp 37–42

Flexner, A (1968) *Universities: American, English, German*, originally published in 1930, reprinted by Polity Press, London

Florida Institute on Public Postsecondary Learning (1997) Final Report of the Library Sub Committee <http://dlis.dos.state.fl.us/dlli/report.html>

Garrison, D R (1993) A cognitive constructivist view of distance education: An analysis of teaching-learning assumptions, *Distance Education*, **14** (2), 199–211

Garrison, D R (1995) Constructivism and the role of self-instructional course materials: A reply, *Distance Education*, **16** (1), 136–40

Giddens, A (1991) *Modernity and Self-identity*, Polity Press, Cambridge, p 1

Hesketh, B, Gosper, M, Andrews, J and Sabaz, M (1996) Computer-Mediated Communication in University Teaching, Department of Employment, Education, and Youth Affairs, Canberra

Higher Education Review (1997) Learning for life: Review of higher education financing and policy – A policy discussion paper [West Committee], Australian Government Publishing Service, Canberra

Hiltz, R (1997) Impacts of college-level courses via asynchronous learning networks: Some preliminary results, *Journal of Asynchronous Learning Networks*, **1** (2) <http://www.aln.org/alnweb/journal/jaln_issue1.htm#turoff>

Jones, B J, Valdez, G, Nowakowski, J and Rasmussen, C (1994) Designing learning and technology for educational reform, North Central Regional Educational Laboratory, Oak Brook, IL

Kulik, C-L and Kulik, J A (1986) Effectiveness of computer-based education in colleges, *AEDS Journal*, 81–108

Kulik, C-L and Kulik, J A (1991) Effectiveness of computer-based instruction: An updated analysis. *Computers and Human Behaviour*, **7**, 75–94

Kulik, C-L, Kulik, J A and Cohen, P (1980) Instructional technology and college teaching, *Teaching of Psychology*, **7**, 199–205

Laurillard, D (1993) *Rethinking University Teaching: A framework for the effective use of educational technology*, Routledge, London

Learning Technology Standards Committee – IEEE (2000) *Draft Standard for learning Object Metadata v4.1* <http://ltsc.ieee.org/doc/wg12/LOMv4.1.htm>

May, M (1998) The implications of the Internet for career counselling and the use of career information, *Australian Journal of Career Development*, **7** (1), 24–29

McGill, I and Beaty, L (1992) *Action Learning: A practitioner's guide*, Kogan Page, London

Mitchell, J and Bluer, R (1996) A Planning Model for Innovation. A report for the office of training and further education on New Learning Technologies:

Case studies, Office of Training and Further Education, Melbourne <http://www.otfe.vic.gov.au/about/model/index.htm>

Moore, G E (1965) Cramming more components onto integrated circuits, *Electronics*, **38** (8), 114–17

National Board of Employment, Education and Training (NBEET) (1996) Education and Technology Convergence, Commissioned Report No 43, Australian Government Printing Service, Canberra

National Board of Employment, Education and Training (1997) Quality in Resource Based Learning, Australian Government Printing Service, Canberra

National Committee of Enquiry into Higher Education (1997) *Higher Education in the Learning Society* (The Dearing Report), NCIHE, Hayes <http://www.leeds.ac.uk/educol/ncihe>

National Information Infrastructure Taskforce (1994) What it Takes to Make it Happen <http://www.pub.whitehouse.gov/WH/html/library.html>

Newman, J H (1947) *The Idea of a University*, reprinted by Longmans, New York

OECD (1996) Information Technology and the Future for Post-secondary Education, OECD, Paris

Pam, A (1995) Where World Wide Web Went Wrong, Proceedings of the Asia-Pacific World Wide Web Conference, Sydney <http://www.xanadu.com.au/xanadu/6w-paper.html>

Patterson, G (1989) The Evolution of the University, Occasional Paper No 2, Department of Management, Massey University, Palmerston North

Phillips, M, Scott, P and Fage, J (1998) Towards a strategy for the use of new technology in student guidance and support, *Open Learning*, **13** (2), 52–58

Polanyi, M (1958) *Personal knowledge: Towards a post-critical philosophy*, Routledge & Kegan Paul, London

Polanyi, M (1967) *The Tacit Dimension*, Routledge & Kegan Paul, London

Rumble, G (1997) *Costs and Economics of Open and Distance Learning*, Kogan Page, London

Schiller, N and Cunningham, N A (1998) Delivering course materials to distance learners over the World Wide Web: Statistical data summary, *The Journal of Library Services for Distance Education*, **1** (2) <http://www.westga.edu/library/jlsde/>

Schön D (1983), *The Reflective Practitioner: How professionals think in action*, Basic Books, New York

Seely, J, Brown, A and Duguid, C P (1989) Situated cognition and the culture of learning, *Educational Researcher*, **18** (1), 32–42

Stephens, K, Unwin, L and Bolton, N (1997) The use of libraries by postgraduate distance learning students: a mismatch of expectations, *Open Learning*, **12** (4), 25–33

Turoff, M (1997) Alternative future for distance learning: The force and the dark side, UNESCO/Open University International Colloquium <http://eies.njit.edu/~turoff/Papers/darkaln.html>

Twigg, C A (1994) The need for a national learning infrastructure, *Educom Review*, **29** (4, 5, 6)

Wagner, P (1994) *A Sociology of Modernity, Liberty and Discipline*, Routledge, London

Wiley, D A (2000) Learning Object Design and Sequencing Theory, Unpublished PhD Thesis, <http://www.opencontent.org/openpub/>

Useful resources on the Web

We offer this list, knowing that it is by no means exhaustive. It is an annotated list of resources that we have found particularly useful. We have limited the list to those sites that we consider likely to be maintained for a considerable time. However, the Web is a dynamic medium and you should not assume that the sites will remain available indefinitely.

General information
<http://www.namss.org.uk/evaluate.htm#General>
Tools for evaluating Web sites and other resources.

<http://www.e-valuate-IT.com/>
Tools to integrate survey reports with the policies, standards and methodologies currently in place at the programme, course or business-unit level. E-valuate-IT also features the ability to analyse and quantify results from open-ended questions, and to generate information-rich reports based upon these results.

<http://www.hpcnet.org/cgi-bin/global/a_bus_card.cgi?SiteID=154797>
Report of the Web-based Education Commission. The Commission was established by Congress to develop policy recommendations geared toward maximizing the educational promise of the Internet for pre-K, elementary, middle, secondary and post-secondary education learners. Dec 2000.

<http://www.ncteam.ac.uk/index.html>
The NCT works on behalf of the Higher Education Funding Council for England (HEFCE) and the Department for Higher and Further Education, Training and

Employment (DHFETE) to manage and co-ordinate two initiatives focused on encouraging innovation and new developments within learning and teaching.

Online journals
<http://www.geteducated.com/onlineguides.htm>
Virtual University Gazette (free) articles and resources for distance education and online learning guides.

<http://www.usdla.org/15_publications.htm>
ED, Education at a Distance, is a journal that is the official publication of the United States Distance Learning Association (USDLA).

<http://www.irrodl.org/current.html>
International Review of Research into Open and Distance Learning

<http://www.aln.org/alnweb/magazine/maga_v4_i2.htm>
The Asynchronous Learning Networks Magazine (ALN Magazine)

<http://www.learningcircuits.org/>
ASTD. A membership organization with a free Webzine.

<http://chronicle.com/infotech/>
Chronicle of Higher Education Information Technology section.

Online books
You may find these books both useful and interesting:

<http://www.usask.ca/dlc/FDLP.htm>
The living book – Flexible Learning for Continuing Professional Education: Models, Issues and Trends. The book is being created by Dr Roy Lundin.

<http://www.coe.uh.edu/~ichen/ebook/ET-IT/cover.htm>
An Electronic Textbook on Instructional Technology.

<http://otis.scotcit.ac.uk/onlinebook/>
An online tutoring e-help book.

<http://www-icdl.open.ac.uk/mindweave/mindweave.htm>
Mindweave: Communication, Computers and Distance Education (1989).

<http://www.ils.nwu.edu/~e_for_e/nodes/I-M-INTRO-ZOOMER-pg.html>
This title is also worth looking at, not only because it uses hypertext to what in our opinion is very good effect – see the links at the foot of each page.

<http://www.geteducated.com/articles.htm>
<http://www.tltgroup.org/>
Articles and guidelines for online learning from private consulting firms

Information on standards
<http://www.learnativity.com/standards.html>
This is one of the most useful sites for obtaining an overview of the way standards in relation to learning management systems are emerging.

<http://www.imsproject.org/>
The site for the Instructional Management Systems (IMS) Project.

<http://ltsc.ieee.org/wg12/index.html>
The site for the Learning Objects Metadata group of the Institution of Electrical and Electronic Engineers, providing the latest information on metadata standards.

<http://www.w3.org/TR/WAI-WEBCONTENT/full-checklist.html>
Web Content Accessibility Guidelines that explain how to make Web content accessible to people with disabilities. The primary goal of these guidelines is to promote accessibility. However, following them will also make Web content more available to all users.

<http://www.qaa.ac.uk/public/dlg/contents.htm>
Distance learning standards by the UK accrediting authority.

<http://standards.edna.edu.au/reference/setting.html>
An Australian site with links to a range of standards organizations.

<http://www.iste.org/index.html>
The National Educational Technology Standards (NETS) Project is an ongoing initiative of the International Society for Technology in Education (ISTE) and a consortium of distinguished partners and co-sponsors.

<http://www.cranfield.ac.uk/docs/publish_code.html>
A code of practice for the publishing of information in electronic format for Cranfield University.

<http://www.learningcircuits.org/2001/jan2001/@work.html>
Accreditation guidelines for online learning organizations.

Information on tools
<http://www.ctt.bc.ca/landonline/>
The most useful site for up-to-date comparative information on integrated electronic learning environments.

<http://www.thinkofit.com>
David Woolley's comprehensive guide to Web conferencing software.

Intellectual property
<http://www.uspto.gov/web/offices/com/doc/ipnii/>
The Report of the Working Group on Intellectual Property Rights, chaired by
Assistant Secretary of Commerce and Commissioner of Patents and Trademarks
Bruce A Lehman, explains how intellectual property law applies to cyberspace
and makes legislative recommendations to Congress to fine tune the law for the
digital age.

**Educational organizations with useful Web sites and links for online
learning**
<http://www.spu.edu/~dwicks/>
<http://www.warwick.ac.uk/ETS/pubsUniversity>
<http://www.mc.maricopa.edu/academic/ctl/DL/>
<http://www2.open.ac.uk/LTTO/internal/tsaa.htm>
<http://www.cdl.edu/html/dist.html>

Australian sites
<http://www.edna.edu.au/>
NET resources and publications.

<http://www.otfe.vic.gov.au/planning/model/index.htm>
A planning model for new learning technologies and case studies of good practice.

Other useful resources
<http://bsd-server.nc.edu/virtcol/ss/learn.html>
An online learning styles questionnaire.

<http://www.ncsa.uiuc.edu/General/Internet/WWW/HTMLPrimer.html>
A beginner's guide to HTML. NCSA was the original source of Netscape and is
super-reputable.

<http://eies.njit.edu/~turoff/Papers/cbdevu.html>
A thought-provoking paper on the costs for the development of a virtual university
by Murray Turoff, Professor of Computer and Information Science New Jersey
Institute of Technology, one of the pioneers of online conferencing.

<http://www.tltgroup/resources/farticles.html>
The Flashlight Project provides instruments for evaluation of the application of
information and communications technology in education.

<http://www.shu.ac.uk/news/releases/oct99/network.htm>
A research report published by Sheffield Hallam University on The Costs of

Networked Learning has revealed that students and academic staff often do not know the financial implications of working by computer at home.

<http://www.useit.com/papers/webwriting>
Jakob Neilsen's site provides information for writers and editors of Web content: Papers and Essays – Writing for the Web. Jakob Neilson is a usability engineer at Sun Microsystems and often-cited usability expert, publishes regular articles about usability and Web trends.

<http://lomond.idol.hw.ac.uk/itdi/>
The Learning Technology Dissemination Initiative was funded between 1994 and 1999 by the Scottish Higher Education Funding Council to promote the use of learning technology and computer-based learning materials in Scottish Higher Education. The LTDI Web site will continue to provide free access to the resources and publications created by LTDI.

<http://www.chea.org/Commentary/distance-learning-3.cfm>
Council for Higher Education Accreditation Resources and articles on distance learning in Higher Education.

<http://info.med.yale.edu/caim/manual/>
Yale Web Style Guide for basic design principles for creating Web sites.

<http://www.ufiltd.co.uk>
University for Industry/LearnDirect (UFI) Handbook for Developers of Online Materials. This extremely comprehensive handbook for Web site and interface design has been used extensively as the quality framework for all online materials available through UFI, a major new UK initiative.

<http://www.w3.org/>
The World Wide Web Consortium (W3C) develops interoperable technologies (specifications, guidelines, software and tools) to lead the Web to its full potential as a forum for information, commerce, communication and collective under-standing. The W3C provides a free 'link checker' service at <http://validator.w3.org/checklink>

<http://www.lrx.com.au>
Learning Resource Exchange (LRX) This consortium will shortly release a set of metadata fields for a local and national catalogue of online learning materials. It will also release a metadata cataloguing tool to enable materials to be added to a database.

<http://www.microsoft.com/office/deployment/ConvFile.htm>
Converting Files Between Different Versions of Office Software: A File Format Matrix. A conversion chart for different MS Office software products.

Index